SMOKE AND
AN EXPERIENC

Pallavi Aiyar has reported from acro
Hindu and the *Indian Express*, the only Chinese-speaking
correspondent to be based in the country. She is the winner of the 2007
Prem Bhatia Memorial Award for excellence in political reporting and
analysis, the youngest ever recipient of the prize. Aside from her work as
a journalist, she has taught news writing to students at the Beijing
Broadcasting Institute and served as advisor to the Confederation
of Indian Industry on China-related issues. Pallavi has degrees from
St Stephen's College, Delhi University, Oxford University and the London
School of Economics. She has recently moved to Brussels where she lives
with her husband Julio, baby boy Ishaan and two Chinese cats, Soyabean
and Tofu.

PRAISE FOR THE BOOK

'*Smoke and Mirrors* is thoroughly entertaining and educative, written
with wit and perception in a lively and evocative style. Aiyar's
observations and experiences helped me to better understand China,
to which I have been an occasional visitor'—Sonia Gandhi, President,
Congress party

'Spurning the usual West-centric perspective on China, Pallavi Aiyar
brings a sharp assessing eye to her intractably complex subject. In
brisk, often entertaining, prose, she exposes the rich paradoxes and
ironies of both "authoritarian" China and "democratic" India'
—Pankaj Mishra

'A deeply insightful and often very amusing mixture of travelogue,
memoir and political analysis . . . offers a perspective on the relationship
between the two countries that doesn't read as a breathless praise-
song to the transforming, medicinal power of globalisation, and that
benefits vastly from the time she has spent talking to villagers, small
traders and economic migrants as much as to CEOs and think-tank
wonks . . . Clever, engaging, reflexive: Aiyar's book will affront
"India Shining" ideologues as much as it punctures the gassy platitudes
of "Chindia" boosters'—Sukhdev Sandhu, *The New Statesman*

'When the obsession with China and India's mutual, competitive, and
thrilling rise comes back into vogue in the West—and it will—we will
benefit from having Aiyar's cultural vantage point and nuanced lens.
She will certainly serve as a better guide to exploring those issues that
don't easily fit into the already hackneyed "Dragon vs. Elephant"
cliché. And when it comes to answering that all-important question of

how these countries are improving the future for their citizens, who better to help us understand than someone who knows them both with the love of a native and the curiosity of a traveler?'—Jeffrey Wasserstrom, *Foreign Policy*

'Aiyar's book is a bridge across two cultures and civilisations, and an important contribution in humanising China and making it more accessible for Indian readers fed on—and presumably fed up of—the daily dose of hyperbole and superlatives that passes for China-watching'—*DNA*

'Pallavi's narrative stands out not only for an engaging style, and telling a story with lots of frills and humour . . . an honest account of the economic superpower with its multiple contradictions . . . A must read'—*The Hindu Business Line*

'Littered with anecdotes and real-time conversations, the book actually demystifies the enigma that is China'—*Economic Times*

'Stunningly panoramic . . . witty, intelligent and makes for very good reading'—*Tehelka*

'With grace and with humour, Aiyar brings to life what would otherwise have been dreary explanations of Chinese culture . . . Don't skip this one . . . a refreshingly different look at a country that few Indians care (or dare) to understand'—*Business World*

'Pallavi Aiyar's *Smoke and Mirrors* deciphers China through unique Indian spectacles in a witty and illuminative account that has flashes of a classic . . . the best comparative narrative on China by an Asian in recent times'—*Asia Times Online*

'. . . entertaining and insightful . . . a landmark of sorts . . . Aiyar seamlessly combines reportage and analysis'—*Hindustan Times*

'. . . a combination of memoir, travelogue and socio-economic treatise . . . manages to be simultaneously intelligent and charming. Aiyar has an easy pen: the statistics are readable and not at all daunting, the historical background relevant and brief, the socio-political observations carried lightly . . . It is the Indian perspective that sets it apart from the other books of the genre and makes it important'—*The Asian Review of Books*

'An Indian window has finally been opened into contemporary China . . . Pallavi Aiyar is the first young Indian to have lived the experience and written about it. She has written a witty, insightful and profound book . . . It deserves to be widely read in India and around the world'—*Outlook*

Smoke and Mirrors

An Experience of China

PALLAVI AIYAR

FOURTH ESTATE • *New Delhi*

First published in India in 2008 by Fourth Estate
An imprint of HarperCollins *Publishers* India
a joint venture with
The India Today Group

Copyright © Pallavi Aiyar 2008

2 4 6 8 10 9 7 5 3 1

ISBN 13: 978-81-7223-846-9

Pallavi Aiyar asserts the moral right to be identified as the author of this work.

HarperCollins *Publishers*
A-53, Sector 57, NOIDA, Uttar Pradesh 201301, India
77-85 Fulham Palace Road, London W6 8JB, United Kingdom
Hazelton Lanes, 55 Avenue Road, Suite 2900, Toronto, Ontario M5R 3L2
and 1995 Markham Road, Scarborough, Ontario M1B 5M8, Canada
25 Ryde Road, Pymble, Sydney, NSW 2073, Australia
31 View Road, Glenfield, Auckland 10, New Zealand
10 East 53rd Street, New York NY 10022, USA

Author's Note: The names of some of the characters in the book have been
changed to protect their identity. In other places I have used either
English names or family names alone, for the same reason.

Typeset in 11/14 Adobe Garamond
SÜRYA

Printed and bound at
Thomson Press (India) Ltd.

For My Mother
Gitanjali

Contents

Acknowledgements

This book was born out of cumulative experiences gathered working in and travelling across China between 2002 and 2007. Those who helped me along the journey in a myriad of ways, big and small, are too many to acknowledge individually, but I owe a debt to them all.

I would like to thank especially all my students at the BBI and my neighbours in Beixin Qiao Tou Tiao *hutong*. Collectively they were my primary guides into the complexities of China. Thanks also to Jian Yi for reeling me in, wriggly fish that I was, and persuading me to make the decision that enabled all that followed.

In China I would also like to thank Prof. Feng Lu, Wang Jinzhen, and Hu Shuli for advice and help over the years. Further, I am grateful to Wu Nan and Ruojing Shan for valuable assistance with my reporting assignments. A big debt is owed to Wang Wanying for his courage of personal conviction, insight and interest in the book.

Thanks also to Mary Kay Magistad for her quick and honest responses to the first draft of the manuscript. A similar *xie xie* is owed to Tuva Kahrs for her fine-toothed comb excavation of parts of the manuscript, even as the indomitable Magnus vied for attention.

An additional thank you must go to Isolda Morillo for language-related help during the trip to the White Horse temple that is detailed in the chapter on religion.

I'd also like to acknowledge the support and assistance of the two CII chiefs I worked with in China—Sunil Kumar Misra and Madhav Sharma.

Finally, my stomach wishes to flag its appreciation of Li Ayi's wonderful chicken curries and samosas that did much to ease the way for the writing of this book.

In the United States I owe gratitude to Sukhdev Sandhu for whetting appetites via his characteristic 'logorrhoeic hyperbolic appreciation' of the manuscript.

I must also thank from the deepest recesses of my heart my brother Shekhar Aiyar for valiantly wading through the manuscript and for excellent and detailed feedback through what I know to have been the busiest period of his life. I am grateful to him, moreover, for much beyond the present book alone. He has been an inspiration to me ever since I can remember.

Last, but far from least, a big thank you to my father, Swaminathan Aiyar, for always having set the bar high and for having pushed me to be the best I could be. His approval of the manuscript did more for my confidence than he can imagine.

In India, I am grateful to N. Ram of the *Hindu* for giving me a broad writing platform coupled with the necessary support for travel and exploration of China. Many of the stories in this book began their lives as reporting assignments for the *Hindu*. Thanks also to Mythili Bhusnurmath for having given me a break at the *Financial Express* and to Tarun Das for an opportunity with CII. Ravi Bhoothalingam has been an invaluable source of support throughout my China life. Prannoy and Radhika Roy have been similarly supportive throughout my working life.

Two of the warmest thanks go to C. Raja Mohan and Krishan Chopra. Raja Mohan not only gave birth to the germ of the idea that grew up to become the book but also put me in touch with my editor at HarperCollins, Krishan Chopra. Krishan believed in the book right off the bat and offered valuable advice through the writing process.

I was also enthused and encouraged by Barun Mitra's unflagging energy and ideas. His thoughtful suggestions and responses to the manuscript were an immense help.

This book would not have been *this* book in the absence of Kiran Ganguli, my friend and mentor since childhood. Thank you, Gang, for buying me books to read and books to write in.

My debt to my mother, Gitanjali Aiyar, for everything I am is overwhelming. It is because of her belief in me that I have been able to take all the important decisions in my life. The book is dedicated to her.

But more than anyone or anything in the world it is to Julio, my great love and rock of support, that I owe China, this book and my happiness.

Prologue

The plane lurched up causing the stewardesses serving drinks to clutch tightly at their trolleys. They looked worn out. China Eastern had only begun flying the New Delhi–Beijing route a few months ago, in March 2002. Before then the world's two most populous countries, neighbours sharing a 3500 km border, lacked a single direct connecting flight. With the exception of a stopover in New Delhi on Ethiopian Airlines' Beijing–Addis Ababa route, the only way into India from mainland China and vice versa had been through a third country like Singapore or Thailand.

Not that there was a crush of people lining up to make the journey. When I arrived at the visa section of the Chinese embassy in Delhi's Shantipath, the quiet was surreal. Snaking queues besieged virtually every other embassy in the vicinity. Beads of sweat dotted the foreheads of visa hopefuls; a combination of sun and stress. But at the Chinese visa section, there was only a gentle hush.

I handed in the letter of employment sent to me by the Beijing Broadcasting Institute, the college that was to be my employer for the next year. It was written in Chinese, filled with impossibly complicated characters, and stamped repeatedly with red seals. The lady at the window glanced at the letter and added more red seals of her own. I was impressed by the practised efficiency of her chop-chop stamping.

A week later I had a visa and before long I was boarding the 3 a.m. flight to Beijing. 'Pork with rice or pork with noodle?' inquired an air hostess a few hours into the journey. She pronounced pork sharply, as if it had no 'r'. I asked for the 'noodle', but had little appetite.

Aside from the fact that the food itself was uninspiring, there was little space in my stomach given the flotillas of butterflies that were crowding it. I was going to China, I thought repeatedly. Repetition usually soothed but in this case it merely terrified.

I had over the last few years lived in Oxford, Los Angeles and London. At the outset of life in each new city I had mostly felt only the pleasant tingle of anticipation. Foreign countries held little terror for me and I believed myself adept at domesticating the unknown.

But it was only when I decided to go to China that I sensed the fear of the truly unknown. None of the cities I had lived in earlier were genuinely new to me, connected as I was to them by bonds of language and colonialism.

But what did I know of China? An alien and seemingly impenetrable language; an inscrutable people; an exotic cuisine. I thought fleetingly of bicycles. Then I reminded myself of the current affairs articles I had religiously been reading to educate myself on my new home.

I was aware that there had been an economic 'miracle' in China. The world's media was abuzz with it. Beijing had won the bid to host the Olympic Games and China had even negotiated entry into the WTO.

There would no longer just be bicycles on the road, I told myself. Expect cars, some fancy ones at that. But beyond that I found it extremely hard to envisage anything about the city that I would be living in for the next year. A large, China-shaped blank existed north of the Himalayas in my mental map of the world.

Over the next five years this blank space would gradually fill up, accumulating details born of friendships, travel and reporting. I would witness first hand the relentless changes and churnings that would propel China into the international limelight. From a country known to the outside world primarily for the excesses of the Maoist period, China would, during my stay there, emerge as the world's fourth largest economy.

The country's rise would have ripple effects across the world. Made in China Jin Cheng mopeds would become the vehicle of choice for young men in places as distant as the fabled trading town of Timbuktu. The bazaars of Central Asia would be filled with the chatter of Chinese merchants. Single towns in China's booming southern provinces would come to manufacture the large majority of the world's supplies of buttons, lighters, spectacles, socks, razors, Christmas ornaments and sex toys.

Over the course of my stay, China would complete the world's biggest dam and highest railway line; begin work on the world's largest airport and museum; introduce the world's fastest train and acquire the world's largest foreign exchange reserves. The country's galloping growth would develop a momentum historically unprecedented and perhaps nowhere envied as much as in neighbouring India.

It would, however, also throw up powerful contradictions as China's often discordant blend of authoritarian politics and liberal economics required of the leadership a tightrope act that could not be expected to last forever. The dichotomous nature of the China I found myself in was a potentially explosive one, where new freedoms and old oppressions, anarchy and discipline, modernity and tradition coexisted without any obvious mechanisms for resolving the tensions that ensued.

Moreover, during this period change and growth would not remain a monopoly of China. India too would begin, albeit more gradually, to benefit from its decade-old reform process aimed at the unfettering of its economy. The term 'Chindia' would thus be coined[1] as a shorthand for talking about the potential of geopolitical and economic interactions between India and China and the implications of these for the rest of the watchful world.

As an Indian living in China at a time when both giant-sized neighbours were undergoing an economic renaissance with repercussions that transcended their borders alone, my experience of China was understandably mediated through the prism of comparison with India.

Differences in the political systems, in the role of women in society, in attitudes to dignity of labour, approaches to food, responsiveness to authority, ancient and more recent history—all these and more, gave me much pause for thought. Over the years, many beliefs I had once considered unshakeable proved in fact to be disconcertingly mutable, as I pondered the relative weight of economic versus political freedoms; of broad roads versus religious persecution; of the freedom to become rich but without the freedom to criticize.

My first year and a half in China were spent learning Mandarin and teaching English. These were days of reflection and wonder as I interacted daily with close to two hundred students who collectively formed my sounding board and guides into the intricacies of a country and society that I was woefully ignorant about.

It was their preoccupations that provided my initial insights into the new China. Part of the first generation of the country's one-child families, the students were both blithely optimistic and unnervingly ignorant. These traits would be put to the test before long, with the outbreak of the deadly SARS epidemic in early 2003.

The students' reactions to the viral disease, in particular the governmental cover-up of the extent of its spread, revealed to me the wobbly foundations upon which the edifice of contemporary

---

[1]The term 'Chindia' was coined by Jairam Ramesh, the Congress party MP. It was introduced in the title of his book, *Making Sense of Chindia: Reflections on China and India*, published in 2005.

China rested. In the event, however, the SARS story was also to point to the surprising resilience of the Chinese leadership and their continuing grip on the minds of the urban educated.

After a year teaching and exploring the tonal intricacies of Mandarin, other paths began to open up to me in the country. I went on to become the first and only Chinese-speaking Indian foreign correspondent in China, reporting for the *Indian Express* and later the *Hindu*.

I travelled across the country from troubled Tibet to booming Zhejiang, encountering a variegated cast of characters along the way: freewheeling entrepreneurs, young monks desperate to escape to India, nationalistic students and cricket-gifting neighbours.

In time I married my long-term boyfriend, Julio, who worked at the European Commission's delegation in Beijing and who was the primary cause for the Chinaward orientation my life had taken.

We had met in London as postgraduate students at the London School of Economics. Julio, who is a Spaniard, was a sinophile and had spent a year learning Chinese at the People's University in Beijing in 1998.

It was in London that I was first introduced to China, through Julio's black-and-white photographs of Beijing's *hutongs*, painfully beautiful in the snow.

A year after we met, Julio returned to Beijing to work and I went on to Los Angeles to continue with my studies. Over the next few months Julio spent hours on book-length emails and marathon telephone conversations persuading me that a move to China would be the smartest thing I could do with my life.

He tried to convey to me the import of the changes China was undergoing. Napoleon had prophesied almost two hundred years ago that once the sleeping dragon that was China awakened, the world would tremble. The dragon had woken up, Julio told me, but at the time it was difficult for me to grasp what he was trying to express. All I knew was that we were in love and that my moving to China would give us a future.

But, I spoke no Chinese and had no background in the country at all. What would I do there? Luckily, just at the time that I began to consider relocating to Beijing, China was being swept by an English-learning craze that had over 375 million Chinese busy learning ABC. This was a number roughly equivalent to the world's entire population of native English speakers. China-related statistics, as I would discover, were never modest.

It was thus that I had been able with minimum fuss to be hired by the Beijing Broadcasting Institute, China's premier college for TV journalists. I was to teach news writing to second-year students of 'English Broadcasting'. The pay was nothing to get excited about, but the job got me a visa, came with an apartment and secured me the grandiose title of *wai guo zhuan jia,* or 'foreign expert'.

'Foreign experts' were foreigners invited to China in the post-economic reform period by the Chinese government, to help impart a variety of skills, felt to be lacking domestically. Comprising doctors, engineers and academics, 'foreign experts' were a standard sight in Chinese cities in the 1980s and '90s as the country continued along its dramatic transition from failed agrarian utopia to factory of the world.

The experts were feted as 'foreign friends' who came to China despite the hardships this ostensibly entailed to help 'build the Chinese nation'. I had unintentionally become part of this patriotically charged set-up, although by the time I moved to Beijing in September 2002 the sheen of simply being foreign in China was already fading.

Once treated with a certain awe, the foreign experts of the new century were no longer considered particularly special. The country had already absorbed much of the foreign technology it once lacked and China's confidence was on the rise. Chinese cities were acquiring a cosmopolitanism unimaginable only a decade ago. Beijing was already home to 100,000-odd officially registered foreigners, with tens of thousands of others illegally continuing to work on short-term business visas procured in Hong Kong.

For decades China had exported swarms of immigrants desperate to find a better life anywhere as long as it was elsewhere. But now it was China that was beginning to import immigrants: French hairdressers, Bulgarian divas, Colombian doctors, Spanish consultants and Indian yoga teachers. China was hot and everyone wanted part of the action. A sense of dynamism and possibility imbued the streets of Beijing and Shanghai. This was the new frontier and it exerted a magnetic pull.

People planned to stay a year and stayed a decade. So it was with me. My initial one-year plan turned to five. I stayed on through the SARS epidemic that swept the country in the spring of 2003; through the first visit by an Indian Prime Minister to China in a decade in the summer of the same year; through the destruction of large parts of Beijing to clear the way for a new Olympics-worthy city of shiny skyscrapers; through sandstorms that turned the skies an angry orange for days and winter blizzards that froze my tropical heart with homesickness.

Over the course of my China life I would see a sharp rise in the number of Indian faces visible in Chinese cities. In 2002, when I first moved to Beijing, the absence of Indians was stunning to me. From Botswana to Fiji, I had always assumed that Indians were, quite simply, everywhere. But as the calm at the Chinese embassy's visa section in New Delhi should have warned me, they hadn't made it across the Great Wall. Yet.

On the upside this meant that the average mainland Chinese had lacked the opportunity to form any category of anti-Indian prejudice. In Hong Kong, where the Indian community was thick and strong, the antipathy of the Chinese towards them was well known. In fact throughout the world Indians and Chinese were natural competitors. They were the traders, the tailors, the shopkeepers, the computer engineers, the model immigrants.

But in mainland China itself, there were few Indians and thus no rivalries. India had already begun obsessing about the successes of its northern neighbour, but China was too busy benchmarking itself against the United States to give India much thought at all. What little the average Zhou knew of India came from Hindi films of the Raj Kapoor era: beautiful actresses, wonderful melodies and dancing. 'Oh, the dancing!' people always said to me, their eyes brimming with nostalgic delight. 'You Indians are so lucky to all be able to dance like that.'

Five years later sarees and dhotis had become standard sights at shopping centres in Beijing and Shanghai. Several hundred thousand Indians began to travel to China annually. Tourists came to gawk at the Great Wall, businessmen to ogle the wonders of Chinese wholesale markets. From virtually nil over 100 Indian companies opened offices in China. Yoga teachers began to set up shop even in smaller second-tier cities. Indian restaurants in Beijing doubled in number and then tripled. Sikh doormen in trademark red turbans began to make an appearance at hotel entrances.

A steady stream of dignitaries, political and military, commenced crossing the border. Memoranda of understanding were signed in defence, energy, culture. 'Chindia' became a buzzword and the average Chinese began to take an interest in India beyond wondering whether all Indian women could dance.

On return trips to Delhi, the same people whose eyes used to glaze over on discovering I didn't live abroad in 'US or UK' but China suddenly couldn't get enough of me. 'But how real is China's growth?' they would ask, greedy for answers. 'How broad are the roads really? Do they eat dogs? Can India ever hope to compete?'

As I sat on the plane, peering through the window for my first glimpse of a new life, I anticipated none of this. I worried instead about whether all my luggage would arrive safely. About what it would feel like to see Julio again. About facing a class full of Chinese teenagers who believed me to be a foreign 'expert'.

Seat back upright, seat-belt fastened, I felt slightly sick as I always did when landing. A few seconds later the usual jarring bump was followed by frantic announcements for everyone to stay in their seats until the plane had come to a complete halt. It was then that all the talk of ancient connections between the great civilizations of India and China began to make sense.

The moment the announcement was made, virtually every Hindi and Chini present scrambled to their feet, jostling to open the overhead lockers, reaching high for their strolleys and boxes. The handful of westerners looked on with barely concealed condescension from their seats. The air hostesses merely looked on in weary resignation. Through the beeps of mobile phones being switched on and the crush of people ducking descending luggage, a recorded message croaked, 'Welcome to Beijing International Airport'.

CHAPTER ONE

Better Fat than Anapple

It was a long trek from the city centre to the Beijing Broadcasting Institute, or BBI as it was commonly abbreviated. The college was located beyond the eastern boundary of the fifth ring road, an area that in 2002 was still more village than city. Peasants from neighbouring Hebei province, brown-toothed and snotty-nosed, sold carrots and cabbage in makeshift shacks that fringed the path running along the college's side entrance.

The glass and chrome temples to Mammon that had begun to dot Beijing's business district were only two ring roads west of the college, but back then the BBI remained cocooned from the material march forward of the rest of the city.

The students hated being marooned in what they saw as the boondocks. Soon, very soon, they would assure me, the subway would connect us downtown. It would only take twenty minutes to reach the nearest Starbucks then, they fantasized, eyes half-closed in frappucino-scented fantasy.

The subway in fact took two years in the opening, by which time I had long flown the BBI coop. The Hebei peasants and their carrots had also been cleaned up by then, replaced by glistening apartment blocks and the inevitable malls. Beijing's embrace of modernity was remorseless, formidable.

By some estimates, half the world's production of concrete and one-third of its steel output were being consumed by the mainland's carnivorous appetite for construction.

In the 1980s Beijing's city limits were marked by a single ring road running along its outskirts. By the time I drove up to the BBI for the first time, three more ring roads circled around the ever expanding boundary of the city and construction on a sixth had begun.

The decrepit red taxi we were riding in just about squeezed in two overstuffed suitcases, Julio and myself. Hung on the rear of the driver's seat was a magazine rack mysteriously exhorting passengers to 'spread window civilization and practice carriage culture'. The six-lane airport expressway spread out ahead of us, silky smooth, light years away from the potholed clumps of tar that passed for roads in most parts of India.

I felt humbled by the road, a phenomenon that would repeatedly revisit me like a persistent mosquito. The sharpest pinch came a few years later when I accompanied a large business delegation from China on a sight-seeing trip from Delhi to Agra. The group was unusually quiet for the first part of the journey, peering out of the bus windows intently. Finally, a middle-aged entrepreneur from Liaoning province cautiously asked me, 'So, when exactly are we going to hit the highway?' We had, of course, been on it for hours.

It was a forty-five-minute drive to the college campus. We drove in through the main gate, past stern-faced security guards framed by a cluster of satellite dishes, their antennae reaching into the sky. Directions for the 'international building', where I had been allocated an apartment, were ascertained. We soon found ourselves pulling up next to a white, bathroom-tiled structure, adorned intermittently with blue plexiglass windows—a style of architecture that I later discovered was considered most chic in the 1990s and afflicted almost every Chinese city of standing.

There was a reception on the ground floor of the building, staffed by two young women in smart uniforms. Julio remained outside paying off the cabbie and taking care of my luggage, so it was left to me to try to obtain the key to my apartment.

After a minute or so of repeating my name and pointing to myself while (rather immodestly) mouthing 'foreign expert', I realized I was getting nowhere. Given that 375 million Chinese were ostensibly learning English I felt mildly surprised that I hadn't as yet encountered any of them.

The women themselves seemed unable to grasp that I did not speak Chinese, convinced that if only they spoke slowly and loudly enough, long dormant Mandarin abilities would awaken within me.

I was growing increasingly desolate when they finally fell silent. A second or two later a slow smile spread across the older one's face. 'Eureka!' she seemed to be thinking. A solution had no doubt occurred to her. I was correct in my assumption, but rather than fetching a dictionary, she began instead to make squiggly patterns in the air with her finger.

Her look of triumph faded after a few moments as I still looked blank and everyone was relieved when Julio appeared to help. The squiggly patterns, it transpired, were the receptionist's attempt to sketch Chinese characters in the air, it being a widely held belief in China that even if foreigners were stupid enough not to understand Chinese, they must surely be able to read it.

In part this belief sprang from the fact that while there were wide differences in the spoken forms of Chinese across the country, the system of writing was uniform. Cantonese and Mandarin, for example, were mutually incomprehensible but almost identical when written. People from different parts of the country were thus used to being able to rely on written characters to clarify meaning to each other, even when their spoken words were not understood. The same logic was extended, somewhat unimaginatively, to foreigners.

With Julio's help I was able without further ado to secure a key to my apartment. It was spartanly furnished but fairly large, comprising two bedrooms, a sitting room, bathroom and kitchen. From the sitting room I had a view of the college's newly constructed sports field. The grass in the field shone bright green, the seats in the spectator's stands bright white. It wasn't open to use yet. The college authorities apparently wanted a semester or so in which to admire their new acquisition unsullied by the sweaty feet of student athletes.

The next morning I walked across to the main teaching building, a four-storey, box-shaped structure, a few minutes before my first class was scheduled to begin. Classrooms were equipped with wooden desks, wide blackboards and an elevated platform for the teacher. The set-up was reassuringly familiar except that I wasn't sitting in the giggly warmth of a gaggle of students at the far end of the room but atop the teacher's platform upfront, exposed and alone.

The students looked at me with mild curiosity. Some squinted through eyes barely visible under carefully overgrown fringes. They were dressed smartly, low-slung jeans and fitted T-shirts revealing well-toned bodies. Only seven years younger than me, I marvelled.

In what I hoped was a friendly yet authoritative tone I introduced myself, speaking slowly, unsure of their language abilities. When I mentioned having studied at Oxford, it drew a gasp of admiration and scattered applause. Encouraged, I ended with what I thought to be the disarming confession that this was the first time I was teaching anything to anyone. A muted groan arose; distinctly impolite.

This was my core group of fifty-odd students: the English Broadcasting majors. Many would remain friends even after I stopped teaching them. Others would re-emerge years later as fellow scribes.

On that first day I was taken aback when a class full of very Chinese students stood up and began introducing themselves as Byron and Montgomery. Others were called Ice and Echo. A dimple-cheeked girl introduced herself as 'Anapple', as in 'an apple'.

One of my favourite name choices was 'Better', a delicate blend, I thought, of arrogance and humility. Better was in fact an affable chap and at twenty-two a couple of years older than the others. As a student he was indeed 'better' than average, but far from the best, making his choice of name most apt.

The climax, however, was when a hirsute lad scrambled to his feet and announced his name as 'Victoria'. He would (wisely) decide to change his name during the course of the next year, twice. He finally settled on Albert.

In China, I discovered, it was standard practice for youngsters to take on western names when they first began to study English. These names were either given to them by their language teacher or self-chosen. Family names were kept on and only given names were anglicized, so that you had Montgomery Hou, Byron Li and so on.

Some chose literal translations of their Chinese names, and so girls called Elegant Wang and Promise Xu were not uncommon. Others had more practical reasons for their choice. 'My name is Fat. I chose this name because I am fat,' announced one portly youth. His classmates nodded in agreement at this statement of fact.

To begin with, I was uncomfortable with this phenomenon of anglicized names. It seemed demeaning for someone with a beautiful Chinese name to have to call themselves Jack or Emma simply to make it more convenient for English speakers to remember.

Later I realized name-changing was a two-way street in China and all foreigners had perforce to adopt Chinese monikers as well. This was because the Chinese language lacked an alphabet. Also, its thousands of characters had just 420 different corresponding sounds. As a result the majority of Chinese words were homonyms distinguishable in meaning only through differences in tone and in the corresponding written characters. The language was therefore unable to absorb foreign words that had sounds lacking a matching Chinese character.

It was, for example, impossible to write Elizabeth in Chinese characters because there was no character that corresponded to that sound. Virtually all foreign proper nouns were thus rechristened in Chinese. America was *Mei Guo*, McDonald's *Mai Dang Lao*, the Olympics *Ao Yun Hui*. Pallavi Aiyar, became *Ai Bei*. Ai because that was the first syllable of my family name Aiyar, and the Chinese wrote their surnames first. Bei meant flower bud, close enough to the 'new leaves' meaning of Pallavi.

Over the next year I taught two-hundred-odd students the 'inverted pyramid' structure of news stories, the art of interviewing, the importance of commitment to deadlines and the mysteries of idiomatic English.

In addition to my main group of English Broadcasting majors I also taught scores of other foreign language students a subject called 'English writing'. The BBI was the chief supplier of employees to China Radio International, the government-owned radio station that broadcast in thirty-eight foreign languages including Swahili and Sinhalese. Amongst my extra charges were students studying Malay, Spanish, Japanese and French. But this was a motley crew and I never grew as close to them as I did to my English Broadcasters.

During the first few months at the college, I was careful to avoid bringing up any topics in class that might have been considered sensitive. My students were of the generation that exemplified the contradictions of contemporary China most baldly. In twenty-first century China economic freedom combined with political authoritarianism in an unpredictable cocktail and while the boundaries of control were no longer as visible as they once were, they existed nonetheless, to be crossed at the transgressor's peril.

The China I lived in was a communist country in name but a strange hybrid in practice. A gigantic portrait of Chairman Mao continued to adorn the entrance to the Forbidden City, the symbolic heart of the country, but housed within the red-and-gold interiors of the palace, a Starbucks coffee house served up caramel lattes.[1] All the English-language explanatory plaques detailing the palace's rich history were sponsored by American Express. The audio guide that assisted tourists as they negotiated the vast interiors of the museum featured the voice of Roger Moore, of 007 fame.

My students sat through compulsory classes in Marxism and Maoist thought, bored blind, fantasizing of little but money. The majority of them wanted to join the Communist Party but only because they believed this would help them get higher status jobs. Young party hopefuls gossiped about the sexual inclinations of classmates, giggling when it was revealed that Kevin was a *tongzhi*, the Chinese word for 'comrade' that had in modern slang become the irreverent euphemism for homosexual.

The students were of the first generation to be born after China's one-child policy was implemented in the late 1970s. They were brought up by fiercely protective parents determined to ensure that their children would never have to face the privations they had themselves suffered. As a result the bulk of them had grown up in sterile, apolitical environments where they were deliberately kept ignorant of knowledge their parents deemed unsuitable.

Instead, parents and teachers alike, constantly reinforced in the kids a sense of determined optimism, regardless of whether it was warranted. Children were told repeatedly that they were lucky. They had choices. They could go abroad. They could make money. And my students, belonging as they did to a class of people who had mostly benefited from China's economic reforms, bought into this story. They were as a whole optimistic, ambitious and very naïve.

---

[1] The Starbucks in question was finally closed in July 2007, seven years after it first opened. The move came after an intensive internet campaign started by a state TV anchor in 2006 accused the coffee shop of 'trampling' on Chinese culture and hurting the image of the historical monument.

In the new China, individual social and economic freedoms were expanding at a giddying pace. People in cities could own property. Private ownership of cars went from virtually zero in the 1980s to 70 per cent of all cars on China's roads by 2005. People no longer needed permission from their work units[2] to travel or marry. These were heady, liberating times.

Of course, you could still be jailed for criticizing the government. You could have your land summarily expropriated by the powerful and be imprisoned without trial for daring to protest. You could be charged with a crime, sentenced to death and executed within the space of hours. This was the nasty flip side to the broad roads and shiny buildings that lined Beijing and Shanghai. China jailed more journalists than any other country in the world. It executed more people than any other country in the world.

These were facts never mentioned in the state media and my students were strikingly unaware of the darker realities of their own country. Many willed this ignorance, consciously avoiding information that might damage their bright, nationalistic world view in which China was getting stronger and stronger and everything was getting better and better.

'My father used to ride a bicycle to work every day even when it was very cold and it snowed. Today we have two cars,' said Flora, one of the smarter students. This was a sentiment repeated ad nauseam in various forms. Parents only ate vegetables, we eat meat every day; parents wore the same drab clothes for years, we have a choice of designers, and so on and on.

---

[2]A work unit, or *danwei*, is the name given to a place of employment in China. Although it remains in contemporary use it has overtones of the pre-reform era when work units were the principal mechanism through which Communist Party policies were implemented. At the time all workers were bound to their work unit for life and in turn each *danwei* provided their workers with housing, child care, schools, clinics and other facilities. The influence of work units on the everyday life of people was substantial and permission had to be obtained from the relevant *danwei* before undertaking travel, marriage, or having children.

To begin with I found this wholesale, uncritical acceptance of the direction that China was taking disheartening. To be in a university with some of the brightest minds of a country and to detect virtually zero anti-establishment feeling was a deadening feeling. Where were the anger and chaos and general contrariness of youth?

'I have a question, Pallavi,' announced Cindy, one of my prettiest students, at the end of a lecture. Preparing to parry queries regarding the agenda-setting function of the press, I nodded in encouragement. 'I was wondering: do you prefer KFC or McDonald's?'

Such were some of the weighty questions that preyed upon the minds of my wards.

After spending weeks getting to know a certain student I finally felt close enough to her to broach a 'controversial' topic. I cautiously asked for her honest assessment of Mao. She seemed to mull it over for a few minutes and then replied gravely, 'I think he was 30 per cent wrong and 70 per cent correct.' I was impressed by this answer. She had obviously given it serious enough thought to have gone as far as to quantify his legacy.

I returned home and promptly told Julio this story, only to have him laugh at my ignorance. 'That's the party line on Mao,' he revealed and indeed the Chinese Communist Party's (CCP) official judgement on Mao was that he had been 30 per cent wrong and 70 per cent right.[3]

It was often like this. My students would repeat official

---

[3]This assessment was first made by the Central Committee of the Communist Party in 1981. After conducting an evaluation of Mao's legacy it concluded that Mao had been correct 70 per cent of the time and wrong for the remaining 30 per cent, although it also emphasized that Mao's contributions were primary and his mistakes secondary. The 70:30 formula went on to become the official party mantra on the subject. See: Jonathan Spence, *The Search for Modern China* (second edition), W.W. Norton & Company, 1999, p. 643.

propaganda with a sincerity that was heartbreaking. Did they really believe it? 'Not really,' said Yee, 'but these things are simply not important to them. The government wants them to shut up and get rich and they are happy doing just that.'

Yee was the antithesis of my students: a five-foot-five dynamo, scornful of his compatriots and scathing of his government. At twenty-six, he was one of the younger teachers at the International Communications department. He had graduated in Peace Studies from the University of Notre Dame in Indiana, and was a big fan of Gandhi, democracy and most radically of all for a Chinese, the Dalai Lama.

I mentioned to him that I had met and interviewed his holiness in Delhi in the days when I worked as a reporter for NDTV. Yee looked at me in admiration and began to ply me with a barrage of questions that I spent the rest of the evening answering.

A few days later a group of four students huddled around me after class. They had heard from Yee that I had met the Dalai Lama, they said. Was this true? I answered yes and asked in return what, if anything, they could tell me about him. There was some shifting of feet and finally one of the boys ventured, 'Well, he's a splittist and was very cruel to the Tibetan people.'

'Splittist' was a uniquely Chinese term meaning someone accused of trying to 'split' the nation; a separatist. It was impossible to pronounce it without a sinister, spitting sound, giving the word particular onomatopoeic depth.

I asked why if the Dalai Lama was indeed so cruel, as they thought, he had been awarded the Nobel prize for peace.

This was met with stunned silence. 'What do you mean, the Nobel peace prize,' asked the boy totally bewildered. I realized that not one of these students had a clue that the Dalai Lama was a Nobel laureate. At first they refused to believe me, insisting that I was mistaken. When research on the internet proved me correct they went quiet and never raised the topic with me again.

The difficulties of teaching news writing in a country where a one-party dictatorship exercised its powers untrammelled by the fourth estate soon became apparent. My first and most difficult task was simply to explain the concept of 'news' as we understood it in India.

In Chinese the word for propaganda, *xuan chuan*, was a neutral one. The information departments of various ministries were thus often translated as propaganda departments, without a trace of irony. When asked to write an essay on the role of the media in society, several of my students churned out pieces that began thus: 'The press is the mouthpiece of the government.' Others were full of sentences that read, 'The government should do more propaganda to educate people about the ancient connections between China and India.'

In China, the role of the press had traditionally been described as that of the *hou she*, or throat and tongue of the government. Even in contemporary China of the miracle economy, the government's legitimacy was dependent to a substantial degree upon the control of information and the suppression of those who attempted to circumvent this control.

Editors who transgressed boundaries were sacked. Investigative journalists found themselves imprisoned under a draconian state secrets act which denied them proper legal representation.

The government marshalled enormous resources trying to tame the information commons of the internet. Over 50,000 individuals spent their entire day monitoring internet traffic. Access to major news sites such as the BBC and Voice of America was blocked. Google searches for banned terms like Falun Gong or even simply 'China, Human Rights' lead to the temporary disruption of online services. Blogs, discussion forums and bulletin boards were all targeted through various measures of state control. Individuals identified for 'seditious' online activity faced detention and arrest.

During the five years I was to spend in China, little would

fundamentally change in this system. Every week the central and regional propaganda departments would continue to issue detailed orders about topics that were off limits to the editors concerned. The topics invariably included the 1989 Tiananmen massacre, the disastrous socio-political experiment of the 1966-76 Cultural Revolution period and the Falun Gong spiritual sect,[4] in addition to more recent developments considered inappropriate. These might include riots in the countryside over illegal land expropriation, unauthorized protests by laid-off workers or vicious crackdowns by the government on unofficial 'home' churches.

Nonetheless, as China continued to open up to the world, the demands of foreign investors for access to reliable information coupled with an increasingly mobile and prosperous middle class meant that some pushing of boundaries inevitably occurred.

A few Chinese-language media, particularly those dealing with economic issues, began to attempt a more investigative and critical style. Even in the official media the self-congratulatory toasts to the progress of China and sagacity of its leaders that were the standard fare when I first arrived slowly began to be tempered by gloomier messages of the need for health care reform and growing unemployment.

But this 'bad news' remained strictly selective and needed first to be endorsed by the party leadership. The most strictly enforced taboo continued to be any kind of criticism of the party itself or of any of its top leaders.

Alternately bored and annoyed by the bland platitudes that made the front page of the English-language *China Daily* newspaper, my only choice for local news, I tried during one class to explain

---

[4] The Falun Gong was a quasi-Buddhist sect which flourished in China in the mid-1990s, developing a devoted following of tens of millions within a few years. Alarmed at the emergence of a disciplined and well-organized grouping of people outside the umbrella of the Communist Party, the government came down on the sect ruthlessly, imprisoning and allegedly torturing members by the thousands.

to the students why in India 'bad news' was considered more newsworthy than 'good news'.

Taking the standard example of a plane crash I waded in. If a plane crashes it is big news, but if a plane lands safely no one gives it a second thought, I said. Bad news is often unexpected and the unexpected makes news. More important, it helps to expose the systemic deficiencies in a society, I continued. It points us to what's wrong with a particular policy or institution, so we can then try and figure out how best to fix it.

My students looked uncomfortable. It was clear they saw this lecture as a criticism aimed at China and by extension at themselves. Coming from a foreigner, this was all the more unpalatable and one of the more nationalistic students of the class, Grace, stood up, her face purple with indignation. She said that while what I was saying might well apply to 'foreign countries', I needed to understand that concepts like freedom of the press were fundamentally unsuitable to a country like China, given the 'volatile' nature of the Chinese people.

I was puzzled by this assertion and asked her to elaborate. The Chinese people, she went on, would get depressed and unproductive if they were constantly confronted with bad news. As a result the economy would suffer and then where would China be? China needed a continuous diet of morale boosters rather than disheartening, bad news if it were to continue to grow rich, Grace concluded emphatically before sitting down.

Over the course of the year my disappointment at the students' lack of activism faded. After all, political apathy was hardly unique to Chinese youth. More crucially, I realized that it was I who had been asking the wrong questions. The students were certainly apolitical, but given China's recent history this should hardly have come as a surprise.

For thirty years of Maoist rule Chinese society had been torn apart by ideology-driven revolution. Millions had died in famine and tens of thousands of others suffered acute deprivation.

Intellectuals had been jailed, the well-to-do ridiculed and exiled to hard labour in the countryside. Children were encouraged to denounce their parents and families were forcibly separated. The individual was relentlessly suppressed and subordinated to Ideology.

For my students the ability to be apolitical was thus a privilege. They were focussed on their careers rather than making the world a better place, but China had just emerged from decades of an attempt to do precisely that and the hubris this entailed was a painful presence in the psyche of the nation.

Also, the students were plentifully rebellious in other ways. They chafed against the strict rules on campus, rules that had originated in an earlier time and were out of sync with the new freedoms sweeping China outside the sheltered world of the college. They complained about their lack of choice in determining what courses to study or where to live. They derided their old-fashioned teachers as brain-dead and claimed their classes were useless in preparing them for their future as TV stars.

Compulsory classes in Marxist thought, which to be fair the teachers dreaded as much as the students, drew their particular ire. They wanted practical knowledge and scorned the traditional Confucian emphasis on theory and rote-learning.

At the time I began to teach at the BBI, it was still against the rules for students to be romantically involved with each other. This was by far the most ignored rule on campus.

Every evening from my sitting room I could see the silhouetted shapes of couples in different corners of the sports field—which had finally been opened up to use—hungrily leaning towards each other. The students may not have been interested in standing up for their political rights but some of that defiance of authority I was looking for was on regular display on the sports field. The driver of China's new Cultural Revolution was quite clearly sexual rather than ideological fervour.

Outside of the campus several hundred sex shops had sprung up all over Beijing. A few years later, while researching a story on changing attitudes to sex, I would visit one of these, rather coyly called 'The Adam and Eve Health Center'. This was the Chinese capital's very first sex shop and had opened its doors as far back as 1993. Wu Ling, the store manager, recalled how when the shop first opened weeks went by without any customers at all.

The few brave souls who did enter were skittish, she said, often running out of the store in embarrassment after a few seconds. A decade later, when I visited, the shop was thronging with clients, openly handling the toys that ranged from plastic vibrating vaginas to S&M gear. Over 70 per cent of the world's sex toys were being manufactured in China by that time with some 10,000 Chinese companies estimated to be involved in the industry.[5]

Sex expos began to be held next door to the more conventional auto expos and condom ads began to be shown on television for the first time. In late 2003, the Chinese authorities formally rescinded a law that required couples to seek permission from their work units before getting married and a while later students were allowed to get married while still in college. But all that was still in the future.

Over time my relationship with the students grew closer. I was only a few years older than them and I think my being Indian helped. I was a foreigner but not of the evil imperialist variety, while at the same time even though I was Indian, I had enough western exposure to lend me an air of glamour. I was thus able to appeal to the schizophrenia of Chinese youngsters who loved nothing more than to spew venom on American foreign policy and its presumed hegemonic intent, while simultaneously gulping down Big Macs and fretting about admission to US universities.

In addition, the students gradually came to see me as a defender of their interests in the face of an unsympathetic and corrupt college officialdom.

[5]Jonathan Watts, 'Sex Is China's Latest Boom Industry', *Guardian*, 25 June 2005; 'Adult Sex Toy Expo Touches Sensitive Area', *People's Daily Online*, 8 August 2004 (htttp://english.peopledaily.com.cn/200408/08/ eng 20040808_152209.html).

My main liaison with the powers that be at the International Communications department, of which I was officially part, was an androgynous-looking woman in her mid-thirties called Dong Li, painful in her sweaty earnestness and awesome in her incompetence. It was clear she hated our weekly meetings, being little more than a puppet in the hands of the higher ups in the department who used her as the main vehicle through which to convey bad news. 'No, we can't buy more books for the students,' she would announce shiftily, her body language oozing misery. 'No money,' was her standard answer to even the most modest of requests. No money for books or computers or foreign teachers' salaries. There was, however, enough money for the department to buy several sleek black Audis, complete with power steering.

'Try and understand,' Dong Li would plead. 'This is the Chinese way.' Corruption was, of course, not unique to China and its universities, but the form it took was particular.

The average teacher at the BBI earned at most 3000 yuan ($375) a month. Teachers were in addition provided simple accommodation and plain food at subsidized rates, a throwback to the times when the *danwei* took care of all the basic needs of employees. Services were paid for largely in kind and the cash fee was thus nominal.

But outside the walls of the college, times had changed. The teachers had friends who were living *la dolce vita,* a life of Chivas and green tea cocktails. China's economic reforms had opened up a world of possibilities for those dynamic, opportunistic or simply well connected enough to take advantage.

One teacher spoke in awe of a friend's boyfriend so wealthy that he had decided to banish the chore of laundry from his life altogether, preferring to buy new clothes daily rather than having them washed. Others had relatives who paid $200 a pop for their children's golf lessons.

Money was everywhere in China, or so it seemed to these teachers, tantalizingly close and yet far away enough to be out of reach. Their opportunity to steal a taste of this extravagant new way of life finally came when in a bid to raise the mainland's global prestige, the Chinese government decided to inject massive resources into select universities. The aim of this scheme, called the 211 project, was to develop one hundred world-class educational institutions in China, transforming the country into an international knowledge hub.

The BBI was selected as one of these key one hundred universities and for the first time in its fifty-odd years long history the college was flush with funds. But money intended for cutting-edge research centres and high-tech labs was funnelled instead into lavish banquets for staff and sexy cars for their departments. Unsurprisingly, China's dreams of emerging as an educational superpower remained unrealized.

I would often surface from my sessions with the unfortunate Dong Li worn out by the futility of the proceedings. Sensing I needed cheering up, the students would send me supportive text messages on my mobile phone. 'Smile, Pallavi. Dong Li is a fat hippopotamus,' read one gem.

On the whole I was closer to the girl students, who enjoyed gossiping about the latest fashions with me. They plied me with questions about bindis and sarees. Gina, a thin-lipped young woman who believed flattery rather than hard work to be the key to academic success, spent much energy on composing elaborate compliments to me. Unfortunately for all concerned, they often backfired.

'Oh, Pallavi, you are so beautiful. Even though you are a little black, we are so lucky to have a teacher with such big eyes,' she would coo.

The common fixation with large eyes amongst my students was disturbing. A cosmetic surgery procedure called 'double-eyelid surgery', which added a crease above the eyes, giving them a rounder look, was almost as common on campus as using mascara. At least three students I knew had their eyes done during the year

I taught them. They were upfront about their reasons: as aspiring TV anchors they needed to be pretty and being pretty in China meant large eyes.

The Chinese media were filled with articles about women from small towns spending all their savings on as many as twenty or thirty nips and tucks. I was repeatedly surprised at the matter-of-fact tone of these reports. There was rarely any discussion of the ethics of this phenomenon, just an objective re-telling in a standardized format. 'So and so was ugly and could not find a job. Her parents and relatives clubbed together to buy her a new face. Now she says she is much more confident of her future.'

This obsession with plastic surgery was all the more striking given that only a few years earlier even wearing make-up used to be condemned in China as a bourgeois practice and beauty pageants were banned as spiritual pollution.

A year after I left the BBI, Yang Yuan, an 18-year-old 'artificial beauty', hogged national headlines for a week when having spent $13,253 on cosmetic operations to win lucrative beauty pageants she was barred from the Miss International Beauty Contest because she had been scalpel-enhanced. She sued the contest organizer on charges of discrimination and lost.

To add a twist to the already bizarre tale, an event management company then stepped forward and proposed organizing the world's first beauty pageant exclusively for women who had undergone cosmetic surgery. The only entry requirement for this Miss Plastic Surgery contest was proof of inauthenticity.

In twenty-first century China authenticity wasn't a word much in fashion. This was a society of red capitalists; of smoke and mirrors. Hypocrisy was elevated to state policy and the face you showed was rarely the face you had. Rich pickings for plastic surgeons.

CHAPTER TWO

Olympian Makeover

The BBI didn't yet have a subway connection, but its seclusion from the feverish activity of central Beijing was already on the wane. A few months before I began teaching at the college an expressway opened connecting the campus directly to what was called the CBD or central business district—the capitalist core of the communist capital.

Here Julio lived in a multi-coloured Lego-like cluster of high-rise apartment buildings called SOHO. This was among the first of what would become a tsunami of glinting high-rises, washing over the CBD and leaving behind the debris of assorted aspirations. In time SOHO would be joined by Park Avenue and Windsor Palace; Central Park would rub shoulders with MOMA and Merlin Champagne Town would compete for clients with Upper East Side.

Prestige oozed from the concrete pores of these monuments to success. Billboards advertising their spacious interiors urged potential homeowners to waste no time in moving in, thereby being able to 'monopolize the CBD and conquer the world'.

But in early 2003, SOHO was largely unrivalled; the upstart Park Avenues of the future were still little more than mounds of dirt, the hapless prey of giant earth-moving machines.

Julio's apartment was one of the more modest in the building; a 90-square-metre, two-bedroom affair, minimally furnished but outfitted with all the standard mod-cons—washing machine, microwave and air conditioners. He rented it for about $1000, double my salary at the BBI.

When I told my students where he lived, they squealed with excitement and begged to be allowed to visit at some point.

Back then Beijing's cityscape was still dominated by the proletarian cement block structures that were the legacy of the Maoist heyday. The uniformity and featurelessness of these drab dwellings prioritized egalitarianism and pragmatism over beauty or individuality. Homes were typically assigned to families by their work units and individuals had little choice over where to live. Thus, for example, all the employees of number five steel factory or number nine car part assembly unit would live together in one large, crumbling compound.

Private property developers only got the green light from the government in the early 1990s, and mortgages, even later.

SOHO was one of the first privately developed 'modern' apartment blocks to appear in Beijing and its ready-to-move-in flats with equipped kitchens, painted walls and bathroom fixtures were unimaginable luxury for people used to the dingy utilitarianism of socialist-era housing.

It was pretty luxurious for me too. SOHO boasted its own clubhouse complete with swimming pool and gymnasium where classes in step aerobics and belly dancing were available every afternoon. At the foot of the compound, a grocery store, stocked with every conceivable imported product from French wine to Swiss cheese, delivered to the apartment 24 hours a day. Next to the store were drycleaners, flower shops, beauty salons and an array of fine restaurants.

A few years on similar sights could be found in the Delhi and Gurgaon of double-digit growth. But in the Delhi I had grown up in, the height of luxury had been a weekend-afternoon ice cream, in a cone, at India Gate.

What was most striking to me, however, wasn't just the existence of an upmarket apartment complex but rather the sterile environs of the compound's surroundings.

In Delhi, even the one of my childhood, oases of air-conditioned, bungalowed privilege had always existed. But the squalour of slums encircled these perfumed enclaves, and despite the valiant attempts of high gates and security guards, penetrated it, in the form of ragged beggars, scavenging stray dogs and the occasional madman with vacant hollows for eyes, driven past sanity by the simple reality of being poor and Indian.

In contrast it wasn't just the interiors of Beijing's plush buildings that gave off the sharp, clean scent of prosperity but the sanitized exteriors as well. China had 1.3 billion people, millions of whom still earned only a dollar or two a day. Yet, nowhere could I find the slums and shanties of Indian cities, the suppurating sores of leprous beggars, the non-stop aural assault of horns, unoiled brakes and sputtering engines as rickshaws, scooters, lorries, tempos, buses and cars bumped and scratched into each other along the scarred roads.

Few signs, in short, of a seething third-world megalopolis on the move.

There were the obviously less wealthy; people with lined faces and cracked teeth, ill-fitting suits and scabby shoes. But I saw no real poverty of the kind that numbs the heart and slams the gut.

In part the reason for this was simple: China was a richer country, its per capita GDP was more than double that of India's, a fact that would remain unchanged throughout my stay.

There was, too, another, less benign reason for the glitter of China's big cities: a Soviet-style internal passport, called the *hukou*. Explicitly designed to restrict the mobility of citizens, the *hukou* ensured that larger cities remained cosseted from the armies of peasants for whom the road to the city represented a road out of poverty.

Since the 1960s Chinese citizens were eligible to receive social services such as education and health care only in the locality they had a *hukou* for. As a result rural migrants who moved to cities lacked access to any of these welfare services, had problems finding housing and were left wide open to exploitation by their employers.[1]

In practice, the efficacy of the *hukou* system in controlling internal migration had been fading away ever since China started economic liberalization. By the time I moved to China, between 150 and 200 million peasants were already estimated.to have left the countryside to work in the cities, supplying the manpower for the thriving factories along China's coast.[2]

Economic reforms and the compulsions of the market meant that the Chinese authorities had to balance competing desires for

---

[1]The *hukou* alone, of course, could not explain the differential migration pressures on Indian and Chinese cities. Migrant workers in India had no access to welfare services either, yet they washed up in the cities in ceaseless floods. An additional reason was the freedom to subsist on the footpath or illegal colonies for migrants in India while they looked for work. Cops could be paid off, local politicians for whom the poor represented a significant 'vote bank' turned a blind eye to illegal encroachment on city land and mafia lords could be counted on to offer a measure of protection. By contrast in China the question of vote banks did not arise and migrants to cities needed to prove they were gainfully employed and apply for temporary residence papers or else face forcible relocation back to their hometowns (at least until 2003). Further, would-be migrants in China enjoyed a far greater choice of locations to move to in search of work than their counterparts in India. Apart from the premier cities of Beijing, Shanghai, Guangzhou and so on scores of second- and even third-tier cities promised significant economic opportunities so that the pressure on the handful of showcase cities was relatively less than on Mumbai, Delhi or Chennai. According to the 2001 census of India, the number of Indian cities with a million-plus population was thirty-five. In contrast 105 Chinese cities had a population of a million or over in 2003, according to the National Statistics Bureau of China.

[2]The World Bank estimates that between 1990 and 1998 migration of workers from rural to urban areas added 2.1 per cent to China's growth rate. See Will Hutton, *The Writing on the Wall: China and the West in the New Century*, Little, Brown, 2006, p. 157.

maintaining and reforming the *hukou* system. On the one hand China's economic growth was predicated on a mobile labour force, but on the other hand the government was keen to ensure that the urban infrastructure wasn't overwhelmed.[3]

In fact when Chinese experts discussed the possibility of modifying the *hukou* system, India and her sagging cities were often pointed to as dystopian visions of what might happen in China were uncontrolled migration allowed. Pictures of Delhi's open sewers and pavement dwellers were broadcast on television while the anchor in the studio asked with a dramatic flourish whether that was what the Chinese wanted their capital to look like. It was, of course, a rhetorical question.

By the beginning of the new century, the *hukou* requirement was no longer much heeded in second-tier cities as the country began to experience the most rapid urbanization the world had ever seen. But, in the bigger showcase cities like Beijing, the rules continued to be stringent. Migrants were usually only allowed to live in demarcated parts of town and to work in specified occupations that tended to be dangerous or dirty.

During my first year in China any person found without proper residence documents could still be summarily arrested and forcibly returned to their place of *hukou* registration under an administrative regulation called 'Measures for Internment and Deportation of Urban Vagrants and Beggars'.

This law, first issued in 1982, was only abolished after an

---

[3]Since economic liberalization the *hukou* had been used by the government to guide labour to certain places and in certain sectors where it was needed most. To begin with, it was only third-tier cities that were opened up to migrant workers, gradually followed by second-tier and finally premier cities. For more see Tom Miller, *Hukou Reform: One Step Forward*, China *Economic Quarterly*, Quarter 3, 2005. For a novel comparison of caste and *hukou* as regulators of labour mobility see Arvinder Singh, 'Labour Mobility in China and India: The Role of Hukou, Caste and Community', in *China and India: Learning from Each Other, Reforms and Policies for Sustained Growth*, IMF, September 2006.

incident in 2003, in which a young college-educated graphic designer, Sun Zhigang, was beaten to death in police custody after being detained for not carrying any residency documents on him. Sun was the employee of a garment company in Guangzhou city but was a native of Wuhan, the capital of Hubei province. He thus lacked a Guangzhou residence permit, a fact that was to cost him his life.

Over the next few years the *hukou* system was incrementally relaxed. But while migrants were increasingly allowed into the cities to work, efforts were made to ensure that they did not spoil the beauty of these metropolises by displaying their malodorous selves too prominently in areas outside of construction sites and other migrant-appropriate spaces.

One Saturday afternoon I was shopping with Cindy, the same student who had inquired tenderly into my KFC-McDonald's preferences, for winter clothes. She was chattering away about wanting to become a sports journalist having been inspired by Beijing's successful bid for the Olympics when rough hands reached out and grabbed my shirt, yanking me sideways.

'Money, money, money. Give me money,' moaned the woman who had grabbed me, in English. Her face was a scar of burnt flesh; her mouth little more than a cavity, puncturing the hideously blistered folds of what was left of her face.

I pulled away and began to search for loose change in my bag, when pretty, petite 20-year-old Cindy slipped off her handbag and started hitting the beggar on the arm, screaming at her to go away and stop bothering 'the foreigner'.

The woman hobbled back and Cindy tugged me in the opposite direction. 'I feel so ashamed that you had to see that,' she said.

Ashamed that I had to 'see' that, rather than ashamed that 'that' existed. My instinctive reaction was to wonder at this shame associated with the witnessing of poverty. In India we simply accepted it as part of life. Our eyes glazed over when maimed beggars tapped desperately on our car windows while we waited at traffic lights in leather-upholstered comfort, but rather than despise them we simply desensitized ourselves to their plight.

Yet, the more I thought about it, perhaps we in India were not so different. I remembered one middle-class acquaintance from Mumbai telling me that the only problem with the city was its slums, so that if you got rid of the slums and their poor inhabitants, all of Mumbai's problems would disappear too—simple.

Communist China had in fact only created what many well-heeled Indians dreamed of: cities where they could move about in large cars on smooth expressways, free of the odours of poverty. Cities where they could live in SOHO and stroll down to their local coffee shop for afternoon snacks of Brie and toast without having to negotiate migrants and vagrants from the countryside, sprawled at their feet, littering, spitting and begging. Cities where an urban elite could be an urban elite, showing off their sparkling environs to foreigners with pride.

Julio's apartment was located just outside the city's third ring road and marked the easternmost edge of the CBD. Further east and you were in the semi-rural surroundings of the BBI. But immediately to the west, the China World Trade Centre, where the investment company that Julio worked for had its offices, loomed over a mesh of elevated roads and freeways. The transition from neglected patches of brown open fields to the über-modern world of international finance was dramatic.

The SOHO apartments stood sandwiched between these two worlds, as did I. During the day my life followed the rhythms of the strictly regimented campus—the bells, the classes, the announcements broadcast across campus on loudspeakers and the long queues for lunch at the university canteen. But most evenings I would head over to SOHO and its creature comforts.

On weekends, I explored the city. Beijing, a word that literally means northern capital, has a history that embraces a motley clutch of characters including communists, Manchus and Mongols. In its tree-lined streets warlords and khans; merchants and scholars; poets and revolutionaries have walked and lived. It was the nerve centre of one of the greatest civilizations of the world for the majority of the last nine hundred years.

Week after week I wandered in search of this history, willing the city to whisper stories of its past into my eager ears. The natural first stop on any such quest was the Forbidden City, thus called because for the five hundred years that it was home to the Ming and Qing emperors, it had been off-limits to commoners.

Today, it was no longer forbidden, but for those without money it might as well have been. It cost 60 yuan, around $8, for an entrance ticket to the palace, a uniform price for locals and foreigners. In India, the entrance fee to the Taj Mahal, the most expensive in the country for a historical monument, was Rs. 20 or less than half a dollar for Indian citizens. That foreigners were charged 750 rupees for entry to the same monument was a fact I had always found discriminatory. But here in China, the government discriminated against its own people. Eight dollars was no longer out of reach for many urban Chinese, but for the country's eight hundred million peasants, the entrance fee would have been prohibitive, excluding many from the symbolic centre of their own nation.

The empty vastness of the palace and its succession of windswept courtyards were a metaphor for both the size of the empire that the rulers of the Forbidden City once reigned over as well as for the boundless power they wielded.

Opposite the southern entrance of the palace stood Tiananmen Square, menacing in its associations, imposing in its size. The ability of large unfilled space to project power and dwarf an individual into insignificance, powerless in the face of Authority, was a lesson China's communist rulers appeared to have learnt well from the country's former emperors.

Communist Tiananmen Square and the Imperial Forbidden City presented an unlikely symmetry, but perhaps not to those who saw contemporary China as merely another avatar of the erstwhile empire, ruled by autocratic emperors in suits rather than robes. Only a section of the Forbidden City was open to the public. A much larger part remained more forbidden than ever. Patrolled by armed guards and encircled by thick, high walls the entire western part of the former imperial palace had been appropriated as the headquarters of the Communist Party into a compound called Zhongnanhai.

Zhongnanhai was impenetrable, opaque. The top party leadership lived and worked here but no commoner was allowed inside. I was certainly struck by how much was changing but sometimes also by how much hadn't changed at all.

From the Forbidden City–Zhongnanhai nucleus of political power, the rest of the capital radiated out in all directions. My first impressions of this wider Beijing were that of a city in the throes of an identity crisis. Massive high-rises were springing up everywhere I looked, but many had a shell-like quality to them, the windowless exteriors resembling hollow skulls with missing teeth and sockets for eyes.

Huge swathes of the ancient capital were being torn down, razed to the ground to make way for a slew of mega construction projects. A platoon of international architectural celebrities had been hired to create what the authorities touted would be a new avant garde Beijing to be unveiled to the world on millions of TV screens broadcasting the 2008 Olympic Games.

The airport, which to my eyes (used as they were to the mouldy environs of Delhi's Indira Gandhi International Airport), was already impossibly modern and sophisticated, was undergoing a further upgradation and expansion. A new terminal designed by British architect Norman Foster was scheduled for completion in time for the Games. When open, it would make Beijing's airport the largest in the world. And the two-billion-dollar expansion was only one of dozens of prestigious projects associated with the Games.

An opera house, a lavish confection of titanium and glass

floating on an artificial lake, designed by French architect Paul Andreu, was being built just to the west of Tiananmen Square. Further north-east, a several-hundred-million-dollar, seventy-floor TV tower began to go up in a gravity-defying 'Z' shape, designed by Dutch superstar architect Rem Koolhaas.

China's official news agency Xinhua reported that in total Beijing would develop some 25 million square metres of property between 2002 and 2008. Hundreds of thousands of city households would be forced to relocate in the same period, their homes demolished to make way for expensive new developments.

A few years later, in 2005, I would visit the newly opened urban planning museum, a swish building in black marble. On its top floor was a gargantuan model of Beijing's intended future look. Apart from the Forbidden City and Tiananmen Square itself, virtually no traces of the city's long past remained. The model showed an entirely new concrete-and-chrome creature with the skyscraper-filled CBD as its glistening heart.

Beijing was no newcomer to change. The communists, as the emperors before them, did much to alter the face of the city and to reshape it in their own image. In the early 1950s the capital's city walls were torn down and blocks of buildings were reduced to rubble to widen avenues and make way for the grim, grey Stalinesque structures so beloved of the architects of the time.

But with the help of modern construction equipment the pace of the current transformation was unbeatable as was its reach, as it pushed into every nook and cranny, bulldozing its way into even Mongol-period enclaves that had so far miraculously remained intact.

'New Beijing, New Olympics' was the motto under which this frenetic building was being undertaken; a motto splashed across the hoardings and banners that festooned the city's neighbourhoods.

It had been only a year since Beijing won the bid to host the Olympics when I arrived in China and it was all anyone seemed able to talk about. Beijing's physical transformation had already begun in the 1990s, but the Games gave it a new purpose and dynamism. The whole city seemed to be on Olympic time, with giant clocks counting down the minutes to the event going up on every street corner.

Weekend music concerts with Olympic themes were a common feature as were more general Olympic cultural festivals. Olympic merchandise flooded shops and high schools held regular Games-related quiz competitions that were televised.

China had lost a previous bid for the Olympics after concerns about its human rights record were voiced and the opportunity to host the 2008 Games was seen as a chance to pull off the public relations coup of the century. It was planned as a grand coming-out party with Beijing as the debutante belle of the ball. It seemed only natural that she would require a brand new set of clothes for the occasion.

Rarely a day went by without an Olympics-related article in the local media. Most often a series of city leaders indistinguishable in their dark suits and large glasses would urge Beijingers to reflect on the importance of the Games for China's image and international standing. One of my favourite exhortations came from Wang Qishan, who was Beijing's Mayor from 2003 onwards. 'We have to have a good Olympics, otherwise not only will our generation lose face, but also our ancestors,' he warned.[4]

The blade-runner-like futuristic cityscape that I saw on display at the urban planning museum remained incomplete during my China-life. The Beijing I lived in was more a work-in-progress, with a continually half-complete feel. Its architectural mishmash of styles lent it an atonal, jarring look. Concrete warehouses peeled in the shadow of zooming skyscrapers; a few unyielding courtyard homes crushed up against bathroom-tiled office-spaces. Bauhaus, baroque and bathroom all jostled together uneasily and the only

---

[4]Xie Chuanjiao, 'The Game Is on Everyone's Lips', *China Daily*, 29 January 2007.

unity the city had was the ubiquity of bulldozers and cranes skewering the haze of construction-site dust. That and the omnipresent Chinese character 拆, pronounced *chai* and meaning demolish.

Chai was probably the very first Chinese character I learnt, so many times a day did I see it painted in big red or white strokes on the walls and doors of the buildings and homes I passed by. Any structure with the character painted on it was doomed. Its presence signified a place on death row and all of Beijing was filled with these marked buildings; less a city and more an execution ground, or so it seemed sometimes.

This imparted a ceaseless impermanence to life in Beijing which made it harder than normal for a foreigner like me to tame the city into familiarity. No sooner had I located a secret little dumpling shop, tucked away in an alley off the beaten path, than the ominous *chai* character would appear on its door and it would be gone forever, sometimes within days.

By the time I left China almost none of the haunts I frequented in my first year in Beijing remained: flower shops, clothing boutiques, restaurants and libraries, all disappeared one by one. It got to the point that I felt a little thrill of relief when I returned to a favourite spot and simply saw that it was still standing.

My students were more equanimous in the face of this flux. I got them to write essays debating whether such dramatic change was desirable. The responses would have made the Buddha proud. Change is in the very nature of being, permanence only an illusion, the majority of them argued, perhaps not quite as philosophically as that but implying as much.

A few questioned Beijing's facelift on aesthetic grounds, saying that the new buildings were 'ugly' and the city that was taking shape lacked 'logic'. But they didn't seem to feel the kind of giddy disorientation I did, living in an environment where nowhere could be taken for granted. The city was changing so rapidly that the municipal authorities resorted to issuing new maps of Beijing every three months.

I was convinced that transformations on this scale must have a serious psychological effect on the people living through them. Only a newcomer, I already found it hard to navigate Beijing's constantly morphing boundaries. For people who had grown up here and whose memories permeated the streets and neighbourhoods now wantonly being torn down, the adjustment, I assumed, must be immeasurably harder.

Yet they seemed to accept their altered circumstances with a quiet grace. Groups of women would appear waving brilliant magenta-feathered fans and pirouette weekend afternoons away on wasted ground, framed by hills of rubble and scaffolding. The area might have been a public park in times past or a willow-lined neighbourhood square, where these women would gather to practise their fan dance. Undeterred by the fact that it was now a construction site, they simply continued with their routine.

Beijing was a surrealist's paradise. Old, bent men in Mao suits taking their caged songbirds for a walk along an expressway; a group of elderly women practising t'ai chi surrounded by bulldozers. These were common sights as I explored the city. The clash of the past and present was certainly highlighted by these juxtapositions, but what struck me most was the fluidity with which the Beijingers I observed negotiated this tension; the lack of visible trauma or resistance.

I was aware, of course, that 'unauthorized' strikes and protests in China were off the cards and that dharnas and hunger strikes, almost banal in their ubiquity back home, were anathema to China's ruling elite.

But the ability of Beijing residents to absorb change wasn't simply a matter of organized protest being outlawed. Change and China had more or less been synonymous for a hundred years by now. The long static, isolationist history of the Chinese empire had in the twentieth century been rent asunder by civil war, revolution, ideology and industrialization. Transformations that in other countries took centuries to accomplish had been telescoped into a few decades in China.[5]

The communists had preached a smashing of the past, a slashing of the umbilical cord of tradition, which they equated with feudalism and imperialism. Religion was condemned as superstition, high culture and art as decadence. It was small wonder that people took this latest turn of events with such composure; it was a serenity borne of practice.

How different, I thought, to India, with its caste-bound, hidebound conventions and temples where priests practised rituals scarcely changed by the millennia. To revolutionless, feudal India, where dalits manually cleared sewage and parents arranged marriages.

India's transition from colonial rule to independence had been overseen by an elite of urban professionals and middle-level landowners so that the country had never experienced the kind of wrenching revolution that propelled China into a modernity that continued to elude India.

Given the hype surrounding the twenty-first century India of malls and metros, reflecting on the country's unchanging nature felt counter-intuitive at first, but when confronted with the reality of twenty-first century China, I could hardly do otherwise.

One Sunday morning Julio and I strolled down the condemned alleyways of a neighbourhood called Qianmen, just south of Tiananmen Square. This was the erstwhile business and entertainment centre of imperial China. The doorways of the shabby, unrenovated homes were liberally painted with the *chai* character.

We often took walks in areas we knew were slated for demolition, trying to imprint their flavour on our minds for posterity. While passing a group of gossiping locals, sipping tea and playing cards at the entrance to one of the old houses, we stopped in our tracks having spotted a pair of impossibly tiny, lotus-shaped

---

[5]For a succinct summary of the communist period, see Jonathan Spence, *The Search for Modern China,* W.W. Norton & Company, 1999, section IV onwards.

feet—the tell-tale sign of a very old woman, old enough to have bound feet, a practice that had been banned for almost a hundred years.

The card players noticed our interest and invited us to join in for a chat. Someone produced a low metal stool; another made space on a torn sofa so I could squeeze in. The old lady was more than willing to show off her feet and seemed pleased at the attention.

Her tongue was thick in her toothless mouth, making it difficult for me to understand what she said, but one of her neighbours helped interpret. The woman, simply called Lao Tai Tai or 'Old Mrs', was over ninety years old. The bones in her feet had been repeatedly broken and bent to achieve the desired size starting when she was about ten. Yes, it had hurt, she said, smiling gummily, a lot. But in those days things were different and you accepted pain as an inextricable part of life.

Lao Tai Tai had moved to Beijing from a village in Shandong province in the years before the communist accession in 1949. In her own lifetime she had seen imperial China change to Red and communist China give way to the multicoloured shopfronts of couture stores.

As the morning turned to noon the sun came out from behind grey clouds, brightening up the winding lanes of the Qianmen neighbourhood that Julio and I sat chatting with Lao Tai Tai in. The old lady turned her wrinkled face up towards the warmth. She said she missed her children—four boys, the oldest of whom was seventy. They had all moved away from the neighbourhood to smarter addresses. On occasion one of them came by to visit her bringing some money, but mostly it was her neighbours who looked after her.

I wondered what would happen to her after the area was demolished and the neighbours forced to scatter and relocate. Instead I asked if she could describe some of the most significant changes she had seen in the neighbourhood over the seventy-odd years she had spent there. 'Changes?' she queried, as though confused by the question. Then mumbled, '*Everything* has changed.'

Her neighbour, our ad hoc interpreter, was embarrassed by her refusal to supply more detail and told us Lao Tai Tai's memory wasn't quite what it used to be.

Conversation with Lao Tai Tai or virtually anyone else in Beijing was made possible only by months of hard battle with Mandarin. As my first encounter with the receptionists at the BBI had portended, English simply wasn't going to help me cut it in Beijing.

It was a miserable, powerless feeling being unable to walk into a shop and ask for a bar of chocolate, or read the menu in a restaurant or ask for help when confused.

Even daily routines I felt I had mastered held undiscovered terrors. I had regularly been taking bus 928 from SOHO to the BBI for over a month without a hitch when one day I boarded the bus as usual only to discover it zooming past the university and entering the expressway that led straight out of the city into Hebei province.

I asked around frantically if anyone spoke English but my query was met with silent bemusement. I was unable to ascertain why we hadn't stopped at the BBI, where we were going or whether we would ever stop, the bus seemingly speeding on forever as we left the college further and further behind. The bus did eventually stop and I took a cab back to the BBI. The fare was steep and I was woefully late for class but most of all I felt shook up by how helpless I had been, disempowered by my lack of Chinese, literally without a voice.

It transpired that bus 928 had two route services: the standard one that I usually took and an express one that went directly, with no stops, to the city's outskirts. The latter was marked by a special character clearly visible at the front of the bus, but being illiterate it had held no meaning for me.

During my first few months in the city I managed to get around primarily by asking Julio to write down useful phrases and the names of places I needed to go to. Body language also helped, although it was less reliable. I remember asking one taxi driver to take me to the 'airport'. When the word elicited only a puzzled scratching of the head, I held my arms out wide, raising them up and down gently in imitation of a plane taking off. He seemed to understand and he motioned me to take a seat. A few minutes later he pulled up in front of a KFC and with a victorious flourish turned around and flapped his arms back at me.

Unwilling to have my planes confused with chickens any longer, I joined evening classes at a private Chinese language school and along with an English accountant and a German travel agent began the long slog of studying a new language.

The two major differences between learning Chinese and most other languages were its tones and characters. Mandarin lacked an alphabet and used instead more than 4000 characters or ideograms. Compared to the twenty-six letters of the English alphabet Chinese characters were an ocean of plurality, but when it came to actual sounds the range of the language was one of the narrowest in the world.

It was a phonetically poor language resulting in an abundance of homonyms distinguishable only by their tones, of which there were four in Mandarin. The first tone was a high flat one, distinct from the harsh downward bark of the fourth tone which in turn varied from the rising upward question-like inflection of the second tone. The third, and what was for many the toughest tone, required first a drop and then a rise, a seamless combination of a fourth and second tone.

The potential for confusion was infinite. *Mai* could mean either 'buy' or 'sell' depending on the tone; *nar* meant 'there' in the fourth tone and 'where' in the third; while *yan jing* in the combination of third and second tone meant 'eyes' but in third and fourth meant 'spectacles'. Gloomily I thought of all the professions

I could never be successful in in China: stockbroker, real estate agent and optometrist.

To make matters more complicated, what I learnt in class was a manicured standardized version of the language, distinct from the Beijing dialect common on the streets. The dialect, called *Beijinghua*, consisted largely of an added, growling 'rrr' sound to the end of every word which made it even harder to distinguish the words.[6] For months conversations between two Beijingers sounded to me pretty much like this:

Beijinger # 1: 'Errr, merr, rrrrrr?'
Beijinger # 2: Khrrrrr!

Gradually I began to make progress and slowly simple conversations in Chinese became possible. The people I chatted most often with were the city's taxi drivers, a chain-smoking group of sage commentators on everything from international affairs to sports.

Their first question on picking up a foreigner was invariably to ask which country said foreigner hailed from. I was to discover a remarkably standardized set of stereotypes that answers to the question elicited. If you were Spanish, as was Julio, cabbies would wax eloquent about the wonders of bullfighting and Spanish football. If you were German they would praise German technology and cars. On occasion, however, there was a sinister twist to this set script. A German friend recalled in embarrassment how when he revealed his nationality to one driver, the cabbie ignored mention of technology and instead flashed him a thumbs up sign while approvingly muttering, 'Hitler! Strong Leader!'

The fact of my being Indian was most often met with an outburst of song. '*Abala Gu*' sang fat drivers and skinny ones, tall

---

[6]The common perception outside of China of the inability of the Chinese to pronounce the 'r' sound applied only to southerners. Up north in Beijing, people rolled their 'r's with felicity.

drivers and stocky ones, as we drove past tea houses and shopping malls, office blocks and grocery stores.

I had heard back in India of Raj Kapoor's fame in the former Soviet Union and my brother had told me of his having picked up the *Awara Hun* riff even on the streets of Lima in faraway Peru. Nonetheless, the ubiquity of the song's popularity in Beijing, was unexpected to me, as was the fact that Hindi films were the primary association that the average Chinese seemed to have with India.

I found that China's love affair with Indian movies went back to the 1950s. This was a love that was deepened in the late 1970s, when Hindi films were amongst the first foreign movies to be shown in Chinese theatres post the Cultural Revolution, their socialist themes having been deemed suitable.[7]

Other than *Awara* and *Do Bigha Zameen,* the 1971 Jeetendra-Asha Parekh starrer *Caravan* had become a smash hit in the early 1980s, playing to house-full theatres in Beijing for years. For an entire generation of Chinese it was this movie that became the main vehicle for information about India.

I was hampered in ascertaining these facts by Mandarin's propensity to alter all foreign proper nouns beyond recognition. It was difficult to figure out that when a taxi driver excitedly nattered on about *Liu Lang Zhe* he was talking about *Awara* or that the *La Zi* whose acting prowess he raved about was Raj Kapoor. I repeatedly heard references to *Da Peng Che* but it took me a long time to discover that this was the name in Chinese for *Caravan.*

The penny only fully dropped when a Chinese friend produced a black-and-white VCD copy of the movie, dubbed in Mandarin. It was a bad copy and the film was incessantly punctured by wavy lines. Sometimes the image would start wobbling just as Asha

---

[7]*Awara*, for example, is the story of a vagabond forced into a life of petty thieving who eventually proves to be more righteous than a high-born judge. The moral of the movie was that birth does not determine character, a theme that would have sat well in the China of the time.

Parekh launched into another song, dupatta trailing behind her bouffant. It reminded me a bit of watching TV in Delhi in the 1980s, when after a while the screen would start wobbling, necessitating an aerial-adjusting trip up to the roof for my father, while we shouted feedback on any improvements from down below.

The upshot of the one-time popularity of films like *Liu Lang Zhe* and *Da Peng Che* in China was that almost every Chinese person I spoke to in the forty-plus demographic asked whether it was true that all Indian women could sing and dance as was shown in the movies. The naiveté of the question surprised me, until I discovered that the Chinese have similar stereotypes about their own non-Han minority ethnic groups, whom they also seemed to conceive of as permanently frozen in mid-folk dance. This was thrown into sharp relief when I visited Tibet, but that was still several years down the line.

Other than Hindi films and their wonderful music and their beautiful actresses with their big, big eyes (the Chinese shared the Indian tendency to add emphasis by repeating a word), the one other association with India that I heard about with some regularity was less flattering. It was a response often conveyed with the slight sneer of condescension, consisting essentially of images of India as poor: bad roads, beggars, shanty towns, and power cuts. The taxi drivers who brought up these grim realities were unanimous in their conclusion: India must enforce a one-child policy.

They would point fingers at me and tell me that India simply had too many people. It was untenable and illogical not to have a one-child policy, if India ever hoped to develop. Struggling with my primitive vocabulary, I tried to talk about democracy and freedom of choice, but my talk was usually dismissed with a wave of the hand and a repetition of India had too many people, with an emphasis on the 'too'.

Apart from discussing their passenger's national traits, taxi drivers also obsessed about learning English, a task that the Olympic

Games had lent a manic urgency to. Across the city cabbies had been handed language audio cassettes by their companies and ordered to learn English or at least a hundred set sentences of it, a number it was hoped would suffice for the needs of the thousands of foreigners that would fill Beijing during the Games.

The cabbies spent large parts of their day listening to the tapes and repeating sentences like 'Good Morning, how are you today?' except that it sounded more like Gooor Morrr, howrr you todarr?' when pronounced in broad Beijing dialect—scary rather than welcoming.

The tribulations of the cabbies were only one manifestation of the much larger phenomenon of English evangelism that the Olympics had engendered across the city.

'Olympic English' classes were sprouting up in every neighbourhood. Armies of senior citizens armed with an official textbook rousingly titled *Don't Be Shy, Just Try* were enlisted to take English lessons every weekend. Regular English-speaking competitions were held in parks and English song performances televised. The Beijing Municipal Authorities announced that it was their aim to have four million of the city's fifteen million inhabitants familiar with their ABC by 2008.

I visited an Olympic English class a few years later as part of a reporting assignment. The class was being held in a neighbourhood called Dong Si, at a local primary school. It was a Saturday afternoon and the classroom was decked out in red banners that read 'Welcome foreign journalist to Dong Si civilized Olympic community'. The students were all retirees, mostly women. They were being taught by a fresh-faced college student who had volunteered her services in response to a city-wide appeal to youngsters like her to do their bit for the Olympics.

The classroom atmosphere was deadly serious as the students struggled to get their tongues in the right position to pronounce the alien words. The main goal of the class was to familiarize the students with an Olympics-friendly sporting vocabulary. 'I'm crazy about shadow-boxing,' said the young teacher from atop her platform. 'I'm crazy about shadow-boxing,' screamed back the fifty elderly pupils. The teacher then decided to break up the sentence to help focus on the pronunciation of individual words. 'I'm crazy,' she exhorted her wards to repeat. 'I'm crazy,' they shouted in reply. I began to fear going crazy myself and beat a hasty retreat.

Voluntary classes for neighbourhood senior citizens aside, English teaching was becoming serious business in China, a country that was increasingly enmeshed in global trade and culture. But English skills, or rather the lack of them, remained a stumbling block in China's projection of itself as a major global player.

A year after I arrived in Beijing the city government made it compulsory for English to be taught from grade 1 of primary school. Previously, children had only begun learning it in grade 5. All university students across the country also had to sit compulsory exams in English to gain admittance. Private English-language schools had begun to pop up across China with price tags reaching up to $2000 a month, but there was still more demand than supply.

As my own students were testament to, young, educated Chinese were already starting to speak the language with a degree of fluency.

But this only made China's continuing inability to get rid of the 'Chinglish' that afflicted the majority of the country's public signs more puzzling. The Chinese could build massive flyovers in months, kilometres of expressways in weeks, but when it came to the smallest of tasks involving labelling in English, they invariably messed up.

I was wowed one winter morning by the electric hand driers and foot-operated flushes of a newly built, obviously expensive public toilet I had wandered into at one of Beijing's busy business districts. But then I read the sign in English above the commode. 'Please remember flush after shitting or pissing,' it read.

Another time, I visited a lovely park just north of the Forbidden City. Unlike the litter-strewn equivalents in India, the park was neat and clean, a fact that had much to with the large, well-located waste receptacles that dotted the gardens at regular intervals. Closer inspection, however, caused bewilderment. The receptacles were divided into two sections, one marked 'Recyclable' and the other 'Organism'. On a nearby wall a plaque asked visitors not to 'scatter seeds of fire'.

A few weeks later I made it across to a museum in north Beijing dedicated to the cultures of China's over fifty ethnic minorities. I was greeted by a sign that welcomed me to 'Racist Park'.

Through the five years I was to live there, the Beijing authorities regularly vowed to rid the city of the scourge of Chinglish. Hotlines were set up for citizens to point out a language-related mistake on a public sign. I tried calling once but the lady who answered the phone didn't speak English, and when I tried to explain what I wanted in my beginner's Chinese, she hung up.

CHAPTER THREE

Coronavirus

The steady cadence of the days at the BBI was soothing. The mini-dramas of my weekly meetings with Dong Li apart, there was little that disrupted the ebb and flow of time on campus. The first class of the day began at eight in the morning. By this time the college radio had already been blasting morning exercise music through loudspeakers strategically placed across the campus for an hour.

The students were kept in class till lunch, which began at noon. The college mess was a massive three-floor affair, but at peak lunch time it was often impossible to find an empty spot at the long tables that cut across the rooms, surrounded by the hiss of steaming noodles and clacking of chopsticks. There were more classes in the afternoon and depending on the day of the week some time off for sports or 'self-study'.

The harsh winter in which temperatures dropped as low as fifteen below zero began to soften into spring. The wind lost its biting edge and a few leaves returned to the starved trees. I had survived my first Beijing winter, a feat I felt quietly triumphant about, but it hadn't been easy.

The coldest city I had lived in before had been Oxford where the temperature rarely fell below zero. Beijing was not only colder but also savaged by winds icy enough to peel off exposed skin from the bone. There were days I was frightened to step outdoors, a confession that caused much mirth amongst my students.

As I was to discover, the Chinese took deep pride in their resilience to cold and the idea that feeling cold at all was an illness seemed to be widespread.

One November, with the first snowfall of the winter only a week away, I remember walking home from class bundled in layers of sweaters and mufflers too numerous to enumerate when I encountered the young lad who ran the tiny grocery store adjacent to my apartment building. He sat outside in his shirtsleeves and nothing else, smoking a cigarette with stunning insouciance.

Flabbergasted, I stopped to ask if he wasn't bothered by the cold at all. 'Cold?' he spat out in disdain. 'Cold?' his tone rising higher in indignation. 'I don't feel even a little bit cold!' he concluded with a superior snigger as he turned away, indicating the end of the conversation.

I, the overclothed object of his disdain, huddled along, feeling weak and deficient, an emotion that would return every winter, when I was regularly subjected to lectures by sundry strangers on the many ways in which I could improve my immune system.

It would typically be a blistering morning, the sun barely visible as angry winds whipped and stung the eyes. Despite the two pairs of gloves I wore my fingers would be numb by the time I flagged down a taxi to take me to SOHO or wherever else I was going. I would get into the warmth of the cab with relief and once sufficiently thawed enough to be able to speak, make an innocuous remark about it being a 'bit chilly', hoping to draw a laugh with my masterful understatement.

Instead the driver would launch into a sermon that made all kinds of assumptions about the lacunae in my diet and exercise regime. The fact that it was minus ten degrees Celsius never seemed to be a good enough excuse to feel cold; the fault was always located in my assumed frailty. 'I'm not sick, I'm just Indian,' I tried protesting, but in vain.

By the time March came around and with it spring, the relief I felt was enormous, given away by the renewed sprightliness to my step as I made my way to morning classes. Even my students seemed touched by the infectious new warmth of the season, laughing more easily and raising more questions.

It was in the middle of this spring-induced contentment that I first began to come across reports of a disturbing new illness that was being described as an atypical pneumonia. There was little mention of it in *China Daily*, but the international media were soon covering the mystery virus regularly.

By late March cases had been reported in places as far-flung as Singapore and Canada but it was south China, in particular Hong Kong and Guangdong province, that were believed to be the epicentre of the disease.

The foreign newspapers I read on the Internet called this disease SARS, an acronym for severe acute respiratory syndrome. There continued to be no mention of it in the local news I read and no one on campus brought it up either, not my students, not Dong Li, nor any of the other teachers.

The lack of any sense of alarm on campus lulled me. Guangdong and Hong Kong were far away and there was no talk at all of Beijing being affected. An American colleague, Daniel, another 'foreign expert', came by one evening to discuss his worries about the virus. Did I feel safe, he asked. Of course I did, I replied sniffily, dismissing his concerns as the overblown paranoia of a westerner. As an Indian, viruses and bacteria held no special dread for me.

In my initial reactions to the news about SARS I was as naïve as the most sheltered amongst my students. This was a naiveté exacerbated by the fact that I hadn't quite yet understood the extent to which information was orchestrated in China. I knew that the media were regularly censored and that criticism of the country's top leadership or discussions of 'sensitive' issues like the Tiananmen killings of 1989 were not permitted.

But the idea that a mysterious disease could be out there, infecting thousands and killing hundreds while a quiescent media were muzzled from reporting on it by a government desperate to avoid bad news even at the expense of putting the lives of its citizens at risk seemed implausible.

As late as 3 April, China's health minister, Zhang Wenkang, gave a televised press conference assuring the world as well as me that Beijing had only a small handful of SARS cases.

It was about a week later that I finally began to wake up to the possibility that the situation in Beijing was graver than that being acknowledged, when investigative reports by foreign media began to accuse the Chinese government of a widespread cover-up of the true extent of the deadly virus in the capital.

These reports followed a letter to the media written by a nationally renowned surgeon called Jiang Yanyong, a Communist Party member and a People's Liberation Army veteran.[1] In the letter Dr Jiang claimed that health workers in military hospitals in Beijing had been ordered by their superiors to keep cases of SARS a secret and that the disease was spreading quickly across the capital, contrary to the government's reassurances.

In the days that followed, other doctors stepped up to corroborate these charges, although most chose to stay anonymous. The usually diplomatic World Health Organisation raised Dr Jiang's allegations with the Chinese authorities and asked for permission to visit Beijing's secretive military hospitals.

---

[1]See Susan Jakes, *Beijing's SARS Attack, Time Magazine* website, 8 April 2003 (http://www.time.com/time/world/article/0,8599,441615,00.html); See also *People Who Mattered 2003, Time Magazine,* Asia Edition, 29 December 2003 (http://www.time.com/time/asia/2003/poypm2003/jiang_yanyong.html).

They were at first denied, although on 16 April were finally allowed to visit a single such hospital. The WHO began to estimate that the numbers of those infected by SARS in Beijing might be as high as two hundred, although the government still insisted that the figure was closer to thirty.

Increasingly jittery, I asked my students for their thoughts on the situation. Their reactions were identical to my response to Daniel's concerns in late March. They smiled in a somewhat patronizing way at my 'foreigner's concerns', dismissing my worries as those of a lily-livered outsider always willing to believe the worst of China, much in the way I had disregarded Daniel's concerns as American paranoia.

'There's nothing to be scared of,' the portly Fat reassured me kindly. The other students concurred arguing that while there may have been a problem in Guangdong, Beijing remained entirely safe.

But I was no longer buying into that line of reasoning. I asked my class what they thought about the reports alleging a government cover-up. The students looked blank. What reports was I talking about?

I brought printouts of stories from the *New York Times*, *Time Magazine*, *Guardian*. Oh! The western media, the students smirked, you can never trust them.

There was little I could say in the face of this unwillingness to even consider that there may be more going on than officially met the eye.

By 14 April, the cumulative number of world-wide cases of SARS had surpassed 3000. Close to eight hundred cases had been reported in Guangdong and Hong Kong was in a state of crisis.[2] But even as concern about the disease around the world mounted, on campus the daily routines continued uninterrupted.

Having only recently completed a loftily titled 'Global Media

---

[2]For a detailed account of the unfolding of the SARS epidemic see Carl Taro Greenfeld, *China Syndrome: The True Story of the Twenty-First Century's First Great Epidemic*, HarperCollins, 2006.

and Communications' degree I was struck by how little difference the availability of uncensored information about SARS on the internet made to the attitudes of both students and teachers. Readings on the new media for my degree had led me to think of the Net as an almost magically emancipatory tool, empowering ordinary people in the face of oppressive authoritarian systems, by enabling them to circumvent officially controlled and imposed versions of the truth.

The Chinese government, also apparently in agreement with such thinking, spent considerable resources in attempting to tame the internet. Given increasingly sophisticated web-filtering technology and the swelling ranks of its internet police, China had achieved a certain degree of success in its aims, but this success was far from complete and information on just about any topic could be located online if the user simply persisted in her search.

Yet, despite the internet, my students blatantly ignored the 'independent' information that was out there, available freely to anyone who looked for it. I was taught a lesson in the basic truth that availability of information in and of itself achieves little, if it is not actively sought out, and my students were certainly not interested in seeking it out—yet.

And then, suddenly on 20 April, the Chinese authorities announced that Beijing had 339 confirmed cases of SARS, a number almost ten times more than the 37 cases made public until then. The Health Minister, Zhang Wenkang, and the Mayor of Beijing, Meng Xuenong, were fired. By 23 April, the official count for SARS cases had doubled again to 693.

Within the space of a few days, Beijing became another city, its traffic-clogged roads and buzzing, busy streets falling silent. Restaurants closed for business, offices made contingency arrangements for employees to work from home, hospitals were quarantined. All primary and secondary schools were suspended for a two-week period. Face masks made a ubiquitous appearance and vast stretches of the city came to resemble a surreal hospital with manic surgeons on the loose.

Rumours began to swish and swoop like malign giant birds, their flapping wings instilling fear. Scornful for so many weeks of the stories I had downloaded from the internet, the students now spent several hours a day monitoring news online. Forwarded text messages on their mobile phones became a major source of information, or misinformation, as was usually the case.

One of the more common rumours doing the rounds via mobile phones was that Beijing was about to be put under martial law, and all entry and exit points would be sealed off. Students began to flee the city returning en masse to their hometowns, despite a college regulation that ordered them to stay put.

The official media urged restraint and calm; the college radio began to broadcast soothing, synthesizer folk tunes instead of the usual brisk exercise music. The music provided the background to a recorded message that played all day on loop. 'Trust the government. Trust the college. You are safe. Let's fight SARS together. Relax and play some badminton. Read a magazine. Trust the government,' a disembodied voice cajoled. But the exhortations fell on deaf ears as the classrooms and dormitories continued to empty out in direct contravention of both college and government rules.

Get out while you still can, Grace begged me one morning. She showed me an SMS she had received a few hours earlier claiming that over 30,000 people had been infected with SARS in Beijing. I responded by showing her another SMS that I had received the same morning. Mine was from the Ministry of Health, which had begun to send out daily SARS information text messages in an effort to combat the rumours that were so rampant.

SMS had become a contested arena, simultaneously used by the government as a channel for promulgating the 'official' voice on SARS and by users to circumvent and disseminate non-official, non-authorized voices.[3]

---

[3]See Pallavi Aiyar, 'Mobile Messages: Chinese Changes in a Time of SARS', *Times of India*, 22 May 2003.

According to the latest update from the ministry there were only around one thousand cases of the virus in the capital, data I showed Grace. She was scornful. Did I actually believe anything that the Ministry of Health claimed, she asked querulously. I countered by asserting that since the 20 April revelation, the government did seem to be doing its best to come clean. Indeed, hospitals and local officials had been given direct orders from the centre to report accurately on SARS and even the media had for once been granted free rein to investigate and report on the disease.

Moreover, the alternative sources of information that most students were basing their decisions on were hardly authoritative, the majority being anonymous SMS senders.

Grace remained unconvinced and a day later packed her bags and left town. This was the same ultra-patriotic Grace who had berated me for suggesting that journalism wasn't always about good news. Her argument at the time had been that the Chinese people are 'volatile' and likely to overreact if confronted with bad news. They would get depressed and unproductive, she had reasoned, unless fed a continuous diet of feel-good morale boosters in the guise of news.

This had struck me then as a singularly unconvincing defence of censorship, but some of her reasoning did now seem to be borne out.

The students were reacting to the situation with ill-considered panic. It was probably more dangerous for them to be flying around the country and exposing themselves to potential virus carriers than simply to stay on campus and get on with their classes, as was being urged by the college. Beijing was a city of 14 million people, and 1000-odd cases of a disease with only a 10-15 per cent fatality rate was hardly a weighty number.

I remembered being at university in Delhi in 1994 when a plague scare swept across India. Pneumonic plague cases began to be reported in Delhi that autumn and the newspapers were flooded with plague stories evoking scenes of medieval horror. In my college we were rehearsing at the time for a production of *Romeo and Juliet*, in which I played the part of the blustering nurse.

Other than a few titters every time Mercutio moaned, 'a plague on both your houses', the pneumonic plague had little effect on our long afternoons of rehearsals, and even longer bus rides back home. Were Indians simply less volatile than the Chinese, as Grace claimed? I doubted it very much. The differences in the manner in which we as students in Delhi had reacted to the plague and my students in Beijing reacted to SARS had little to do with volatility in either of our national characters, and lay instead in the fact that in India we had a free press.

The plague scare had been debated to its bare bones by pundits of all shades in the Indian media. For weeks we had read about the slow spread of the disease across the country. There were no surprises when the first cases began to be reported from Delhi. We had had the time to absorb and assess the information.

In contrast, China's censored media at first contributed to an artificial calm and then in the aftermath of the government's sudden disclosure of cover-ups and lies, were no longer considered credible by their audience.

The paternalism inherent in China's political structure had created a society where people had become used to being treated like children, protected by a government that always knew best. Faced with the abrupt reality of having been lied to by this government, coupled with the fact of a rapidly spreading deadly virus, panic was but the natural reaction amongst my students. They felt let down and the resultant resentment and shock ran deep.

In India the inept handling of a public crisis would hardly evoke shock. If anything efficiency and honesty in our government would be more likely to provoke surprise, used as we were to a norm of corruption and deceit. Our vaunted free media and democracy had not rid the system of dishonesty as much as simply got us used to it as a fact of life. The constant stream of exposés of the grimy dealings of elected politicians had little power to incite passionate indignation. At most they elicited some disapproving clucking or a long-drawn sigh as one pondered the sad state of affairs in the country before moving on to the latest cricket scores.

But in China the rare public admission of governmental deceit rent a hole in my students' otherwise go-go world view in which everything was getting better and better, with everyone getting richer and richer. This issue moreover had implications that were far more democratic than most. The SARS coronavirus was class-blind. It could infect cosseted university students as easily as ragged migrant workers. The government's cover-up affected my students and their families directly and they were distraught, the certainties that protected them suddenly giving way.

The manner in which the students violently oscillated from complete trust in the authorities to hysterical suspicion gave me a glimpse of how volatile Chinese society really was. Not in the way that Grace had implied, in that it had little to do with anything intrinsic in the Chinese people as a race. But in a society that had constantly been twisted and pushed towards dramatically new directions without participatory mechanisms that could give the affected people themselves a say, volatility was but to be expected.

The tensions within Chinese society had little release so that the whole country was like a pressure cooker, calm on the top but boiling inside. India with its riots and strikes appeared on the surface to be far more chaotic and unstable but in the long run had developed the institutional mechanisms that enabled it to create, albeit creakily, a slow, broad-based consensus.

To the naked eye as it looked upon Beijing's orderly expressways in contrast to the bedlam of Delhi's roads, it may have seemed counter-intuitive, but India in fact enjoyed the kind of social stability that was for the Chinese authorities a paramount but elusive goal.

So nervous was China's government about bringing to the surface the instability it was aware simmered just below that the initial cover-up of the SARS virus was driven by the fear that admitting the real extent of its spread would unleash these forces, and thus take away the only legitimacy that the ruling party had left.

The Chinese Communist Party's legitimacy no longer lay in its founding ideology of communism, as my bored students who used their classes in Marxism to catch up on lost sleep testified. This was a party that had stormed to power on the basis of a philosophy that it was now busy blatantly undoing, even as the rhetorical gymnastics of its leaders tried to prove otherwise but fooled few.

The CCP had not been elected, nor did it have any intentions of allowing elections in the near future. However, ruling by large-scale coercion was an option that was also unviable. Over six hundred foreign journalists were now resident in China. Millions of Chinese citizens were wealthy, educated and increasingly worldly. It was far harder for the CCP to roll out the tanks and survive in the twenty-first century than it had been in 1989.

The government's legitimacy was thus dependent on the uninterrupted illusion that the CCP's continuing rule was essential to and beneficial for all sections of Chinese society. This single party purported to represent equally the interests of the workers, the peasants, the military and the entrepreneurs.

The manifest contradictions of Chinese society were to be reconciled by the sage decisions of the party's leadership. All Chinese had already tangibly benefited from these policies and were thus enthusiastic supporters of the party, as it heroically strove to achieve its noble aims.

This was the official story and it bore a kernel of truth.

Hundreds of millions had been lifted out of poverty since China began economic reforms and the country's leaders, autocratic as they were, had steered this process with both vision and a measure of courage. It was a story that many of the Chinese I spoke to understandably bought into.

But there were also many who did not. Twenty-five-million-plus workers had been laid off from China's state-owned enterprises. These casualties of the reform process coupled with powerless peasants, whose lands were regularly taken away by corrupt officials for sale to real estate developers, formed a formidable front of disaffected workers and peasants, once the mainstay of support for the CCP.

The party had been more successful in co-opting the white-collar urban elite and entrepreneurs of all shades; people like my students and their parents, for whom the future shone much brighter than the past. But the SARS cover-up had angered even this group of believers, threatening the CCP's legitimacy where it was considered most secure.

This had been a scenario the authorities were anxious to avoid but were forced to confront by the unexpected and unknown coronavirus that caused SARS.

The worst-case outcomes that the SARS epidemic engendered included a China where millions were infected, causing a total collapse of the country's already ailing health care system. Others predicted an economic meltdown and widespread social instability. If any of these putative catastrophes had come to pass, it is doubtful that the CCP could have emerged unscathed and with its authority intact.

As it transpired, the virus proved easier to tame than at first thought and the epidemic was limited to thousands rather than the millions once feared.

By the end of May the World Health Organisation had lifted its travel advisory against non-essential travel to Hong Kong, Singapore and infected cities in Vietnam and Canada.

A month later, on 24 June, Beijing too was declared safe for visitors. By mid-July the epidemic was definitively declared to be under control across the world.

For the CCP, it was a close call. At one point in late April, disaster appeared imminent. That it was avoided owed much to luck, with SARS proving less virulent than imagined, but it also owed something to the shrewd handling of the crisis by the authorities once they finally came out and made a clean break.

Hu Jintao had been anointed President of China only a month

before the SARS crisis reached a head in April. Until then few knew much about this enigmatic new leader either within or outside of China. SARS was to become the canvas on which Mr Hu's first widely scrutinized actions unfolded.

These were actions that proved astute. The prompt sacking of the health minister and the Beijing mayor located the responsibility for the disaster in these two sacrificial scapegoats, while absolving Mr Hu himself. The President was able to distance the central leadership from those lower down the pecking order who were blamed for having hidden vital information from their superiors.

Once again, there was, no doubt, some truth in these claims. In a hangover from the Maoist period there was a proclivity in China for subordinates in the official hierarchy to please their superiors with good news, regardless of the facts. During the Great Leap Forward of the late 1950s, for example, the central government was inundated with statistics from the provinces claiming bumper crops and miraculous yields when in fact upwards of twenty million were dying of famine.[4]

Realizing the urgent desire for transparency felt by the distraught public, Mr Hu then lifted stringent censorship rules on the media, allowing them for the first time to report somewhat freely on the epidemic. The Ministry of Health was ordered to give daily televised press conferences in which local reporters were able to ask some genuinely tough questions. Dr Jiang, the whistleblower, was feted as a hero.[5]

---

[4]See Jonathan Spence, *The Search for Modern China* (second edition), W.W. Norton & Company 1999, pp. 544-553. See also Jonathan Spence, *Mao*, Phoenix, p. 146.

[5]See 'A Chinese Doctor's Extraordinary April in 2003', *People's Daily Online*, 13 June 2003 (http://english.people.com.cn/200306/13/eng20030613 118182.shtml). However, when a year later, in 2004, Jiang wrote to the National People's Congress suggesting that it was time for a revaluation of the events of the 1989 Tiananmen protests he was arrested and 're-educated' and since his release has dropped out of public life altogether.

Mr Hu repeatedly pledged greater transparency and openness going forward. Lessons had been learnt from the mistakes of the past, he said, mistakes that would never be repeated. For many analysts around the world the new President began to look like a potential democrat, giving hope that China's economic openness might soon be matched by a degree of political reform.

Over and above Mr Hu's earnest rhetoric and the partial freeing up of the media what impressed me most about the government's response was simply its efficiency. Overnight up-to-date information on the latest developments began to be sent out over all mobile phones. Even at the height of the panic public transport continued to run unhindered. Most miraculously of all, a 1000-bed hospital purpose-built for the treatment of SARS was constructed in a northern suburb of Beijing in seven days.

There were reportedly a minimum of 4000 construction labourers working non-stop at the site between April 24 and 30. At peak times there were up to 7000 workers simultaneously engaged in building the giant hospital with the help of 500 massive construction machines. The hospital was operational within days of completion, 1200 medical staff having been transferred from military hospitals nationwide to man it.[6]

In Delhi it took almost three years to build a twenty-metre underpass that connected the western part of my neighbourhood, Nizamuddin, to the eastern section. Apparently the developer ran out of money after a couple of months and the entire project became the subject of litigation. The road remained in a permanently dug-up state, and the congestion the underpass was meant to ease only became worse.

The feat of the seven-day SARS hospital was thus what stayed with me most vividly, long after coronavirus fell out of daily vocabulary. Used as I was to the three-year underpass, it seemed almost preternatural.

---

[6]See 'Xiaotangshan: Beijing's SARS city', *Asia Times* Online, 15 May 2005 (http://www.atimes.com/atimes/China/EE15Ad04.html).

Returning to the action on campus in the immediate aftermath of the 20 April revelations, one afternoon a few days later, there was a knock on my apartment door. I opened up to reveal Dong Li in all her nervous magnificence clutching a giant crate of what turned out to be orange juice. 'The department wishes you stay healthy,' she beamed sweatily as she handed over the crate. Its weight came as a shock and I almost dropped it. By the time I got a secure grip, Dong was already departing. 'Drink orange juice and try not to go out more than necessary. Play badminton,' she added as a parting shot, her voice trailing off as she jogged down the stairs.

This was the extent of the department's communication with me on the SARS situation. Other than the orange juice I was pretty much left to my own devices, although Dong did call again a few days later to clarify that I should conduct classes as usual without paying heed to the absentee population. 'They (the absentees) will be punished appropriately,' she said ominously. 'No need for you to bother about them.'

In truth I was bothered less by the absentees than the constant smell of vinegar I was having to learn to live with. The idea that vinegar helped guard against SARS was gaining quick currency across the city and the college janitors had been ordered to rub down all the building surfaces with a mixture of vinegar and water several times a day. My apartment stank of it, as did the classrooms.

The price of vinegar skyrocketed, as much as by 50 per cent, according to some reports I read.

The college was put under partial quarantine. No outsiders were allowed in and although we could leave if we so chose, the department 'strongly discouraged' us to do so. Orange juice and badminton, they repeated often. Stay put, drink your orange juice and play badminton.

As the days went by and the apocalyptic visions conjured up by the rumours circulating on our mobile phones did not come to pass, there was a palpable sense of release on campus. My classes were three-quarters empty and the few remaining students were keen to take advantage of this. They would persuade me to play word games with them in class or simply gossip; academic advancement could wait.

Everywhere people did begin to play badminton as the government urged (this being deemed good for the immune system). It was the first sign I noticed of the return of faith in the wisdom of the authorities.

My mobile phone that had for many days only brought news of gloom and doom began to light up with a few jokes. I woke one morning to my phone's beeping. A student had sent me this SMS:

At times when you cry, no one sees your tears,
When you worry, no one sees your pain,
When you are happy no one sees your smile,
Try coughing, they'll all look at you.

The students were learning to smile again. Their tense, worried looks softening. The girls began to sport custom-made face masks in bright reds and greens. One had a Snoopy pattern on hers, another produced a Burberry rip-off. A new emoticon began to do the rounds over SMS. It was a smiley face, wearing a mask.

By mid-May I began to go out a lot more. The roads were still relatively free of traffic and for once it was a pleasure to drive through downtown Beijing.

Julio and I were visiting an old, historic neighbourhood north of the Forbidden City on a sunny Sunday when we came across a poster that left us befuddled.

It pictured a man, sitting down to a meal in western style, with fork and knife in each hand and napkin tucked into his shirt-front. Before him was a shiny, round plate on top of which sat what was unmistakably a fluffy, smiling cat. A big red slash ran across the picture, indicating that the activity portrayed was a forbidden one.

The poster was obviously exhorting its audience to desist from eating cats. I was aware that some Chinese ate dogs, but I hadn't been aware that cats were considered as chow too, and even if they were why was the government suddenly advising people not to eat them?[7]

The answer lay in the fact that by late May research teams in Hong Kong and the mainland had announced detection of a SARS-like virus in the masked palm civet cat and racoon-dog.

Wildlife has traditionally been consumed in China for both food and medicinal purposes. It was thus no coincidence that many of the diseases that have jumped from animals to humans have originated in China, in particular its wet markets in the south, where live animals are sold and slaughtered in densely packed bazaars.

The news that the SARS virus may have originated in certain species of wild dogs and cats rippled across the country leading to the formation of vigilante groups who rounded up all the dogs or cats they came across on the streets and bludgeoned them to death. Hundreds of pets were killed in Beijing alone.[8]

Dogs had always occupied a precarious space in China. Not only were they eaten in the winter, their meat considered warming and health-giving, but they had also been subject to numerous extermination campaigns during the Maoist era when they were deemed a threat to public hygiene.

A few years later, in 2006, rabies scares across the country would lead to similar scenes. In July of that year the local government of Mouding County in southwest China's Yunnan Province killed 54,429 dogs after three people died in a rabies outbreak. All dogs in the area were ordered killed regardless of whether they were strays or pets and without mind to whether or

---

[7]See 'Stricter Measures to Stop Wild Animal Eating', *People's Daily Online*, 26 May 2003 (http://english.people.com.cn/200305/26/eng20030526_ 117241.shtml)

[8]See Oliver August, 'Fearful Chinese Slaughter Pets in SARS Hysteria', *The Times*, 10 May 2003.

not they had been vaccinated.[9]

Once again there were reports of mob attacks on dogs out for a walk with their owners. The pets were clubbed to death with sticks on the spot.

I was instinctively revolted by these atrocities even though somewhere in my mind I heard a voice accusing me of bourgeois sentimentalism. Attacks on dogs were hardly the most appalling of the instances of mob violence I had been exposed to.

I was eight years old when the assassination of Prime Minister Indira Gandhi by her Sikh bodyguard sparked riots in which the homes of our Sikh neighbours were burnt to the ground. My brother's best friend's father, a sardar, was shot in the head and left for dead. The bullet had lodged in his turban and he survived.

I had grown up surrounded by stories of mob attacks: on Hindus and Muslims and Christians and even representatives of the Delhi electrical service unit. 'Irate mobs' were a fixture in Indian newspapers, thrashing and burning.

But I didn't recall animals being the object of these murderous, raging mobs. In China the mobs massacred dogs and justified it on the grounds that they spread rabies or SARS. There were around 2500 cases of rabies on average in China every year. In India there were 30,000. Yet we worshipped our rabies-carrying monkeys and when the municipal authorities attempted to round up stray dogs, activists rechristened them 'community *kuttas*' deserving of protection for the role they played in the community.

Perhaps our mobs in India simply had too many competing objects at which to direct their ire and had no energy left for the dogs. In China, on the other hand, protest was carefully managed and only permitted for a limited range of issues, one of which

---

[9]Rabies scares and culling of dogs continued for several months that summer. See Jonathan Watts, 'China's Rabies Outbreak Triggers Second Dog Cull', *Guardian*, 4 August 2006.

happened to be dogs (the only other I could think of during my five-year stay in the country were the Japanese).

China was a country where ordinary people were offered few opportunities for the release of their frustrations, of which there were many. Frustration at having their home bulldozed, at being unable to afford the privatised health care that was now the norm, at having their wages withheld without cause—the potential list was a very long one.

When proffered the opportunity to vent these frustrations, even if it was only on dogs, it is perhaps unsurprising that there were so many takers.

By mid-June the majority of students had returned to campus, appearing in class flashing sheepish grins. They looked well rested and fed, the result of some six weeks of unbroken attention from their doting mothers.

Yes, they had overreacted, they admitted. The government had been right after all and they should have stayed put. But their penitence was patently half-hearted. Everyone had enjoyed the unscheduled holiday.

Despite Dong Li's sinister warnings of the 'appropriate' manner in which the absentees would be dealt with upon their return, the college seemed to have decided it best to ignore their disobedience and save face. If all concerned pretended that no rules had in fact been broken, then the college's authority remained intact, a charade that suited the students fine.

Instead of being punished, they were given extra classes to help them catch up on the work they had missed out on. Final exams were only weeks away and the holiday was emphatically over. Badminton playing came to a halt, as did class-time gossip. The books were out and with everyone focussing on the exams SARS began to recede into the background almost as suddenly as it had first appeared.

The domestic media were once again busy devising odes to the sagacity of the country's leadership, their brief period of freedom over.[10] There were no signs of a major democratic awakening either among the people or those in power. President Hu Jintao emerged from the crisis stronger. The economy in 2003 was to grow at a spanking 9 per cent, making a mockery of the dire predictions of economic meltdown that SARS had given rise to.

Yet, for a brief while, the contradictions in China's underlying political economy had been exposed. Economic liberalization and loosening social controls sat uneasily within an autocratic political system. The two faces of contemporary China chafed at each other producing bubbles of tension that had thus far remained isolated and small enough to cause only a barely audible pop on bursting. It was the CCP's primary concern to maintain this status quo and prevent the bubbles from merging into larger, more powerful forces, a concern that remained unchanged throughout my China stay.

But back in Beijing in June 2003, my attention shifted to what analysts around the world were heralding as a 'historic' moment: the first visit in a decade to China by an Indian Prime Minister; a visit that was later seen as a watershed in a bilateral relationship that would soon begin to loom large on the global imagination.

---

[10]John Pomfret, 'China Tightens Grip on What Press Can Print', *Washington Post*, 22 June 2003.

CHAPTER FOUR

Hindi-Chini Buy Buy

At the height of the SARS crisis, I sat in my apartment surrounded by bottles of orange juice and realized that I was plum in the midst of the biggest international news story of the moment. For months I had been teaching my students how to sniff out and sell a good yarn but instead of practising what I preached in class, I was whiling away the time spending moody afternoons gazing out of my window at the badminton-playing hordes outside.

The realization galvanized me into action and I shot off emails to NDTV, the television company that were my former employers, and a couple of the major English-language broadsheets. Soon I was penning Op Eds describing life from the trenches of SARS and being interviewed on the phone for NDTV's evening news bulletins.

The previous year had been a quiet one for me, teaching and learning Chinese, and I recognized now that it had been a time of preparation. Almost without my having noticed, China had sucked me in and although I had agreed to come here only reluctantly, I no longer wanted to leave in a hurry.

China was complex on a continental scale and during the year I had come to catch tantalizing peeks into this complexity in which the old and new, past and future surged and crashed against each other in the process of change. These glimpses left me hungry for more.

Once the extent of the spread of SARS in Beijing was revealed, several of our expatriate friends had upped and left, returning to their homes, leaving virus-ridden China behind. But to Julio and me, Beijing had become home, made more so by the fact that as a couple we lacked a natural home elsewhere. Delhi was mine, Madrid his, but Beijing was ours.

My Chinese was progressing and I was able now to wield a pair of chopsticks with some felicity. Moreover, my first SARS-inspired forays into journalism, reporting on China for an Indian audience, were exciting, pointing to possibilities outside of the campus. I began to think seriously about committing to China for a few years.

The aptly named Middle Kingdom was at the centre of the world's attention and I was one of the few Indians in a position to exploit that centrality. The timing was perfect, although I wasn't to know at the time just how perfect.

In the summer of 2003 we were still a year or two away from 'China' as a story becoming the 'China *and* India' story. India seemed stuck at five to six per cent growth rates and the elephant's lumbering stroll forward was only ever compared to the dragon's fiery ascent to highlight the widening chasm between the two neighbours.

Not only was China's economic performance on a different plane to India's, the shadow of the 1962 war continued to cast a pall of gloom over their bilateral ties. Lashings of pride and deeply entrenched prejudice on both sides of the Himalayas meant that a concept like 'Chindia' would have been laughed out of the room at the time.

At the end of 2002 bilateral trade stood at a paltry $5 billion; direct flights between the neighbours had begun only a few months earlier after a gap of three decades. When New Delhi tested a nuclear bomb in 1998, the defence minister pointed to China as the chief security threat impelling India to go nuclear. China's missile and nuclear assistance to its 'all-weather' ally Pakistan and India's engagement with the 'splittist' Dalai Lama were further complicating factors.

Eight rounds of border talks between 1981 and 1987 and an additional fourteen Joint Working Group meetings between 1988 and 2003 had failed to result in even a clarification of the Line of Actual Control along the 3500 km Sino-Indian border.[1] The Hindi-Chini Bhai Bhai bonhomie of the1950s had long degraded into the reality of Hindi-Chini Bye Bye, or so the joke went.

It was in this context that the China visit of Atal Bihari Vajpayee, the first Indian Prime Minister to travel to Beijing in a decade, took place. Mr Vajpayee was also one of the first world leaders to visit Beijing in the aftermath of the SARS epidemic. He touched down at the Chinese capital on 22 June, two days before the WHO lifted its travel advisory against Beijing.

Less than twenty-four hours later two major joint declarations had been signed and announced, establishing the framework that was to guide bilateral relations for the years to come. China implicitly recognized Sikkim as part of India for the first time while India explicitly acknowledged that Tibet was part of China's territory. Special representatives were appointed to seek a political solution to the border and territorial disputes. A new trade target for $10 billion by 2005 was set and Indian mangoes were given the green light for export to China.

I was able to watch the prime ministerial visit to Beijing up close, an internet news portal, Rediff, having commissioned stories on the trip from me. I wasn't officially accredited as a journalist but Rajdeep Sardesai, a former colleague at NDTV and part of the press corps accompanying the Prime Minister, managed to call in a favour and get me a media pass.

---

[1]The Sino-Indian boundary as claimed by India, that is, including portions disputed with Pakistan and China, stands at 3488 kilometres.

For the two and half days that Vajpayee spent in Beijing I thus became 'Puneet', an NDTV cameraperson who never made it across but for whom a media pass had nonetheless been issued.

As Puneet, my first stop was the leafy environs of Peking University, where the Prime Minister was to address a gathering of China's brightest young minds. The hall was packed to the rafters. It was a large space but I was only able to squeeze in right at the back. When Vajpayee appeared on the stage, the distance dwarfed him, accentuating his frailty. He shuffled towards the podium and when he began to speak his voice was weak. The students strained to hear him despite the amplification of the mike.

Vajpayee read out from a set text. He talked about the historical ups and downs of Sino-Indian relations; of the two countries having emerged recently from one of these cyclical downturns and being engaged now in the delicate process of recovering trust and understanding.

The speech read well on the written page but Vajpayee delivered it with little flourish, making no eye contact and taking no questions at the end. Instead he finished reading, thanked his audience and shuffled off the stage, the event over as abruptly as it began.

Outside the hall, I met with a few Hindi-language students at the university. One of them, a moon-faced girl who asked me to call her Asha, said she had thought the speech okay but wished it had been in Hindi. The students went on tell me that they had chosen to study Hindi at university in the hope of it helping them find a job at the South Asia section of the foreign ministry or perhaps in one of the Indian companies that were beginning to operate out of China. It was, however, slowly dawning on them that English might have been more useful, even in an India-connected line of work.

Why don't all Indians speak Hindi, Asha asked me grumpily. I replied that India had a proud multilingual tradition that embraced many languages and that it was difficult to prioritize one of these, Hindi, over others like Tamil or Telegu.

I was aware even as I uttered the words, that China had achieved just that: a prioritization of Mandarin over all other languages and dialects. The growling roughness of the northern accent remained distinct from the sibilant susurration of the southern, but almost everyone across China spoke some Mandarin. The fact that all Chinese languages shared at least a common written basis helped, but making Mandarin speakers out of Cantonese or Shanghainese people couldn't have been an easy task.

But then the Cantonese and Shanghainese didn't vote, unlike the Tamils and Telegus in India. And difficult as it must have been for the southerners to swallow the linguistic superimposition of Mandarin, the logic that a country needs a common language to give it a coherence seemed by now to be self-evident in China.

The Hindi-major Peking University students remained baffled in the face of my explanations for why Hindi had failed as a national language and why many would argue that this failure wasn't necessarily a bad thing.

Well, what did I think, Asha finally asked me.

I had no easy answer for the question, it being one that forced me to think about an even more fundamental question: What did I think of the idea of India: a country without a language, without a centre, lacking singularity except in being singularly diverse?

I had been brought up on the 'unity in diversity' propaganda that children across the country were fed in classrooms. I thus grew up feeling fierce pride in India's particular brand of syncretic secularism where rather than a separation of religion and state we were taught an equal respect for all religions. I loved India's all-encompassing schizophrenia in which Angrezi, Gujarati, Bengali, and Punjabi sang 'I love you' in Amitabh Bachchan movies. In the Delhi of my personal geography the ghosts of Ghalib and Lutyens, of Lodhis and Sufis rubbed up against each other in companionable accommodation. Nizamuddin and Lodhi Garden, Rashtrapati

Bhavan and Chandni Chowk: this was the Delhi I grew up in.[2]

We were a country of 22 official languages and over 200 recorded mother tongues, of lily-white Kashmiris and coffee-hued Malyalis, of fish-eating Bengalis and herbivorous Gujaratis. In our 'Hindu' country, there were almost as many Muslims as in all of Pakistan. Our cultural inheritance included fire-worshiping Zoroastrians, and Torah-reciting Jews. With no single language, ethnicity, religion or food, India to an outsider was understandably implausible. Yet, its existence, messy and confusing though it may be, was fact.

What was the idea of India? I wanted to believe that in essence it was a capacity for tolerance and diversity.[3]

But such beliefs did not survive unscathed through my passage into adulthood. Even within my relatively sheltered world of privilege and good intentions I had not remained blind to the reality of what India could be. A country where hatred and bigotry seeped into ordinary people turning them into killers and rapists; where for periods of time Hindus and Muslims and Christians and

---

[2]Nizamuddin, the area I grew up in, is a south Delhi neighbourhood home to both the shrine of the renowned fourteenth-century Sufi saint, Hazrat Nizamuddin Aulia, as well as Mughal emperor Humayun's tomb. Only a kilometre or so away is Lodhi Garden, where various buildings including tombs and mosques dating from the Lodhi dynasty are set in a leafy park. The Lodhis were an Afghan dynasty who ruled parts of north India from 1451 to 1526. A ten-minute drive north is the President of India's residence, Rashtrapati Bhavan. It was designed by the British architect Edward Lutyens in a style that mixed colonial and Indian elements. Intended originally to serve as the British Viceroy's palace, it was officially opened in 1931. Chandni Chowk, a wholesale and retail market in the heart of Old Delhi, dates back to A.D. 1650, when it was built to serve the needs of the Red Fort. It was designed partly by the Mughal emperor Shahjahan's daughter, Jahanara.

[3]This was a sentiment summed up by Jawaharlal Nehru in *Discovery of India*, where he said India was an 'ancient palimpsest on which layer upon layer of thought and reverie had been inscribed and yet no succeeding layer had completely hidden or erased what had been written previously'.

Sikhs stopped seeing each other as human. Where far from the tolerance I had once believed India's historical diversity to have engendered, difference only bred insularity and prejudice.

No other nationality seemed to have quite as many ways in which to categorize people, making an 'other' of almost everyone. In India we differentiated on caste and sub-caste, region and religion, gender and colour of the skin.

In the face of this realization, the China of one language, of one major ethnicity, of one political party did not seem as unattractive as it might once have seemed to me. Perhaps China with its centralized imperial system stretching back hundreds of years, uniform script and standardized pagoda architecture did make more sense as a country than India.

Living in China I often encountered moments like these, where an innocuous question sent me scurrying off into a maze of thoughts from which I emerged even more uncertain of my moral and intellectual compass than when I entered. I found myself asserting ideas that did not behove the liberal I thought I was.

Many times it was authoritarian China that seemed to offer greater social justice for its people, freedom for its women, protection for its poor. China's people may have lacked a 'voice', but so did most Indians. India's poor had a vote, but this did not always equal a voice.

I thus remained tongue-tied in response to Asha's question and the students sensing my unease were polite enough to change the subject. 'I like your Prime Minister,' said one of the boys, a pimply youth, taller than average. 'He reminds me of my grandfather.'

My next glimpse of Vajpayee was on the following evening at a reception hosted by the outgoing Indian ambassador, Shiv Shankar Menon.

The majority of the invitees comprised the 300-strong Indian community in Beijing at the time. As they nibbled on dainty samosas and sipped fizzy orange drinks, the atmosphere was thick with anticipation. For most of those gathered it was to be their first face-to-face meeting with their Prime Minister.

When Vajpayee arrived a few minutes later, he looked more at ease than he had the day before. Beaming an avuncular smile, he did a round of namastes around the room before spending some time chatting with Mrs Guo Kotnis. Mrs Kotnis was the almost ninety-year-old Chinese wife of Dr Dwarkanath Kotnis, a member of an Indian medical mission sent to China in 1938 to provide assistance in the face of the Japanese invasion. Dr Kotnis died while still in China, in 1942, and he remained the most potent symbol of the Hindi-Chini Bhai Bhai sentiment that had grown fainter and fainter over the decades.

His ageing wife was always trotted out on any major occasion that put Sino-Indian ties in the spotlight. And although I was cynically aware of her 'uses' it was difficult not to be moved by her love story. She had only known the doctor for four years as a young girl and in the middle of a war. Guo had also been a medical practitioner with the Eighth Route Army. I imagined the flush on her ivory-toned cheek the first time the doctor brushed her palm lightly with his fingertips . . .

Now, over sixty years later, gnarled and bent with age, she gifted a Bengali translation of a book about her husband's short life to Vajpayee. 'I love my India as much as I love my motherland China' the inscription in the book read. There was something that touched me about this hopeless bit of sentimentalism.

I remembered the feeling a few years later when I chanced upon an old photograph of the 1938 Indian medical team at a museum housed in Madam Sun Yat Sen's home in central Beijing.

The photograph was faded, bleached and I could barely make out the faces of the five young doctors. But the angle of their raised heads spoke somehow of hope and innocence. Dr Kotnis died at the age of thirty-two. It's not clear what he died of, although it was probably malaria, endemic in China at the time.

Back at the reception, as the evening progressed and enough orange squash was imbibed, events took a boisterous turn. One of the Hindi professors from Peking University, the Vice-Dean of the department that Asha and the other students I had met the day before belonged to, broke through the crowds that surrounded Vajpayee and announced in loud, flawless Hindi that he had translated the Ramayana into Chinese. He would be honoured to translate one of the Prime Minister's poems as well, he said, and soon the entire room was egging on Vajpayee to recite a poem.

The Prime Minister allowed himself to be persuaded without too much difficulty. He cleared his throat and with one arm raised, recited:

> *There was a time in the past when the poet used to sing a beautiful melody,*
> *But then came a time when the poet refused to sing any more*
> *And now finally the poet is singing a new song, again.*

This is an unlovely, rough translation into English of the PM's impeccable Hindustani rendition and given that the poem appeared to be both spontaneous and about the rather prosaic topic of Sino-Indian relations, it was a worthy enough effort and met with uproarious applause.

The reception lasted an hour and the next day the Prime Minister flew to Shanghai and from there back to India. He had only been in Beijing for two and a half days but something shifted after this trip.

Partly, it was the timing.

A few months later the investment bank Goldman Sachs came up with what would become one of the most quoted forecasts for emerging economies, the BRIC report. According to the report, India, China, Russia and Brazil were the four countries that would emerge as dominant economic powers by 2050.[4] This was one of the first instances of the 'and' that would later become common when talking about 'China *and* India'.

---

[4]Dominic Wilson and Roopa Purushothaman, *Dreaming with BRICs: The Path to 2050*, Goldman Sachs Global Economics Paper No.99, October 2003.

Before long, taxi drivers in Beijing began to ask me about India's software prowess. Those who used to only talk to me about Hindi movies started to inquire about the benefits of introducing private competition in India's telecommunications industry.

In October of 2003 the Confederation of Indian Industry (CII) organized its first ever 'Made in India' show in the Chinese capital in which over a hundred Indian companies participated. The underlying message of the show, CII's Director General, Tarun Das, told me, was that India Inc was no longer running scared of China. 'This is all about Indian industry getting a new confidence. We are ready now to engage with China rather than run away,' Das said during an interview on the eve of the show, in the Sheraton hotel's airy lobby.

On one level his words proved prophetic. From 2004 India began to average a growth rate of 8 per cent and the shift in the perception of India that had begun a year earlier solidified. India was 'discovered' anew by the West. Suddenly no conference on global business was complete without an India and China section; every major investment bank and consultancy company around the world produced comparative studies and forecasts while the western media went into overdrive with analyses of implications for the world were a formidable combination of Chindia to emerge.

I remained painfully aware throughout that much of the 'China and India' growth story was over-hyped and lacking basis. China continued to outclass India on virtually every parameter of economic or social growth. In 2005 Indians were jubilant when foreign direct investment (FDI) into the country hit $5.5 billion; the same year actual FDI into China was worth $72.4 billion. That year India spent $28 billion on infrastructure development compared to over $200 billion by China. China's share in global exports remained six times that of India.[5]

---

[5]Chetan Ahya, Andy Xie, Stephen Roach, Mihir Sheth and Denise Yam, *India and China: New Tigers of Asia, Part II*, Morgan Stanley Research, June 2006, p. 40.

Even more tellingly, when it came to providing its millions of poor with drinking water, telephone lines and schools, China continued to be in a different category altogether from its southern neighbour. According to UNICEF, by 2006 India still had fifty-seven million children who suffered from malnutrition compared to only seven million in China.[6] World Bank estimates for 2005 put youth illiteracy in India at almost 25 per cent. In China the corresponding figure was only one per cent.[7]

Moreover, the notion of China and India combining strengths to emerge as a united economic colossus, Chindia, remained at best fanciful. In 2005, China's total trade volume was worth $1.4 trillion. Sino-US bilateral trade reached $204.7 billion and Sino-Japanese trade, $189.4 billion. India was merely the 16th largest exporting nation to China that year and the 13th biggest importer of Chinese products.[8]

Indian investment in China stood at $130 million by the end of 2005. In contrast, US businesses had actually invested $51.1 billion in the mainland by then. Chinese investments in India were even less impressive. According to the Indian government, FDI inflows to India from China between August 1991 and October 2005 worked out to a staggeringly low total of $2.03 million, although Chinese statistics put the figure higher at about $47.35 million.[9]

The most hyped idea of all, the coming together of Indian software and Chinese hardware, demonstrated how rhetorical artifice had somehow managed to obscure reality. By 2005 there was not a single case in which Indian software had been employed in the

[6] *The State of the World's Children 2006: Excluded and Invisible*, UNICEF: http://www.unicef.org/sowc06/fullreport/full_report.php

[7] *World Development Indicators 2006*. 'Youth' is defined as the 15-24 age group.

[8] This is data I received from the Indian embassy in Beijing based on statistics compiled from relevant Indian and Chinese ministries.

[9] Ibid.

production of Chinese hardware and no Indian software firm had invested in Chinese hardware companies in order to control a vehicle for the distribution of their product.[10]

But although the case for Chindia, and India-China comparisons more generally, was more often than not overstated, 2003 was a watershed year for the Sino-Indian engagement.

It was as if someone had lit a match under bilateral trade, which simply rocketed up. By the end of 2003, trade had touched $7.6 billion; in 2004 it zoomed upwards by 79 per cent to $13.6 billion; by 2005 it was at $18.7 billion and in 2006 it crossed $25 billion. By the time I left China, the mainland was well on track to becoming India's largest trading partner. In this latest twist in the Sino-Indian tale, Hindi-Chini Bye Bye had once again morphed to emerge in its latest avatar of Hindi-Chini Buy Buy.

And although Chinese investments in India remained tiny, Indian investments in the mainland began to grow and diversify markedly from 2003 on.

All the big names in Indian software—TCS, Infosys, Wipro and Satyam—and several smaller ones—IGate, Newgen and Zenzar—set up shop one by one.[11] Later, auto component majors like Sundram Fasteners and Bharat Forge entered. Mahindra and Mahindra set up a joint venture to make trucks; the wind-energy firm Suzlon established a $60 million factory to manufacture wind turbines in the eastern city of Tianjin. Half a dozen Indian banks opened up representative offices and in 2006 the State Bank of India got a licence to begin commercial banking operations. Later in the same year the first Indian law firm, Remfry and Sagar, set up office in Beijing and was doing brisk business within months.

---

[10]Arthur Kroeber, 'China and India: Myths Exploded', China Economic Quarterly, Volume 10 Issue I, First Quarter 2006.

[11]These Indian IT companies, however, struggled to gain access to the domestic IT market in China. Their operations were largely confined to servicing global clients on the Chinese mainland. The much heralded India-China cooperation in IT thus remained largely unrealized.

Manufacturing facilities, research and development centres, banks and legal services: the economic engagement across the Himalayas was certainly thickening and this was a phenomenon visible to the naked eye.

The numbers of Indian faces on Beijing's streets spiked. In my first year I was constantly amazed at the absence of Indians, people I had imagined to be as ubiquitous as curry, which is available everywhere from Birmingham to Kuala Lampur. My amazement proved relatively short-lived. Within a year of my having moved to China, both curry and the Indians to accompany it became increasingly common.

In 2004 390,000 Indians visited China, up 44 per cent from 2003, the largest increase of visitors to the mainland from any country, according to the China National Tourism Administration.

By 2004 there were close to ten Indian restaurants in Beijing serving up aromatic rogan josh and butter-thick dal makhani. This was almost double the number of such restaurants that had existed when I arrived in Beijing in late 2002.

I began to notice large advertisements for familiar names like NIIT and Aptech go up all over the city. By 2006 when I visited Aptech's headquarters in Beijing the company had already established over two hundred training schools in fifty-seven different Chinese cities.

Its joint venture with Peking University had maintained the number one slot in the IT training market in China for four consecutive years.

At the training centre I visited in Beijing, more than two thousand students from across China were enrolled in study towards degrees that would qualify them as either software engineers or network administrators.

These were students who wanted to work in India one happy day in the future or at the very least for an Indian software company in China. They may not have known it but they were pioneers; modern-day Xuan Zangs, young Chinese seekers of

Indian knowledge.[12]

If there really was to be any future Chindia, it was kids like these that would give it substance. But even here there were signs that such a future was far from assured.

Ren Yuan Jin, a 23-year-old, blew perfectly formed smoke rings into the air as he considered my question. Would he want to work in India? Not really, he replied eventually. He'd rather work for an American or European company. India was good at software but the country was crowded and dirty. Ren Yuan Jin preferred to move to the States, if possible, or if that didn't work out, he'd stay on in Beijing.

But while only a few Chinese and mostly aspiring software engineers at that had begun to orient themselves India-wards, all manner of Indians were flocking to China's cities in the hope of finding their fortune or at least making one.

China's star was on the ascent and a rising star exerted a magnetic pull. The Beijing I found myself in had a frontier feel to it. People from around the world came here to start afresh and find a better life.

On weekend nights, Beijing's bars were like the tower of Babel. Africans, Americans, Australians, Japanese—it was as if all the world's nationalities had gathered in this one Chinese city to quench their thirst. This was a thirst for action, for opportunity, for growth and twenty-first century China offered just that.

Amongst my friends in Beijing were Filipina film-makers and Bulgarian singers; Kiwi bartenders and Ugandan students.

It was ironic that even as stories of poor Chinese immigrants asphyxiating in the back of trucks in frantic attempts to smuggle themselves into other countries were filling column space in world media, foreigners from other countries were flocking to China like cats to cream.

---

[12]'Xuan Zang' is the modern romanization of the name that in India is more commonly known as Huein Tsang. For more on the seventh century Buddhist monk's journey to India see Mishi Saran, *Chasing the Monk's Shadow: A Journey in the Footsteps of Xuan Zang,* Penguin, 2005.

Beijing's universities were teeming with foreigners, poring over Chinese characters, practising their tones, determined to master Mandarin and with it a ticket to a bright future. I was startled to learn that the numbers of Chinese students going abroad to study and those of foreign students choosing China to study in equalled out as far back as 2001.

In 2002, the year I touched down in Beijing, 86,000 foreign students from 175 countries had enrolled for programmes in universities across China. By 2005 this number had increased to 141,087.[13] The Ministry for Education statistics showed that in the same year only 118,500 Chinese students were studying abroad.

Taking their place in this crush of fortune-seeking hopefuls from elsewhere were a handful of Indians: yoga teachers, photographers, restaurateurs, cooks, medical students, hotel doormen and anything-for-a-buck free-spirited adventurers.

Of these categories the most numerous were aspiring doctors, for whom China was fast becoming a Mecca of medicine. From 2004 onwards over twenty medical universities across China began aggressively to recruit medical students from India. Tuition fees ranged on average from $2000 to 3000 a year, so that hundreds of Indians unable to either find or afford a place at medical colleges back home were converging on China's shores in a bid to get a coveted MBBS.

Scenic Hangzhou, bustling Chongqing, remote Dali, cities most Indians had never heard of, were suddenly teeming with youngsters from small-town India. Across China universities were waking up the realization that tapping into the vein of aspirant Indian doctors was a lucrative business.

In early 2006 I visited Tianjin Medical University on a reporting assignment. There were around 250 Indian students studying there at the time and the university authorities were keen

---

[13]See Wang Qian, 'China Sees Rising Influx of Foreign Students', China.org.cn, 9 July 2006 (http://www.china.org.cn/english/2006/Jul/ 174007.htm).

to recruit more.[14]

The Dean of the International Exchange Department spent the better part of an hour assuring me of the high standards that the students accepted needed to meet and in turn the high quality of teaching they received.

Students needed a 70 per cent mark in their high school leaving exams, he said. Once admitted to the university all their classes were taught in English by Chinese professors with international qualifications.

Later in the day I attended an organic chemistry class comprising second year students from India. The class began conventionally enough but within fifteen minutes dozens of listless, whispering boys in the back row began to browbeat the teacher into declaring a break.

To be fair to the students, the teacher was a male version of the sweaty Dong Li. He exuded nervousness and paused every few seconds to mop at the perspiration on his forehead with a grimly clutched handkerchief. His English was incomprehensible even to my attuned ear and he had an unfortunate stutter, whether a permanent affliction or a temporary one born of stage fright, I wasn't certain.

He begged the students to be quiet. A break wasn't due for another hour, he reasoned weakly. The clamour at the back of the class only grew louder.

After years of teaching and attending classes in China, where students bordered on the deferential and classroom etiquette was deeply ingrained, the chaos of this class was a shock. You could take the kids out of India, but not India out of them, I mused.

After class, different groups of students came up to me to explain what had been going on. I met with a clutch of 19-year-old girls from Andhra Pradesh. They wore long skirts and kurtas. Bindis dotted their foreheads and their oiled hair was fragrant.

---

[14]See Pallavi Aiyar, 'Made in China Indian Doctors', *The Hindu*, 17 May 2006.

Kohl-darkened eyes opened wide expressively as they talked about all their classes being regularly interrupted in this manner by the 'Punjabi' boys.

The Punjabi boys in question were in the meantime yowling in the distance like cats on heat. They kept running up to me and shouting 'hello' loudly, right in my face. This was familiar behaviour to me from Delhi where sexually repressed young boys—and given the mores of Indian society, there were legions of these—would spend their days trying to get any kind of reaction whatsoever, from any girl, whomsoever.

It transpired that contrary to the dean's claims, the university accepted virtually any student that applied as long as they could pay. There were no cut-off percentages and little quality control. The classes were taught in Chinglish and only a small percentage of their professors held international degrees. The students worried about being able to pass the screening test required by the Medical Council of India, a necessity if they were to be able to practise back home.

The list of complaints was long, yet everyone I talked to wanted to see the degree through. It wasn't perfect here, admitted Manpreet Kaur, a buxom 20-year-old from Chandigarh, but it was better than in India. Back home everything was so corrupt that all the places at medical colleges were bought up even before the entrance exams, she said bitterly. At least in China, they had a chance.

Other than these Made in China Indian doctors, the second most populous guild of Indians in China that was to emerge during my time there was that of yoga teachers.

It was late in 2003 that a Chinese acquaintance I knew from the tango classes Julio and I had enrolled in came up to me at the start of one of these classes and without warning folded her hands in a namaskar stretched up high over her head while solemnly intoning, '*Om Suryaya Namahe.*'

She giggled at my surprise and went on to tell me that she had begun taking yoga classes from the 'cuuutest Indian teacher'. He was 'really authentic', she said, and pressed a business card into my hand.

The card was for a Yogi Mohan and his alliteratively named Yogi Yoga centre. I had in fact begun to notice advertisements for yoga classes sprouting up in the classified sections of local magazines for a while by then but hadn't given it much thought. Most of the teachers were either Chinese who had learnt yoga exercises off videotapes or Americans from California.

Now that an Indian teacher was in town, it piqued my interest. I called Yogi Mohan that afternoon itself and he welcomed me to attend a class the following day.

I arrived a little late and the class had already begun. Yogi Mohan, dressed in a blindingly white kurta pyjama, was standing in the Surya Namaskar pose, like a finely chiselled Chola bronze. His chocolatey eyes were framed by long, sweeping lashes, his rosebud mouth revealed a row of perfect white teeth when he smiled. Yogi Mohan was, in short, a looker.

I was evidently not the only one to think so. The room was filled with adoring women panting and sweating as they inhaled and exhaled in unison, with eyes that never seemed to leave their teacher.

After class we sat down on a park bench outside for a chat and Yogi Mohan told me a little of his story. He had been born in a small town in Garhwal and had moved to Rishikesh as a teenager. In Rishikesh Mohan began to study yoga in earnest and was soon teaching it as well. His students were almost exclusively foreigners, he said, and mostly women.

He didn't have much to complain about. He had imagined the rest of his life would play out in a largely similar way: slowly, quietly, in hour-long sessions, to the rhythm of the Ganga.

In April of 2003 all of this would change when a stylish young Chinese woman swept into Rishikesh and Mohan's life.

Yin Yan, who was China Editorial Director for the fashion

magazine *Elle*, was spending an extended vacation travelling across India. She made a stop in Rishikesh and stayed long enough to develop a yen for yoga, the result of her one-on-one classes with Mohan.

Yin Yan returned to China a few weeks later and noticed a steady increase in interest in yoga amongst her friends. The Chinese in her social circle were both rich and stressed out. They exercised regularly to keep fit and de-stress. They also yearned for a vaguely defined spirituality, something to give their lives meaning beyond the materialism they were surrounded by. There was more than a hint of American suburbia with its self-involved angst, retail therapy and quiet desperation amongst the moneyed circles in China's big cities.

Yin Yan decided that yoga was the perfect two-in-one fitness-cum-spirituality solution China's new rich were looking for. Her mind made up, she got on the phone to Mohan and asked him to come over to Beijing at her expense. If he agreed she would put up the capital necessary to start a high-end yoga boutique.

I met Mohan around two months after he landed in Beijing. At the time the Yogi Yoga centre had enrolled around three dozen regular students.

Mohan had a shy manner when speaking and diffidently asked me if there were any supermarkets in Beijing where he could buy Indian food.

The next time I met him was almost exactly three years later, in August 2006. By then yoga had caught on across China like wildfire and my editor wanted a related feature for the Sunday magazine section of the paper.

I dug up Mohan's old visiting card and gave him a call. The mobile number I had for him still worked. He was pleased to hear from me but we had problems scheduling a meeting. He rarely took classes these days, he said, his was more of a managerial role now.

When we finally caught up a week later he told me that Yogi

Yoga had expanded to fifty-one centres across China, ten of which were self-owned, the rest franchised out. They had 3500 students in Beijing alone and some 10,000 in all China.

Mohan had brought thirty other 'yogis' from India to staff all these centres and more were coming in every month. 'Rishikesh is empty now,' he said smiling. 'I am bringing people from Bombay, Rajasthan, Jammu, everywhere.'

Did he have any problems persuading people to relocate to China? It was, after all, an unknown quantity for most Indians; a country where they didn't speak the language or have any family.

Mohan smiled and opened his palms outwards in a gesture signifying that what he was about to say was obvious. There was money to be made here, he said. These yoga teachers could make a future for themselves in China. In India they would live out their lives in disguised poverty. Never quite sinking into destitution but engaged in a constant, numbing struggle to keep their head above water.

No one in India cares about yoga, Mohan said. But in China they are willing to pay $20 for one class. Was it a problem persuading teachers to make the move? No.

More than 150 million Chinese continued to subsist on a dollar a day or less. Tens of thousands of these were still willing to risk their lives attempting to smuggle themselves into the West.

Yet it was the same China that Mohan and many other Indians like him were beginning to look to for their chance to move up and on. It was a topsy-turvy world I found myself in. China's convulsive growth over the last decade was throwing up opportunities for anyone smart or lucky enough to spot them. Hitherto rigid boundaries were bursting open and the dust had not as yet settled.

China's newly affluent were hungry for the novel and after decades of isolation from the rest of the world, the novel was usually equated with the foreign. Brown may have been the new Black on the catwalks of Milan and Paris, but in Beijing yoga was the new t'ai chi.

It was this demand for the exotic and foreign that created widening possibilities for the intrepid Indian. Over the years I noticed an increase in Indian managers at restaurants across Beijing. These were not Indian food restaurants but Mexican, Italian and in one instance even Chinese. I talked to some of these young men.

Shashi, the manager of Gold Barn, an upmarket nouvelle Chinese food eatery in the CBD, confessed that the reason he had been hired was primarily to give a foreign face to the restaurant. It was considered an alluring touch of glamour. 'The Chinese like foreign things, ma'am,' he said.

Shashi earned $1500 a month in China. He was in no hurry to return to Delhi where he used to make a tenth of that as a waiter in a five-star hotel's coffee shop.

In the Beijing of today, waiters could become managers and yoga teachers, businessmen.

But not everyone was as lucky.

A few years later I was travelling in Zhejiang province as part of a group of foreign journalists reporting on the province's private enterprises.

During the trip we visited Wenzhou, a city famous in China for its entrepreneurial people, who had made it the centre of the country's light manufacturing industry.

We pulled up at the Wenzhou Dynasty hotel after a longish bus ride from a neighbouring city. I got off the bus and stretched my legs, enjoying the feeling after the cramped journey. We had woken early that morning and I was drowsy. As I blinked away the sleep from my eyes a burly Sardar complete with flaming red turban shimmered into vision.

He came running up to me grinning widely and began to speak in Punjabi-accented Hindi. 'Can I help you with your bags, madam? Are you from India? How long will you be staying?' the questions bubbled and gushed as he took over my suitcase and handed it to a bell hop.

Were I to have been in nineteenth-century Shanghai the

appearance of the said gentleman would have hardly warranted comment. Until the communist accession in 1949, there had been hundreds of Sikhs in that city. Colloquially known as *Hong Tou A-San*—a reference to their red turbans (*hong* means red in Mandarin while *tou* refers to the head), they were either part of the police or served as watchmen at banks and hotels.

But in the intervening years the mainland's Sikh population had virtually disappeared. Most left for Hong Kong, others returned to India. Communist China, particularly after 1962, was no longer a welcoming place for the *Hong Tou A-San*.

Since China's reform and opening up, however, the ghosts of the country's past were fast being resurrected. In cities like Shanghai, American and European businessmen could once again be found crowded in hotel lobbies and in a manner not very different from the taipans of old complaining about the lack of creativity amongst the locals.

The classifieds of newspapers in Beijing were filled with advertisements seeking amahs to look after children and bars with names like Suzie Wong overflowed on weekend nights with single white men flashing loaded wallets and scantily clad, tired-faced Chinese women helping them unload the wallets.

After decades of communist-imposed austerity on the general populace, the decadence of the pre-1949 years was making a comeback.

And now the *Hong Tou A-San* were gradually reappearing too. At lunch that day in Wenzhou, the conversation at the table turned to all the unlikely places people had spotted Sikh doormen in recent months. Beijing, said one observant scribe, had had a couple of *Hong Tou A-San* for several years, welcoming guests at the Presidential Plaza Hotel in the city's west. Sightings in Shenzhen, Hangzhou, and Shanghai were also mentioned.

I met Surinder Singh, the Wenzhou Dynasty doorman, later that evening. He was virtually unrecognizable when he appeared in the lobby without his doorman outfit and, to my surprise, sans turban.

Surinder, it transpired, had cut off his hair years ago, but the hotel had insisted that he would lack a certain *je ne sais quoi* without a *pagdi* and so he continued to wear one during work hours.

We sat down on an overstuffed velvet sofa and he repeatedly told me how happy he was to have met an Indian, so unexpectedly and so far away from home. I discovered that the 27-year-old wheat farmer from a village close to Amritsar was overwhelmingly lonely; a loneliness made worse by his inability to share his unhappiness with anyone. Surinder spoke no Chinese and very little English.

A high school graduate, Surinder had heard of the job opportunity at the hotel through a friend who had been an employee at the same establishment. The job paid $500 a month plus board and lodging, considerably more than he made helping his parents in the fields.

But with only four months having passed since his arrival in Wenzhou, he was already thinking of packing his bags and returning to India. 'I just need to save up enough for a ticket,' he said bitterly.

Surinder finished work at 4:30 in the afternoon, at which point hours of unrelenting boredom awaited him. Unable to talk to anyone he spent the time alone in his room, watching TV and salivating over memories of sarson ka saag.

'Madam, the food problem here is too much for me. I just can't take it any more,' he despaired. Surinder was not alone among Indians in China with food troubles, but in Wenzhou, unlike Beijing or Shanghai, he had little choice in the matter.

His happiest time of the week, Surinder told me, was on Sunday, his day off, when he was occasionally able to meet up with the only two other Indians he knew in the city, both yoga instructors.

Surinder clutched my hand like a drowning sailor when I stood up to take my leave, but the next day he was smiling widely again as he waved our departing bus goodbye.

CHAPTER FIVE

Mr Wu and Family

In August of 2003, my contract with the BBI expired and I decided against renewing it. The college had been a fine training ground for a novice sinologist, but it was time to start ranging further afield. There were adventures awaiting me outside of the campus and I was straining at the bit to wade right into these.

The prospects of meeting adventures in SOHO, however, were dim. The most excitement we had there was watching the gridlocked traffic on the third ring road. As the sun set, the headlights of all the cars would switch on, and the expressway would transform into a slow-moving constellation of stars.

Julio and I decided to move to one of the fast-disappearing, winding alleyways of a *hutong* neighbourhood. These neighbourhoods, some of which dated back to the Mongolian Yuan dynasty, formed the stubborn heart of the Old Peking; a Peking that despite some heavy-handed treatment from municipal bulldozers refused to give in totally to the New Beijing of tall skyscrapers.

Large swathes of *hutongs* were being demolished to dress up the Chinese capital in its Olympic clothes, but clustered around the Forbidden City, a core of these anachronistic neighbourhoods defiantly lived on.[1]

The *hutongs* were essentially willow-lined villages hidden away from the surrounding urban sprawl and were one of the few organic connections that Beijing retained with its past.[2] Too narrow for supermarkets, hutongs relied on street vendors and corner shops called *xiao mai bu* to provide residents with their daily needs: candied crab apples, knife-sharpening services, coal for the freezing winters.

In imperial times the *hutongs* were where the grand and rich resided, in opulent traditional-style courtyard homes called *siheyuan*, or four-sided yards. Blood-red lacquered doors were flanked on either side by marble-hewn guardian lions, their faces turned up in snarls ferocious enough to scare aware intruders from both the spirit and mortal worlds.

Inside the high, grey-brick walls of these *siheyuan*, complex family dramas played out, as generations of the same family and the servants that catered to them lived under a single roof much in the same style as India's joint families.

Pomegranate trees hung heavy with sweet red fruit in the courtyards. The south facing pavilion was usually the largest and reserved for those members of the family with the highest status: patriarchs, sons and first wives.

The main pavilion was flanked on either side by a series of chambers used as kitchens, libraries and guest rooms. If the owner was wealthy enough to afford concubines the *siheyuan* would likely consist of several interconnected courtyards, around which were housed his primary family, concubines and servants in descending order of importance.

The tinkle of women's laugher, the flurry of servants preparing succulent banquets, the clatter of horse hooves as guests rode up

---

[1]For more on Old Beijing see M.A. Aldrich, *The Search for a Vanishing Beijing*, Hong Kong University Press, 2006.

[2]See the website of Beijing Cultural Heritage Protection Centre (http://www.bjchp.org/).

from neighbouring cities for a visit: *siheyuan* were the quintessence of glamour, wealth and privilege in imperial China.

They were thus amongst the most obvious targets for the communists. From 1949 onwards *siheyuan* across Beijing were summarily expropriated and handed over to work units which then allocated accommodation to workers. Homes that had for centuries housed the extended families of the city's elite were transformed into dilapidated shacks that often squeezed in a dozen families, five or more to a room.

The red lacquer on the once ornate gates of *siheyuan* was stripped away; families built ad hoc shacks of corrugated iron and tin upon the wide expanse of the courtyard spaces; the marble-hewn lions were condemned as symbols of feudalism and smashed into little pieces, their ferocious snarls that had once frightened away even the most evil of spirits proving inadequate in the face of communism.

Gradually the *hutongs* ceased to give off the scent of elegance. This aroma was instead replaced by the odour of communal toilets. The majority of *hutong* residents lacked private facilities and had to use instead the plentiful public loos that dotted each neighbourhood at regular 100-metre intervals.

For the younger, wealthier, snootier Beijinger the *hutongs* were no longer a favoured address. Their cramped quarters were decaying, their narrow lanes unsuitable for cars, their lack of central heating inconvenient in the winter and their shoddy plumbing an embarrassment.

None of these observations were disputable and if I had grown up in one of these homes it is more than likely that I would have left for SOHO's double-glazed, centrally heated comfort at the first opportunity.

But as a foreigner the chance to live in the *hutongs* was a window to a world that remained rough-edged and uncosmopolitan, and very much Chinese. The *hutongs* were where one headed to hang out with the *laobaixing*, a Chinese word that literally meant 'the old hundred names' but was used more generally to designate the 'common people'—the average Zhou on the street. And although *hutong* homes were mouldy and crumbling, these neighbourhoods had genuine charm. Unlike the equivalent in Delhi—the narrow alleys around the Red Fort—*hutongs* were, on the whole, clean. They were crowded but not suffocatingly so, and best of all, they were quiet. Aside from the intermittent cry of a street vendor, *hutongs* were oases of aural peace, devoid of the constant hammering and drilling of New Beijing.

I loved the communality that infused the *hutongs*. Over-full quarters forced people out to the streets and through the changing seasons residents bundled together outdoors, exchanging gossip, playing mahjong, quaffing beers on steamy hot summer nights or just watching the world go by.

Finding an appropriate home in the *hutongs*, however, was a challenge. Aside from the toilet-less, shared spaces where the *laobaixing* resided, a few grand *siheyuan* in the imperial style survived, but these were the exclusive preserves of high officials and military grandees. Those at the top of the party hierarchy had never lost their taste for elegant courtyard homes and a number of these had remained discreetly preserved.

The gates of these *siheyuan* were guarded on the outside by the marble lions of old but on the inside by armed police bearing semi-automatic weapons. The compounds were surrounded by higher than average walls with only the antenna of satellite dishes peeping out and no one able to peep in. These were mini-forbidden cities for mini-modern-day emperors, patently out of reach for Julio and I.

What we were looking for was in fact what was hardest to find: a modestly renovated, small size *siheyuan*, with private bathroom. There were a few of these around, rented out primarily to foreigners, but demand far exceeded supply.

We found a real estate agent who specialized in locating courtyard homes and spent the next couple of weekends visiting the *siheyuan* that Tracy, the agent, took us to see in her shiny black Hyundai.

Nothing was suitable. They were either too expensive or badly located. One *siheyuan* that had only been refurbished a month ago featured pink crushed-velvet sofas and gigantic flat screen televisions. But the toilet was a hole in the floor of a closet-sized space with the shower directly above, so that the only way to bathe was by planting your feet on either side of the toilet hole.

When our agent told the landlady our reasons for passing on it, she was dejected. 'Foreigners are always fussing so much about toilets,' she muttered.

The next courtyard we visited had the opposite problem. The landlord, obviously *au fait* with the toilet fetish displayed by foreigners, had transformed the majority of the rooms in his house into sparkling temples to cleanliness. Everywhere, gilt-edged taps gushed streams of water into translucent glass basins and alongside numerous commodes stood glistening enamel urinals which the landlord kept urging Julio to try.

Finally one exhausted Sunday we pulled up into a *siheyuan* somewhat smaller than the ones we had been looking at but perfectly located. It was only a ten-minute bike-ride away from the European Union's Beijing delegation, where Julio had recently begun to work.

Picturing what the house would look like if we decided to rent it was a little difficult. The current occupant was the NGO Greenpeace, which was using the space to mount a month-long exhibition on the endangered forests of the world.

What would be the bathroom was thus filled with hanging green vines and life-size models of various species of great apes were swinging from these.

But we liked the layout of the house and the courtyard itself was lovely, a large poplar provided a shady canopy under which to sip nimbu pani on a summer's evening.

Major work was required before we could move in, though. I

wanted the walls painted a mango yellow, and the skanky toilet, even without the apes, was in definite need of a facelift. Most of all we needed to have a heating system installed, something the *siheyuan* conspicuously lacked.

'But why do you need heating?' the poker-faced landlord, Mr Wu, asked when we informed him of our needs. 'Err, temperatures fall to fifteen below in the winter,' I countered. 'You can always wear more clothes,' Mr Wu suggested.

And so it went. The negotiations were painstaking but two months later we were ready to move in.

The phenomenon of trendily renovated *siheyuan*, rented out to foreigners at what to the *laobaixing* would have been heart-attack inducing prices, was a relatively new one and most *hutong* dwellers had had limited interaction with foreigners.

The arrival of my Spanish husband and Indian self to live in Beixin Qiao Tou Tiao *hutong* thus caused understandable consternation. Seeing the crowds that gathered the day we moved in, one might have been forgiven for thinking the circus had come to town and indeed many of our neighbours seemed to view us as an amusing and exotic species of animal.

Little Wang from next door stroked my husband Julio's arm lovingly the first time they met. He fingered the cloth of Julio's shirt in wonder. 'Foreigners!' he exclaimed repeatedly, in a tizzy of delight.

The much treasured, recently remodelled toilet inside our home had a window high up that opened on the street, across which was situated the local *xiao mai bu*. Jolly mahjong gatherings took place outside this store, stretching late into the night.

On my first morning using the facilities, I picked up the word 'Indian' or '*Yindu*' drifting in through the window and began to pay more attention to the animated conversation emanating from the *xiao mai bu*. 'Oh! So she's Indian?' queried a baritone. 'Must be, I think,' replied an alto. 'But the husband? He's not dark enough?' came back the baritone. 'Yes, she's black but he's white. Must be from different countries,' concluded alto.

In SOHO I had chafed against the bubble-like nature of my existence and yearned for more interaction with the neighbours. Life in the *hutongs* was certainly going to give me that.

But even more than the neighbours it was our landlord who became a permanent fixture in our *hutong* life. The *siheyuan* was charming but with Yuan dynasty charm came Yuan dynasty plumbing, and barely a week went by without a burst pipe, blocked sink, leaking faucet or dripping drain.

All of these received the personal attention of Mr Wu. We pleaded in vain for professional plumbers and electricians but our pleas only met with Mr Wu's raised hand, palm spread wide to deflect our concerns. No need for a plumber, he would say. Why do you need an electrician? I am much better than plumbers and electricians.

And so every time the courtyard got flooded in *hutong* sewage or plunged into darkness, the light bulbs having all fused in union, we had to give Mr Wu a call. He would usually arrive within an hour or so of the summons, atop his trusty moped. Some days he would bring along his wife and son.

Mrs Wu seemed to love these visits to our courtyard. She was a neatly dressed lady in her late fifties, her hair always swept off her face and caught in a bun with a net. While her husband busied himself around the house with wrenches and hammers, she liked to wander around the courtyard, commenting on little details with approval. 'Lovely colour,' she would exclaim of some new acquisition.

The landlord himself had less appreciation for our aesthetic sense. '*Bu hao kan*! Ugly!' he had said straight off the bat when I pointed to the mango yellow colour I wanted for the walls at the paint shop.

A retired official from the Ministry of Railways, Mr Wu was an enigma to us at first. We knew little about him although his upright posture showed his liking for early-morning callisthenics. This was a taste he shared with the majority of *hutong* residents of a certain age.

Sheltered by the weeping of the willows that lined their alleys from the sweeping changes that were creating the viscerally modern 'New Beijing', the remnants of a collective culture lingered on in the *hutongs*; a hangover from the communism of a bygone era. This collectivism was articulated by the physical space of the *hutongs* themselves. In the narrowness of their lanes and closeness of their homes the *hutongs* were a celebration of the collective over the individual. There was no room for privacy here, physical or mental.

This shared 'culture of the masses' meant that even in the dead of winter the majority of the middle-aged and elderly would wake up at the first glint of dawn and spend an hour or so engaged in group exercises.[3] There was a startling unselfconsciousness to these collective workouts that stripped them of exhibitionism and bestowed on the participants a wonderful solemnity.

As an occasional spectator, my favourite among the myriad forms of morning exercises was group dancing. Husbands and wives who had been together so long their eyes barely registered the other's presence would shuffle along in unison in a locally modified version of the waltz. Sometimes there would be two old men dancing together, widowers, locked in an embrace that had once held a wife or a lover, but not for a long time.

The downside of Mr Wu's participation in these early morning pursuits was his penchant for arriving at our courtyard unannounced and unsolicited, confident that we would be awake, showered and welcoming of these crack-of-dawn visitations. He was inevitably disappointed.

The episode would usually begin with a persistent knocking that pierced straight through the pillow I buried my head in to drown out the sharp rapping. The pillow was never any match for Mr Wu's perseverance. I would finally emerge from my bedroom, groggily cross the courtyard and throw open the main door to reveal the energetic Mr Wu, who in contrast with my pallid

---

[3]This is a phenomenon that has been commented on by a wide number of observers, even those new to China. See, for example, Pankaj Mishra, 'Getting Rich', *London Review of Books*, Vol. 28 No. 23, 30 November 2006.

countenance would literally be glowing in a post-exercise euphoria.

We would stare at each other for a few seconds in mutual, horrified disbelief. Mr Wu was invariably amazed at finding his tenant still half-asleep at as late an hour as half-past seven in the morning.

He tended to recover from his shock quickly enough though, and would bustle past me without much in the way of explanation, busying himself with examinations of various crevices in the house. Every time I plucked up enough courage to ask him what he wanted he would pre-empt any speech on my part with his signature raised palm. 'Don't worry about me,' he would say solemnly. 'You must be very busy. Go away and do your work and just ignore me.'

I would spend hours cowering in my study trying to do as instructed and ignore the fact that my landlord was for some mystifying reason manically sweeping the courtyard. After this same scene had played out over half a dozen times, I reached breaking point.

One brave morning I marched up to Mr Wu in mid-sweep and politely asked him to desist from mopping my courtyard. I would do it myself, I told him, or the maid would when she got in, a few hours later.

'A courtyard must be swept clean every morning,' opined Mr Wu in sanctimonious response. At almost sixty he moved around with surprising sprightliness, teasing out fallen leaves from troublesome corners. I tugged at the broom gently, in a bid to disarm him. But Mr Wu clung to it tenaciously with an iron grip that once again belied his advanced years. I tugged harder, Mr Wu hung on. Finally using every ounce of strength I could summon, I wrenched the broom away, falling backwards flat on my bum in the process.

'Please, Mr Wu. Let *me* do the sweeping,' I begged, sprawled out on the floor in most undignified repose. Slowly he nodded in defeat. 'If there's nothing else I can do for you,' he said courteously, 'I'll take my leave.'

As we got to know Mr Wu better, we were able to put together bits of information gleaned off him to reach the startling conclusion that despite his humble appearance our landlord was a millionaire. It transpired that he owned not one but four *siheyuan* in the choicest of locations around Beijing. The one we rented off him for $2500 a month was the smallest and least prepossessing of these.

The going market rate for the kind of homes Mr Wu owned was around $3800 per square metre. On this basis our courtyard alone was worth $760,000.

Mr Wu was born in 1946 into a wealthy merchant's family. His ancestral home was a large *siheyuan* in the western part of Beijing. 'It had a pond and trees and rockeries as high as a mountain,' he told me once, his usually stern countenance softened by nostalgia. After 1949 his family home was expropriated and he lived out the next decade in a dank, cramped, one-bedroom apartment. But the worst was still to come.

Given his bourgeois background Mr Wu was branded a class-enemy and exiled to the countryside for 're-education' through hard labour during the Cultural Revolution. He was to spend over ten years in the windswept grasslands of Inner Mongolia shovelling manure.

The Mr Wu I knew was deeply dignified and cultured. He spent his evenings practising calligraphy and his days immersed in books detailing the intricacies of traditional Beijing architecture. His eyes lit up when explaining to us how different styles of doorways to *siheyuan* indicated the differing ranks of the occupants.

Everything Mr Wu represented—education, privilege and urbanity—would have been anathema in the days of the Cultural Revolution. I imagined him tortured by the incessant taunts of the villagers he had been made to live with for over a decade. 'Intellectual!' they would have spat out with contempt. 'Capitalist roader!' they would have accused, scowling.

Or perhaps I was wrong and the villagers had been kind. I never knew because Mr Wu rarely elaborated on his time in exile.

Mrs Wu was more forthcoming. She would sometimes tell us

about her resentment at her own ruined youth, whispering despite there being no one else around. Her family had been Kuomintang loyalists and while most of her relatives fled to Taiwan along with Chiang Kai Shek, her parents stayed on in mainland China, left with little save their pride.

This was a pride Mrs Wu desperately hung on to and whenever we met she rarely lost an opportunity to remind us that she was 'from Kuomintang people'. Most of the Chinese we knew, including Mr Wu, were guarded when talking of either their own or China's past, but Mrs Wu seemed impelled by a force beyond her control.

The Cultural Revolution interrupted her education and like her husband she spent the better part of her youth exiled in the countryside. 'I am uneducated,' Mrs Wu would tell us in sad confession. But then she would toss her head defiantly and add, 'But I am from a cultured family, not peasant riff-raff.'

In the early 1980s Mr Wu returned to Beijing and was able eventually to get a job in the railway ministry. He worked until retirement as a mid-level bureaucrat. His was an ordinary life and he was happy enough but at night his dreams were punctuated with memories of his ancestral family *siheyuan* with its rockeries and ponds and courtyards filled with chatter.

He took to walking around Beijing's remaining *hutong* neighbourhoods on the weekends, scouting around for a courtyard home to be had on the cheap, which he then intended to renovate. It wasn't long before he found one. In the late 1990s few people wanted to live in *hutongs* and the lack of protection afforded to private property made the land even less valuable.

For Mr Wu it was a fortuitous move. By the time we moved into Beixin Qiao Tou Tiao, a bill aimed at the protection of private property was set to be passed by the National People's Congress, China's legislature. *Hutong* neighbourhoods like ours had been declared protected historical zones and the value of *siheyuan* was shooting up as straight as an arrow. In short, Mr Wu was suddenly very rich.

Yet despite his wealth he continued to eschew fancy cars in

favour of a moped and fixed leaking toilets himself. When he took us out for a meal, Mrs Wu would carefully have every bit of leftover food packed in a take-away bag for them to eat later at home.

In India, where even our maidservants refused to clean the toilet, pointing out in injured tones that they were not jamadars, the idea of a millionaire landlord coming to a tenant's home to unblock a backed up commode would have been as likely as a drove of pigs sprouting wings and taking flight. Yet, Mr Wu did just that, on more than one occasion.

One of communism's lingering legacies in China was a basic belief in the dignity of labour and to me it was this belief that created the broadest gulf between India and China; a chasm ultimately much harder to bridge than that of GDP growth rates or flashy infrastructure.

This realization struck me first during a conversation with Cindy, my KFC-loving, beggar-despising student at the BBI. We were sitting together one afternoon at the apartment in SOHO, sharing a pot of freshly boiled green tea. Cindy was helping me out with the research for a story I was working on.

As we took a break, Cindy ran her fingers through her stylishly cut hair and looked around the freshly vacuumed apartment thoughtfully. Did I have an *ayi*, she asked? *Ayi*, a word that meant auntie in Mandarin, was the standard epithet for 'maid' in China.

I answered that I had someone come in thrice a week for a few hours each time, to do the laundry, clean the house and cook a simple meal or two. What did I pay her, Cindy inquired next.

I paid $100 a month but my *ayi* had several other clients besides me and I estimated that she made from $300 to 500 every month.

It was Cindy's next question that left me speechless. Could I help find her mother a job as an *ayi*, she asked. The idea that a university-educated, obviously well-off young girl clad in Levis jeans was interested in finding a job as a maid for her mother was almost as improbable to me as that of a millionaire landlord fixing toilets. I hadn't, of course, met Mr Wu yet.

Cindy went on to explain that her mother had recently retired and was anxious to move from Changsha, the city where she lived, to Beijing. Mother and daughter missed each other and were looking forward to being together again. But Cindy was concerned that her mother would get bored without a job. 'My mum's a great cook,' she said. 'She'll make a good *ayi.*'

I never did find a job for Cindy's mother, but I thought about her request often.

In India I had grown up surrounded by servants. We had a maid who made up the beds and set the table and another who cooked and washed the dishes. There was a gardener who came by in the mornings, and a young boy who would arrive on weekend afternoons to polish the brass. The boy was the son of the neighbourhood 'press wali', the lady who ironed our clothes with an old-fashioned coal-heated iron. Last and least in terms of status, we had a jamadarni, who cleaned out the toilets every day.

This might sound like a life of haute luxury but in fact I came from a middle-class background. I was already in college by the time we could afford to have an air conditioner installed in the house to run on the days that the temperature soared to almost 45 degrees Centigrade. It was cheaper in the India of the time to have a full-time maid than pay the electricity bills for an air conditioner.

Our maids lived with us. They had a room each in the 'servant's quarters' to the back of the house. Their rooms were big enough to fit in a bed and perhaps a cupboard but over the years the space had to stretch to accommodate much more than that. In these tiny lodgings would be housed the possessions and dreams of a lifetime.

The cook lived with her husband and two sons; the bed-maker and table setter, with her husband, three daughters and later, one son. Sometimes a relative of one of the maids would visit and stay over for the night. The elasticity of the rooms was infinite.

We were 'good' to our servants; my mother drilled into me the need to be polite to them. We paid for the medical expenses of their families and made sure their kids went to school. We bought them presents on special occasions and allowed them into the bedroom on Sunday mornings to watch the latest episode of the Ramayana, the televised version of the Hindu epic that was wildly popular in the 1980s.

But when we watched TV together, the servants sat on the floor, while my mother, the 'memsahib', my brother, 'baba', and I, 'baby', lolled back on the bed or sat cross-legged on chairs.

In all the years our servants worked for us, and they still do at my mother's home, not once did they sit down at the dining table with us for a meal; not once did we ask them to. We inhabited two different planes of existence, the servants and us, separated by language—we spoke English to each other and Hindi only to the servants—and wholly different choices. While I fretted about whether to choose Cambridge or Oxford in the event of being offered scholarships to both, the table-laying maid, not much older than I was at the time, fretted about whether or not to give in to her husband's demand for another, fourth child, in the hope of it being a boy. It was.

In China, communism had collapsed the feudal hierarchies that had once created similar parallel worlds between those that served and were served.[4] In Mao's China landlords lived as peasants

---

[4]It should be kept in mind, however, that in classic communist style while everyone was equal in Mao's China, some were more equal than others. Thus while feudal hierarchies might have been flattened, new party-based hierarchies of power and privilege took their place. For an account of the luxury and corruption that characterized Mao's own 'imperial court' see an excellent account by his personal physician: Li Zhisui, *The Private Life of Chairman Mao: The Inside Story of the Man Who Made Modern China*, Chatto & Windus, 1994.

and intellectuals did the bidding of the illiterate. This flattening of Chinese society was achieved through force and as the dead light of Mrs Wu's eyes hinted at when she talked of her past, at a terrible human cost. Yet, in the end it had propelled China into a modernity that seemed an epoch away from the caste-bound, class-enforced social hierarchies that persisted in India.

When I wrote a story along similar lines for a newspaper, friends from Delhi were outraged. How could you write such things about India, they asked me accusingly? 'We are *good* to our servants.'

My story had focussed on differing attitudes on either side of the Himalayas towards the dignity of labour. At the article's centre were a series of interviews I conducted with neighbourhood toilet cleaners.

Gandhi had identified toilet cleaning as key to revolutionizing society. He stressed repeatedly that in a society's approach to private and public sanitation lay its commitment to true freedom and dignity. If he was correct in his beliefs, then it was authoritarian China, not democratic India, that had in fact achieved self-respect for its citizens, my article argued.

My argument was backed up by conversations with sanitation workers like Yu Bao Ping, the cleaner at the public loo in a neighbouring *hutong* to ours.

The 38-year-old was originally a rice farmer from Anhui province. He moved to Beijing in early 2004 and landed the toilet-cleaning job soon after. He was lucky to have got such a good job in Beijing, he told me. Compared to the backbreaking labour of farming, the toilet business was a cinch. It gave him a stable income of around $100 a month and most important a chance to broaden his horizons in the big city.

Before moving to Beijing he had been afraid of life in a city where he knew no one, but thanks to the toilet he had made many friends. Most of the homes around Yu's toilet, as in other *hutongs*, lacked private facilities and so the majority of those in the lane used the communal toilet. 'Everyone in this neighbourhood comes through these doors,' Yu said, smiling.

When I said goodbye to Yu Bao Ping, he shook my hand with confidence and invited me to come back a few weeks later. His wife would be joining him soon and he wanted to introduce us. She had apparently never met a foreigner before. I thought of India where in some parts of the country people would still rush off to take a bath if they accidentally touched a bhangi.

I realized that Yu who cleaned out flush toilets with running water performed a function far less degrading than the hundreds of thousands of night soil workers in India who continued manually to handle human refuse on a daily basis. They were identifiable most of all by the smell of shit that clung to them; a smell that never left them as they spent their lives amidst the bacteria of a society that shunned them. Yu Bao Ping was spared this.

But manual cleaning of toilets had a long history in China too and it was only fairly recently that *hutong* loos had been outfitted with proper plumbing. In my conversations with the toilet cleaners, they all admitted that it was not a stigma-free job.

Lou Ya, the cleaner at a toilet near Beijing's historic Drum Tower, said she knew there were people who would view her work with revulsion. Although she had little time for them—'I'm not stealing and I stand my own two feet'—there were moments when Lou wished she didn't have to spend her days cleaning other people's 'big mess'. But then she would think about the story of Shi Chuanxiang, take a deep breath and keep going.

I had never heard of Shi Chuanxiang and hurried home to investigate this obviously inspirational figure for toilet cleaners. I discovered that he was one of the 'model workers' of communist folklore. Model workers were exemplary figures chosen by the party from the country's vast working class; a practice intended to instil in citizens a respect for manual labour.

Shi had spent more than forty years of his life shovelling and carrying human refuse from hole-in-the-ground public bathrooms when he was designated a 'model worker' and subsequently received by Liu Shaoqi, the President, in 1959. He became an idealized figure and people across the country were exhorted to learn from Shi. His story was compulsory reading in elementary schools even today.

What influence it had in today's China was debatable. Despite having imbibed Shi's story at a tender age it was obvious that Chinese youngsters were not running off en masse to take up toilet cleaning. The revolutionary fervour that had impelled their parents had long dissipated. In the old China joining the ranks of those who chose to emulate Shi was a way of publicly flagging the volunteer's correct class credentials. In the new China a platinum credit card was the preferred manner to signal the owners' participation in the correct class.

By the time I moved to Beijing, China had long emerged from the vortex of revolution and was well into the process of settling back into a semblance of its class-divided pre-communist days. What was once one of the world's most equal societies was fast transforming into one of the most unequal.

In Beijing it was common enough to see black-toothed construction workers, squatting on their haunches and gulping plain rice, taking shelter from the harsh mid-day sun in the shadow of a BMW.

Powering the motor of China's showy cities was a vast underclass of migrants, performing the services and jobs city folk wrinkled up their noses at. So it was with toilet cleaners. Not one amongst those I interviewed was from Beijing.

But despite all the re-emerging inequalities of class and circumstance, a little of the dignity that the country's painful tryst with communism had conferred on labour persisted.

The stigma attached to cleaning toilets was thus far from visceral. To the toilet attendants I spoke with, it was simply a job; not the best they could have hoped for but preferable nonetheless to many others. Some of the cleaners had worked previously as construction labourers. They were happier mopping the floors of a loo than sweating away at building sites. One young woman had been a waitress. She quit in favour of the toilet job because it was less stressful.

I got little sense that these were people condemned to cleaning toilets for life. Lou Ya wanted to be a hairdresser some day. Yu Bao Ping planned to save enough money to return to Anhui with his wife a few years later and start up his own business.

Unlike in India, 'servant' in China was more an adjective than a noun. It described a job that someone did rather than defining the essence of who they were.

In part this difference sprang from the fact that servants in China were richer. As I had told Cindy, Li Ayi, my maid, made almost $500 a month, more than what many of my students would go on to earn as journalists or white-collar workers in offices. Moreover, all migrants, no matter how poor, had rights to a plot of land back in their village and were thus rarely destitute.[5]

But another, equally crucial factor that distinguished the serving classes in India and China was education. Our cook in Delhi was illiterate, as were almost half of all Indian women. By contrast Li Ayi was a middle-school graduate and during the Cultural Revolution had even taught at a village primary school for a few years. Yu Bao Ping, the toilet cleaner, had two years of high school behind him.

In 2003, only 68 per cent of Indians over the age of fifteen were categorized as literate compared to 95 per cent for China.[6] Female illiteracy rates in China were around 13 per cent compared

---

[5]These land rights were, however, use rights rather than ownership rights. Following the break-up of the 'people's communes', the early 1980s saw a household responsibility system implemented in the countryside. Under this system while all land remained collectively owned, individual households were given long-term leases for the production and management of allocated property. The lease period is usually thirty years.

[6]*World Development Indicators, 2005*, World Bank.

to well over 50 per cent in India.[7] This was despite the fact that in India the definition of literacy was much less stringent, often restricted to the mere ability to write one's name. In China, by contrast, being counted as literate required the ability to write 1500 characters.

The systematic denial of an education to women or those of certain castes was one of the most insidious atrocities that a society could commit against its own people. Perpetuated over generations it robbed those discriminated against of a belief in their own worth as human beings. Illiteracy deprived people of their ability to function independently and narrowed their choices to the point where bondage was often the only option.

It was perhaps the greatest failing of the Indian government that it had been unable to ensure a basic education for close to 300 million of its citizens.

In China the party, for all its autocratic, power-clinging tendencies, had done a far better job than democratic India in ensuring an education for its people.

Moreover, the communist revolution had ensured that everyone of a certain generation had cleaned toilets and swept floors. The new rich that drove Mercedes and vacationed in Paris had parents who had scrubbed and washed as much as my *ayi* did today.

Youngsters like my students would talk of the suffering their parents endured during Mao's reign and the fact that they themselves

---

[7]However, it should also be kept in mind that matters in India have improved sharply over the last decade with recent drives to improve education beginning to pay off. For example, of the 200 million children in the 6 to 14 year age group about 42 million were not in school in 2000. Following a drive to bring them back initiated by the government in 2005 this number fell to 9.5 million—See Chetan Ahya, Andy Xie, Stephen Roach, Mihir Sheth and Denise Yam, *India and China: New Tigers of Asia*, Part-II, Morgan Stanley Research, 2006, p. 36. Again, while only some 48 per cent of adult women in India were literate, the figures for female youth literacy were a full 20 percentage points higher at 68 per cent, pointing to significant improvements. See: Sandra Lawson, David R. Heacock, Anna Stupnytska, *BRICs Monthly Report*, Goldman Sachs, 12 June 2007.

were spared the same trials with open relief. But even though servant's work was for them something to be avoided, they were aware that the line separating them from it was far from inviolable; it had been crossed only a generation ago.

In India, the same line was thick, almost sacred, its solidity preventing identification between those on either side and thus reinforcing their separation.

Not all the credit for the comparative fluidity of this line in China belonged to communism. China had historically been a more egalitarian society than India.[8] The examinations to the imperial civil services, for example, were theoretically open to anyone, underpinned by the idea that merit rather than birth was the correct criterion by which to determine a person's future.

It was in the absence of caste that the original seeds of the relative social mobility in China lay. Caste's boundary walls in India had always been higher and more forbidding than those of class in China.

Mr Wu's wise investments in *hutong* homes had ensured that his son was amongst those quickly scaling up the class ladder. At twenty-seven, little Wu, as his parents affectionately referred to him, was the embodiment of a 'little emperor', an overindulged only child.

Every penny that Mr Wu scrimped to save over the years was spent on giving his son the opportunities he himself was denied. Thus Mr Wu rode a moped but gave his son a spanking white Fiat to drive around in. Our courtyard was rented out in the son's name and the money earned in rent spent on the construction of another, more elaborate *siheyuan* that would be little Wu's to live in, once ready.

Little Wu had no job or income of his own. His parents told us he was studying English and often urged him to practise his linguistic skills with us. He never did. 'Oh, little Wu is a shy boy,'

---

[8]See P. Kuhn, 'Chinese Views of Social Classification', in J. Watson (ed.) *Class and Social Stratification in Post-revolution China*, Cambridge, 1984.

his mother would explain in embarrassment at his inability or unwillingness.

While Mr Wu rushed around the house, unflagging in his energy for stoppering leaks, little Wu, who often accompanied him, usually took a turn on the hammock chair we had in the courtyard.

He snapped out of his lethargy on the occasions he caught his mother whispering to us about her suffering during the Cultural Revolution. 'Why do you always have to bring up boring history,' he would snap, 'especially in front of foreigners? Why do you give foreigners a bad impression of China?'

One day as the Wu family was about to leave, the latest plumbing crisis successfully resolved, Mr Wu asked Julio for a favour. 'You've seen little Wu drive,' he said chattily. We had indeed and Julio nodded in acknowledgement. 'He's a very good driver,' continued Mr Wu. 'Perhaps your embassy could hire him as a driver?'

It was difficult to judge who looked more flabbergasted, Julio or little Wu.

CHAPTER SIX

Hutong *Days*

In China the red banner with large white characters had been the standard channel of communicating governmental directives and concerns to citizens ever since the communists came to power more than half a century ago. In turn citizens themselves used these banners to flag their collective commitment and support for government policy. Collective aspirations, collective commitment, the very thoughts of people were assumed and expressed as collective through these red banners.

So powerful was their presence that they seeped into metaphor. Only a few decades ago citizens were regularly urged to 'raise high the red banner of Mao Zedong thought'. Red was a potent colour in China—traditionally the colour for good luck and celebration and in more modern times the hue of revolution.

The *hutongs*, in many ways the last bastions of the collective culture of communism, were filled with the gnomic utterances of large white-character-on-red-backdrop banners. Three issues loomed larger than others on the banners that dotted my neighbourhood: the Olympic Games, care for the elderly, and dogs.

'Abide by the Dog Rules', one large banner cryptically announced, stretched out between two sturdy trees, only a few metres down from my courtyard. Next to it another urged residents to 'Visit the elderly; Bring happiness to them'.

The *hutongs* were disproportionately peopled with retirees and their pets; the ever-dwindling younger generation having taken off for swankier addresses. China's experiment with demographic engineering through its one-child policy had created one of the fastest ageing populations the world had ever seen. 'The Middle Kingdom Goes from Red to Grey', the headline of one media report catchily summed up, a summation that a quick walk around the *hutongs* was enough to confirm.

It was a marked contrast to Indian cities where the streets were swarming with adolescents and their pent-up energies and frustrations. In our *hutong* it was the elderly, men and women, who were out in full force, laughing toothlessly, kissing their dressed-up Pekinese dogs and exchanging news of their absent children. This visibility of old age was for me remarkable, particularly so for its gender-blindness.

In Delhi, retired men taking brisk morning walks or attempting to touch their toes over rounded bellies were common enough sights, but elderly women tended to remain confined behind closed doors. They had passed their best-before date and were expected by society to quietly and invisibly live out the rest of their time left in prayer or looking after grandchildren.

Where Chinese and Indian societies were similar was in their traditional reliance on large families as social insurance for the care of the older generation. But in China the one-child policy had abruptly disrupted this pattern, precipitating unprecedented age-related fiscal and social challenges. And while the central government grappled with devising pensions and adequate health care for the swelling ranks of senior citizens, in the *hutongs* this rupture found expression most visibly in the acquisition of pets.

The yapping of Pekinese was thus the primary aural backdrop to my *hutong* life, punctuated by the occasional anxious warning to '*Bao Beir*' or '*Xiang Pi*'—to 'avoid the bicycles' and 'keep to the

The main administrative building of the Beijing Broadcasting Institute, where the author took up her first job in China, teaching English.

The entrance to the author's house in a Beijing *hutong*.

The author (centre) with her students at the BBI.

The courtyard of the author's home. The courtyard, with its fruit-bearing pomegranate tree, became in many ways the fulcrum of her life in Beijing.

The courtyard, after a snowfall.

Li Ayi, who caught on fast to cooking Indian food, samosas included.

Little Wang, good to have around, despite his penchant for odd presents.

Julio, the author's husband, enjoying the snowfall. For the author herself, winters proved an ordeal—temperatures drop to 15 below zero.

The *hutongs*—old-style neighbourhoods in the heart of Beijing—are home to many elderly people. Dancing offers a panacea for loneliness.

Card players in the *hutong*. Retirees form a sizeable number of the inhabitants in these localities.

One of the pleasures of living in a *hutong* was the friendliness of its residents. Some of the neighbours, taking a break.

Glistening new malls and offices in the new Beijing. *(Inset)* Beijing is a city that is in a continuous process of reinvention. One fallout: as old gives way to new, a constant need for new maps, not to mention reorienting the mind.

One of the things that strikes one about China when comparing it with India—the respect for work, no matter what it is.

Young Beijingers at a mass English class. Learning English is the new buzz, specially in view of the Olympics. Some 375 million Chinese are stated to be learning English.

Yogi Mohan—from a modest start this youth from small-town India has gone on to run a chain of yoga centres in China.

American suburbia in China: The average house of a peasant in Huaxi village, the richest village in China.

It's always a pleasant surprise to see a compatriot in a foreign land. Surinder Singh went from Amritsar to China, but the transition wasn't easy.

The author with Shi Yongxin (right), the abbot of the Shaolin temple, famous for the style of kung fu that originated there.

The Baimasi abbot, Yin Le (right), at the spot where an Indian-style stupa is to come up. Baimasi is the birthplace of Chinese Buddhism and marks a seminal moment in Sino-Indian ties, as it was built to house two Indian monks way back in A.D. 68.

The entrance to Baimasi. It draws about 2000 visitors a day.

Hui women at a class in Arabic in Ningxia Hui region. The region is home to a large number of Muslims, who show a renewed interest in Islamic doctrine with the lifting of curbs imposed during the Cultural Revolution.

side of the road'. Bao Beir or Baby, and Xiang Pi or Eraser, were the beloved pets of Old Lady Zhou and Old Lady Qi,[1] two of our neighbours. Further along the *hutong* Old Lady Fang had a treasured poodle, Guai Guai, whom she dressed up in pink wool in the winter.

'Ma Ma' she would patiently repeat to Guai Guai throughout the day while pointing at herself, as if secretly cherishing the hope that one morning Guai Guai would open his mouth and eschew his usual bark in favour of a 'Ma Ma' in perfectly enunciated Mandarin.

For my *hutong* neighbours pets were quite obviously child-substitutes; someone to care for, someone to kiss on the nose. Owning a dog in Beijing was, however, no stroll in the park. Aside from the dangers of dog-extermination mobs that a SARS or rabies scare could spontaneously engender, pet dogs were also victims of bureaucratic rules that limited their number, size and breed.

In a manner akin to the one-child policy, a one-dog policy in Beijing confined each family to a single pooch. Moreover, the pooch had to be small. Over forty breeds including Dalmatians, terriers, collies and Labradors, were illegal in the capital, branded as dangerous by the city authorities due to their large size.

Every dog also needed to be registered at what was for many *hutong* dwellers a prohibitive cost. Until 2003 the fee for a dog licence was $600, followed by an additional yearly registration fee of $250. New regulations subsequently slashed these rates but the initial registration still cost $120.

The red banner that adorned my *hutong*, admonishing residents to 'Obey the Dog Rules', no longer seemed so cryptic.

But far outnumbering the dog and care-for-elderly-people banners were those dealing with the Olympic Games. The red of

---

[1] In China the prefix *lao* meaning old or *xiao* meaning young is commonly used before a person's family name to indicate the generation they belong to. Thus our landlord was called *Lao Wu* while his son was *Xiao Wu*. In the *hutongs* the *lao* were in abundance but the *xiao* few.

these banners seemed to have a special sheen as though touched by Olympic sunshine. 'I Will Participate in the Olympic Games; The Olympic Games are Good for Me' announced one. 'My Games, My Contribution, My Happiness' proclaimed another. My favourite simply said: 'Welcome the Games; Be Civilized.'

The campaign to create 'civilized neighbourhoods' was part of the government's strenuous efforts to transform the capital into an Olympic-worthy city. Elsewhere in Beijing this was being achieved through building snazzily designed opera houses and sporting stadia, but in the *hutongs* the municipal authorities had wisely zeroed in on the public toilets.

Hutong loos had long transcended the functionality of mere toilets. They were public spaces where residents gathered to share gossip and chattily exchange news of the latest developments in their bowel movements. What coffee shops were to Paris, W.C.s were to *hutongs*.

But despite their social significance, the majority of *hutong* toilets consisted of a series of un-partitioned pits in the floor with no flushes or running water. The mess of numerous users would then pile up until the evening, when a pump truck made the rounds of the alleyways, sucking up everything from the pits and carrying it away.

In the winter of 2004, Beijing hosted a meeting of the WTO. Unlike the more well known world trade organization with which it shared an acronym, the World Toilet Organisation focussed on toilets rather than tariffs. For three whole days more than 150 washroom heavyweights from nineteen countries, including academics, sanitation experts and toilet designers, thronged Beijing's loos, examining, discussing and suggesting ways of transforming them from the fetid to the fragrant.[2]

In the summit's aftermath the city government announced that it would spend $10 million a year until 2008 on rebuilding and

---

[2]See Pallavi Aiyar, 'China Prepares its New Revolootion', *Indian Express*, 16 November 2004.

upgrading *hutong* bathrooms into what the local media dubbed 'luxurious lavatories', suitable for use by even the sniffiest of foreign athletes.

A star rating system was devised for public loos, ranging from one to four stars, depending on the facilities made available. The loo bang opposite our *siheyuan* underwent its makeover only a few weeks before we moved in. To the disappointment of our neighbours it had only warranted a one-star construction, tucked away as it was in a cul-de-sac, few foreign visitors were likely to chance upon it during the Games. The chief improvement in the new one-star toilet, I ascertained, was the introduction of foot-operated flushes.

'Oh, it's much better than before,' said the mild-mannered and balding Mr Zhou, one of the fifteen-odd inhabitants of the plot to the right of our courtyard. 'At least the smell has gone.'

Stricken by thoughts of the 'smell' the unrenovated, flushless loo would have sent wafting over into our courtyard on a hot summer's day, I sent up a silent thanks to the Olympic God. 'It used to stink of rotten eggs,' Mr Zhou continued with scatological glee, but then his expression darkened. 'But ours is nothing much compared to some of the other new ones.'

Indeed, only a few minutes away at the head of neighbouring *Ju'er* or Chrysanthemum *hutong* a full-on four-star luxurious lavatory had been constructed as far back as 2002, predating the WTO summit. This loo had been built soon after Beijing won the bid to host the Games and it was to become the prototype for other post-WTO summit toilets in the area; the kind that Yu Bao Ping and Lou Ya would eventually work in.

Infrared-automated flush commodes, electric hand driers and signs in English, Chinese and Braille decorated the building. As the first four-star toilet in the area, the *Ju'er* lavatory had quickly become a major attraction, drawing in customers from as far as four *hutongs* away. Mr Yang, the local bicycle repairman, set up shop outside the loo to capitalize on the crowds. On most nights impromptu barbeque parties took place at the toilet's doorstep, organized by the entrepreneurial Old Wang, who owned the cigarette and beer shop opposite.[3]

A few stained couches, their insides spilling out, were set up. Others brought folding chairs. Mahjong sets and chess boards made an appearance. Soon a motley crew of regulars at the toilet entrance emerged and the locals jokingly began to call them the 'W.C. *Julebu*' or the W.C. club.

In the days when we were still looking for a suitable *siheyuan*, Julio and I had lived in a small duplex apartment in *Ju'er hutong* for a while. We had attended more than a few of these W.C. club gatherings and even after we moved to Beixin Qiao Tou Tiao we returned on occasion for a drink at the *Ju'er* toilet.

On the last few occasions we visited, however, the club had lost its former panache, the chief organizer, Old Wang, having moved away. Wang's dilapidated *hutong* apartment had become slated for demolition and he had little choice but to leave the alleyway his family had lived in for half a century.

For the W.C *Julebu*, as for many other communities in the city, the Olympic Games had proved to be a double-edged sword. Improved toilets built in the name of the Games certainly represented a major improvement in the quality of *hutong* life but between a third and half of all the *hutongs* that once crisscrossed their way across the capital had been demolished to pave the way for the 'New Beijing, Olympic Beijing' that the red banners promulgated.

Under China's legal system all land was publicly owned and individuals leased their homes for a set number of years. If the state decided that the land where a particular property stood better served the 'public interest' in some other way a large *chai* sign would be painted on the property and the residents given a few

---

[3]See Peter Hessler, 'Hutong Karma', *The New Yorker*, 13-20 February 2006. The author, who lived in *Ju'er hutong* for several years, details the feel of life in the *hutongs* and also follows the adventures of the W.C. *Julebu* and Old Wang.

weeks to move out before the wrecking balls bashed it in. Crucially, the definition of public interest remained vague. A multiplex cinema was in the public interest of some, not to mention the public that was very interested in golf courses. And so over the rubble of the *hutongs* mega malls, high-rise apartment complexes and entertainment centres were born. For real estate developers and their local official friends the *hutongs* were a cash cow to milk dry.

I brought up the issue of the wanton demolition of these neighbourhoods during an interview with an official with the Beijing Organizing Committee for the Olympic Games (BOCOG) in late 2005. The official in charge, Sun Weide, was dismissive. Not all the *hutongs* had historic value, he said. Most of them were just slums, unworthy of preservation or renovation.

'You foreign reporters always go on about what a pity it is to clear away the *hutongs*, but have you asked the *hutong* people themselves what they want? They would themselves much rather live in clean apartments with their own bathroom and better facilities,' he said.

'I would never leave the *hutong*,' Old Lady Fang, the proprietress of the *xiao mai bu* opposite our courtyard, had said to me only a few days before this interview. 'Not even if they paid me a lot of money.'

On this last count, Old Lady Fang could rest assured. It was extremely unlikely that anyone would pay her a lot of money to vacate. Although the law provided for compensation in the event of expropriation of property, the amount of this compensation was in practice well below its market value.

The *hutongs* were on prime land, the very centre of the city. They were the home of *lao Beijingren*, or long-time Beijing people, the inheritors and safe-keepers of all that made the city unique: the growling accent, the warming street snacks, the sense of being connected to the *hutongs* by roots that ran deep. So strong was their identification with the city that they often described themselves simply as *lao Beijing*, or 'old Beijing', dropping '*ren*', the word for 'people', altogether.

The compensation that the majority of these *lao Beijingren* received for their *hutong* homes was at the most enough to buy them a two-bedroom flat in one of the new developments outside of the fifth ring road. Cast out symbolically and literally to the periphery of the city that had once defined their very essence, they were made painfully aware that there was little place for them in the 'New Beijing'.

Estimates of the number of households forced to relocate in the five years leading up to the Olympics varied between 350,000 and 500,000.[4] In this mass displacement of hundreds of thousands of people the cruel fangs of China's autocratic regime were exposed as was its sharp variance to the workings of the system in India. One of the hardest things for a government to do in India was to displace human beings.

Powerless in so many ways, degraded and disregarded in many others, India's poor nonetheless had a vote, so that however downtrodden they may have been as individuals, the 'vote banks' they comprised collectively had a power that their elected officials could disregard only at their own peril.

The irony of democracy was that the same people who may not have had enough to eat or clothe themselves adequately had the ability to hold up the biggest of hydroelectric power plants and stall the most vaunted of special economic zones.

In China the *lao Beijingren* had no vote and no choice. With neither an independent media nor an impartial judiciary, channels of protest were in short supply for these people. Most simply accepted their fate and moved away from the friends and neighbours who had punctuated their *hutong* lives to live out the rest of their time within the confines of a distant apartment in quiet isolation. They had been at the receiving end of the capricious whims of an

---

[4]Andrew Ness, 'Blue Skies for the Beijing Olympics', *China Business Review*, March-April 2002.

authoritarian state before; theirs was a resignation borne of experience.

For some, however, the state-sanctioned violence to their homes proved too bitter a pill to swallow in silence. A wave of suicides and attempted suicides rippled across the city. In September 2003 a Beijing resident, Wang Baoguang, set himself on fire while forcibly being evicted from his home. Less than a month later a *hutong* dweller, 43-year-old Ye Guoqiang, jumped off a bridge in the Forbidden City to protest the demolition of his family's home and restaurant to make way for a shopping arcade. He survived the fall only to be arrested and jailed.[5]

Beating, intimidation and jailing were common outcomes for those who like Ye attempted to draw public attention to their plight. A more common form of protest was thus a simple and obstinate refusal to leave.

Every once in a while I would spot a wrecked block of low-rise flats with pyjamas drying on the balcony of a lone surviving apartment. As a symbol of defiance the pyjamas would be imbued with a heroic quality, David against Goliath, the powerless *laobaixing* against the might of a real estate tycoon.

These were families that lived on in their homes even after the electricity was cut off and the taps ran dry. They stoically withstood the bullying of thugs sent around to 'persuade' them to depart. Wrecking balls smashed neighbouring homes to smithereens but they continued to dry their pyjamas out front among the ruins.[6]

In the end, however, they always left. If they were lucky their compensation was considerably upped to achieve their exit. Not everyone was lucky.

What was it that drove these people to cling to their homes

---

[5] *China: Human Rights Defenders at Risk*, Amnesty International (http://web.amnesty.org/library/index/engasa170452004).

[6] There was a special term for these houses in Chinese, *ding zi hu* or 'nail house', borrowed from a popular Chinese expression in which a 'nail' is a person who sticks out by refusing to submit to authority.

against all odds? Why weren't they simply relieved to be able to move to centrally heated apartments with good plumbing and leak-free roofs, as the BOCOG official had suggested they were.

'Because it would be so lonely,' replied Old Lady Fang simply.

In their layout and composition the *hutongs* were a celebration of the communal over the individual. The architecture of the new high-rises that replaced these neighbourhoods achieved the polar opposite. Private toilets meant greater convenience for the individual users. 'But where would we meet to chat and find out how everyone was doing,' explained Old Lady Fang. 'Who would we joke with?'

Staircases would be hard on arthritic knees and indoor heating would militate against the elderly congregating in the afternoon sun to soak up its precious warmth. The visibility of old age in the *hutongs* that had struck me with such force would gradually fade and eventually disappear behind closed doors, as was usual in so many other parts of the world.

New Beijing was a formidable foe, fed fat on money and unthinking of its own consequences.

After my chat with Old Lady Fang I took a quick walk around the surrounding *hutongs*. A couple of middle-aged men were sneaking a quick snooze on ripped-up beds put out on the alleyway for precisely that purpose. Further on a flock of older women peeled sunflower seeds, sitting on the doorstep of one of their homes. They waved to me as I walked by. '*Chu qu?*'—'Going out?'—they asked.

I imagined the New Beijing equivalent—IKEA stores and bowling alleys—and felt soft waves of nostalgia that were alien to me. I had never thought of myself as a sentimental pastoral-type. But *hutong* communities were vibrant and viable. They could be adapted and upgraded for modern times. Their demolition was both unnecessary and unethical given that so little serious attempt had been made to consider other alternatives.

When I returned home that afternoon little Wang from next

door was stretched out in a makeshift hammock, blocking the entrance to my main door. On his left he had a turtle in a glass jar, on his right, a cricket stuffed into a woven bamboo box. Unsure of how to proceed, I tried stepping over him, at which point he woke up, mortified to have been discovered napping at my doorstep.

I hastened to assure him that it was quite all right and began to make my way in but overcome with guilt little Wang pressed his pet cricket into my hands, insisting I take it as a gift. Less than fond of green, singing insects, I pushed it right back towards him, claiming I couldn't possibly accept such a generous offer. A struggle ensued as we both tried to force the hapless cricket into the other's bosom, until he cried out 'Please! I want to be your friend. Take it!'

The cricket was discreetly released into a friend's garden the next day but I thought of it often, as a symbol of friendship so openly offered and of a *hutong* way of life that I had quietly fallen in love with.

CHAPTER SEVEN

Chicken Feet and Jain Diets

By mid-2004 I was writing in earnest but a freelancer's income was always in need of supplementing. I thus agreed to take up a position as a part-time consultant for the Confederation of Indian Industry (CII). For me it was a welcome opportunity to earn a regular salary while learning more about the Sino-Indian economic engagement from the ground up. For the CII, whose China office was in Shanghai, the services of a Beijing-based consultant were useful.

One of my first tasks in this new position was to attend the inauguration of the China factory of Indian auto component major Sundram Fasteners. This was in fact the first of what would later become several, Indian-invested manufacturing plants in China. The plant was located in Haiyan County, part of the booming province of Zhejiang, and was a two-hour drive from Shanghai.

It was arranged for me to fly to Shanghai and then drive to the factory site along with Sunil, Director of the CII's China operations. I arrived at the CII office in Shanghai on schedule, where I was introduced by Sunil to Nigamji, the local representative of an Indian bank. We would all be driving to Haiyan together.

We settled into the car, Sunil in the front, next to the driver, Nigamji and I in the back. Over the next two hours it became clear that Nigamji was a man of opinions, ones that he was wont to share. His salt-and-pepper hair slicked back with Brylcreem and his trousers riding high above his ankles, the bank representative waxed eloquent on 'the Chinese race' and its shortcomings for virtually the entire journey with an unselfconsciousness that was terrifying.

Nigamji was unhappy with the lack of diversity in China. 'In India we are so varied, we look so different, have different languages, dress differently, but the Chinese are just all the same,' he alleged.

Next on Nigamji's charge-sheet of crimes was the *Chini admi's* or Chinese man's passion for baijiu, a local liquor, gallons of which were consumed during business dinners. 'They like to drink and smoke and Pallaviji you know how difficult it is for us Indians to adjust here.'

'The Europeans, of course, enjoy themselves here,' he continued, revealing the egalitarian nature of his prejudices that were far from confined to the Chinese alone. 'They also like to drink and smoke. Many even marry Chinese girls and the food is fine for them, because they like non-veg in any case.'

Nigamji's confidence in my sharing both his values and opinions by virtue of also being an Indian was total. I was soon to be married to a European (Julio and I had decided to take the plunge and set the date for spring 2005). I liked to drink on occasion and smoke and eat non-veg, but patently none of this had even momentarily occurred to the man. Throughout his journey-long discourse Nigamji thus continued to smile beatifically at me, completely un-put-out by my increasingly strained expression.

Although at first uncomfortable with having the role of audience for the exposition of his *Chini admi* theories thrust upon me, I cheered up a bit after deciding to look upon the whole experience as an anthropological exploration into the reaction of the middle-class, middle-aged Indian male (the bulk of the country's business community) to Chinese culture. This was a reaction that was bound to have an impact on the hoped-for smooth development of Sino-Indian economic cooperation.

In interviews given by business and political leaders on either side of the Himalayas the fashion was to expound at length on the similarities of the two ancient and neighbouring civilizations. Buddhism was inevitably alluded to.

But it was through Nigamji's conversation that an essential truth first became clear to me. Despite all the feel-good rhetoric that flogged the ancient connection of a religion that was now all but dead in its country of origin, Indians and Chinese were in fact largely culturally untranslatable to each other.

Nowhere was there less mutual comprehension than in attitudes to food. In India, elite Brahmins delineated their status by increasingly finickier food choices: no meat, no garlic, no onions, no non-vegetarians in the kitchen. In China, the greater the variety of things you could afford to eat, the meatier and the weirder, the higher was your status.

In India, even non-vegetarians would only eat certain animals and then only certain parts of those animals. So chicken was okay, but not chicken feet. Lamb was fine, but not the intestines. Prawns were good, but not octopus. To an average Chinese such discrimination was deeply mystifying.

In the ensuing years I became a regular at banquets organized by Chinese hosts for visiting trade delegations from India and on occasion I had the unhappy task of trying to explain the requirements of a Jain diet. Saying that the Jain guests did not eat root vegetables was so outside of the average Chinese person's experience of the world that their eyes simply glazed over and they often acted as if they hadn't heard. I realized that for them it was such an unlikely request that ignoring it was the only way in which they could deal with it.

Watching their Indian guests sniff suspiciously at their soup for traces of animal stock, harried trade officials would lean across to me and wail in distress, 'You Indians. You don't eat anything!' A few minutes later, having just been confronted with chicken feet a la mode, one of the Indian delegates would tap me on the shoulder and whisper in disgust in my ear, 'These Chinese. They eat everything!'

On the evening of the Sundram Fasteners plant inauguration the local officials of Haiyan County organized a banquet for the Indian guests to mark the occasion. I sat sandwiched between Nigamji, who seemed to have taken a strong liking to me, and an Indian embassy official.

As the dinner progressed, course after course of exotic and expensive foods made an appearance. With each new dish Nigamji blanched ever paler. By the time a bowl of soup with floating sea slugs made an appearance, he was positively white.

As the dinner drew to a close the Chinese officials began to get boisterous. They had been quaffing substantial portions of baijiu through the evening and now the vice-mayor took it upon himself to go around toasting every individual present.

'*Ganbei*'—'Bottoms up'—he said, and drained his small glass clean, staggering on to the next toast. How do you say 'cheers' in Hindi, asked a young Chinese translator seated at my table. I wracked my brains and was forced to admit it didn't have an equivalent. 'Then what do you say to each other when you drink?' he asked back.

'Well, we don't really drink much,' I replied, 'Or at least we're not supposed to.' I thought about the coke and orange juice parties the Indian embassy was so adept at hosting and sighed.

I looked around. All the Chinese were flushed and a little drunk. They oozed baijiu-induced goodwill. 'To India! *Ganbei*!' one toasted. 'To Friendship! *Ganbei*!' another added.

In the meantime the majority of the Indians sat around in prim disapproval, stiffly partaking of a tiny sip from their wine glasses if absolutely forced to. As they dabbed the mouths that had hardly eaten anything with napkin corners, a barely concealed look of disdain lurked behind their forced smiles.

I was to become used to these cross-Himalayan food-related faux pas. In August of 2004 I accompanied a ninety-member strong Chinese business delegation to New Delhi and Calcutta to participate in CII-organized conferences. In Calcutta the hosts had arranged for the guests to sample the city's Chinese food, famous across India.

As the restaurant's best paneer manchurian and garlic chilli chowmein were served up for the guests, one of the delegates, who had been tucking away quite happily, turned to me and without a trace of irony announced, 'Best Indian food I've had here.'

But the cultural faux pas were not limited to food. Indian businessmen visiting China bearing corporate gifts were often embarrassed to discover that a large number of the officials and entrepreneurs they had meetings fixed with turned out to be women. Emergency requests to headquarters in India had to be sent for gender-neutral supplements to the ties they had brought with them as gifts.

Just as old age was more visible on Chinese streets than Indian ones, so were women. Women bus drivers and conductors, taxi drivers and police officers were a common sight in Beijing.

The Chinese capital's airport was also the only one I had seen in the world where the security check, complete with manual patting down, was performed on both male and female passengers by women.

In contrast, much of daily life in India was conducted on the assumption that women were in constant need of having to protect their modesty from ravaging, savage men.

In Indian airports not only were security checks for women conducted by women but in a separate cubicle curtained off from the world. Not only did women not drive buses in India, in many cities they sat in specially partitioned sections of the bus reserved exclusively for ladies. India may not officially have had a purdah system but invisible purdahs lingered in myriad ways.

Understandably, for Chinese women visiting India, a culture shock was in store. During the CII trip to India the entire delegation was taken on a one-day sightseeing trip to the Taj Mahal. We had only been on board the bus to Agra twenty minutes or so when one of the female participants who had been staring out the window turned to me and remarked, 'There are a lot of men in India.'

I looked at the scene she had been surveying and sure enough the streets were full of men, mostly young—some leaning carelessly against bus stands, others holding hands in companionable lethargy, still others hurrying about their business riding two-wheeler scooters and bicycles or hanging on dangerously to overcrowded buses.

The Chinese woman cleared her throat as though afraid of being impolite and hesitantly added, 'Where are the women?'

I looked out once again. There were no women riding two-wheeler scooters and bicycles. There were no casual clusters of women loitering around aimlessly, laughing up at the sun. There were no women, period.

After a few seconds of intent peering, I finally spotted a female municipal employee sweeping up leaves. 'There's a woman,' I said, pointing her out in triumph to my Chinese friend. She gave me a strange look.

There were many occasions during the week in India on which I was at the receiving end of these strange looks from the delegates. 'You have separate ladies lines to buy railway tickets?' 'These people sleeping on the road are allowed to be here?' 'You can really have as many children as you like?'

One reason for the comparative gender empowerment of women in urban China was the one-child policy. Freed from the burden of raising several children Chinese women were better able to participate in the workforce and in fact comprised 45 per cent of the working population in cities, considerably higher than the world average of 35 per cent.

Still, I was never quite sure what I thought of the one-child policy myself. It was clearly undemocratic and the idea of the state dictating what I had grown up believing to be a deeply personal choice was objectionable.

I had occasion to ponder the policy at length when in the fall of 2006 I was nominated by the Indian government to participate in a large Indian 'youth delegation' touring China for two weeks as part of an inter-governmental exchange programme.

The delegation brought together a motley group of people whose lives would only improbably have crossed back in India. It included doctors, parachutists, students, jugglers, Panchayati Raj members and dancers.[1]

The one-child policy was much discussed by the delegates given how it cut to the core of the divergent realities of contemporary China and India. The doctors and students I discussed the issue with thought the policy was simply too much of an infringement on individual human rights to be justified.

Next I talked with the magician Raffan. At five-foot-nothing he was a ball of nervous energy, constantly chewing Paan Parag and drawing attention to himself with impromptu renditions of Hindi movie song sequences. Raffan, it transpired, already had two wives and nine children, all by the age of twenty-four. He'd grown up in the slums of west Delhi and married his first wife at the age of fifteen. '*Hamare mein aisa hi hota hai,*' he said—'It's just the way it is in our community.'

Unsurprisingly perhaps, Raffan was also against the idea of a one-child policy.

Of all the different groups of people that formed the delegation it was only the women members of the Panchayati Raj contingent that saw the policy in a positive light. These village-level representatives of women from the poorest of areas of Chhattisgarh

[1]Pallavi Aiyar, 'An Exercise in Strengthening Relations', *The Hindu*, 20 October 2006.

and Rajasthan and Haryana argued that the one-child policy was an empowering measure.[2]

'If in Haryana we also made it compulsory to have only one child, what couldn't the women achieve,' said Preeti Choudhary, a Zila Parishad member from Faridabad, near Delhi, as we drove along a smooth highway on the outskirts of Xian.

But the one-child policy was a two-sided coin, particularly in a country with a deep traditional preference for male children. Thus even as it allowed women in cities more time to focus on their careers, in the countryside in particular it meant the regular aborting of female foetuses by parents hell-bent on ensuring that their one child was a boy.[3] Most analysts in the field agreed that China's sharply distorted sex ratio of 117 to 119 boys for every 100 girls was in no small measure the result of the Chinese state's attempt at demographic engineering.

In Preeti's state, Haryana, the sex ratio for some districts was over 130 boys for every 100 girls,[4] even in the absence of a one-

---

[2]The one-child policy in fact applied to less than half of China's population. In most rural areas, if a couple's first child was a girl they were permitted to have a second. Ethnic minorities were exempt from the policy as were couples in which both partners were only-children themselves.

[3]Stories of forced abortions to ensure compliance with the policy were common in China. Suicide amongst young rural women in China was also extremely high. Fifty-six per cent of the world's female suicides are in China, according to a study by the World Bank, Harvard University and the World Health Organisation. See: Elizabeth Rosenthal, 'Study Links Rural Suicides in China to Stress and Ready Poisons', *New York Times*, 29 November 2002. See also Maureen Fan, 'In Rural China, a Bitter Way Out', *Washington Post*, 15 May 2007.

[4]See Census of India 2001. In China however, the worst sex ratio for newborns aged zero to four had reached 163.5 boys to 100 girls by the end of 2005 in Lianyungang, a city in Jiangsu Province. See Xinhua, 'China Warned of Risks of Imbalanced Sex Ratio', *China Daily*, 24 August 2007.

child policy. Prescribing the policy for Haryana in the hope that it would facilitate gender empowerment would be foolhardy.

The long strides that Chinese women had walked from the days in which their feet were broken and bound to produce a tiny foot considered beautiful to men could not simply be attributed to the one-child policy. As with attitudes to dignity of labour, equality of the sexes was part and parcel of the rupture with the country's past that the communists aimed to create.

Under Mao, who famously declared that 'women hold up half the sky', women were for the first time given the right to divorce and own land. Foot binding was stamped out and the practice of bride sales and concubines made illegal. Women continued to suffer from the privations and strictures of the period as did men, but for the first time people were educated into a strong belief regarding gender equality.[5]

In the vast hinterland bride sales never totally vanished and even today the practice continues to exist in the remote countryside. Concubines in the traditional sense may have ceased to exist but in the new China of re-emergent wealth and privilege, the practice of keeping mistresses had also re-emerged, as had prostitution.

Nonetheless, the communist revolution did cause a fundamental, albeit violent, break with the feudal past and along with it a feudal mentality. In India's revolutionless present, on the other hand, feudalism and modernity have continued to walk hand in hand.

Thus the dowry system was not just a remnant of history that persisted in the remoter villages but a thriving practice in the largest of cities. This was not to deny that at the same time an alternative reality of powerful women lawyers, journalists and

---

[5]See Sandra Lawson, David R. Heacock, Anna Stupnytska, *Women Hold up Half the Sky*, BRICs Monthly Report, Goldman Sachs, 16 May 2007, according to which India does worst of all the BRICs on all gender-related parameters evaluated. China does best on two: political representation at 20 per cent (India is 8 per cent) and labour force participation which is more than twice as high as India's.

politicians also existed. In India's present of dowry deaths and female prime ministers, shunned bhangis and untouchable Presidents, there was a fluid intermingling of the medieval and modern. The same could be claimed of China as well. However, the proportion of the two ingredients in the countries varied: a greater measure of the medieval in India and a dash more of the modern in China.

By pointing this out I do not mean to suggest violent revolution as the sole solution to the kinds of social ills that have persisted in India over the centuries. What was true was that the longer I lived in China the less black and white I was in my judgements regarding not only the country's past but also its present. I realized further that this was a present that did not make for a simple fit with India's.

But although the cultural gap was wider than sometimes assumed there were certain points where it narrowed. I lived in one of these points—the *hutongs*.

In the manner in which *hutong* life mixed long-preserved traditions and more modern elements it approximated the social fabric that makes up Indian cities. In these neighbourhoods, kabadiwallahs relaxed after a hard day's work collecting junk by watching the latest DVD on their newly acquired players; street-food vendors ordered in fresh supplies on mobile phones; and cycling itinerants attached hastily assembled motors to their bicycles to make pedalling unnecessary.

So although the *hutong* equivalent of the always male local paanwallah in Delhi, the *xiao maibu* owner, may have been a woman, there was nonetheless a rhythm to life in these historic neighbourhoods that matched that of my childhood. The same modes of address—auntie, granny, brother—that embraced strangers, transforming them into family and the same sabziwallahs screeching out a list of vegetables.

These were similarities that resulted from both the *hutongs* and the middle-class Delhi neighbourhood I had grown up in having retained the shadow of the village. They were essentially rural cityscapes. They were also cityscapes under siege.

In Olympic Beijing the *hutongs* were the last vestiges of a past that was rapidly being flattened into an all-embracing, ahistoric, almost tyrannical present. I was fortunate to have found myself a life in them before this process was complete.

In the evenings I would sit writing in my study, looking out every once in a while at the courtyard to appreciate the redness of the hanging fruit on the pomegranate tree. The hoarse cry of a street vendor cycling by would waft in. 'Ventilator cleeeaner,' he would shriek, every other word elongated in emphasis. 'I can clean your dirty ventilatooors.'

CHAPTER EIGHT

Factory of the World

Days turned into months almost without my noticing. When summer gave way to fall, the trees took on a fiery orange hue and the nip in the air brought out coal vendors on their tricycles in full force. Little Wang from next door wore a jacket in the evenings when he took his turtle out for a stroll and Old Lady Fang wrapped up Guai Guai in pink wool.

Once winter set in, the trees turned skinny, their scraggly, gnarled trunks and branches almost obscene in their nakedness. Old men still took their songbirds out for an afternoon walk but covered up their cages in thick insulating cloth to protect them from the harsh winds that whooshed in from Siberia. In spring the first blossoms drew swirls of colour in the sky and in summer the large poplar just outside our courtyard fanned out to form a natural umbrella to shade us from the strong sun.

But the *hutongs*, enchanting as they were, were not the reason that China was capturing headlines across the world. Global attention was rather focussed thousands of kilometres south of the *hutongs*, where forests of factories hummed along non-stop in the boom towns along China's eastern and southern coast. The Pearl river delta and the Yangtse river delta together formed the heart of the 'China Miracle', journalistic shorthand for the unprecedented economic transformations that had reshaped a backward and poor agrarian society and wrought it into the world's fourth largest economy.

This was a world of vertiginous statistics, where millions and billions rolled off the tongue in a constant flow. Single towns churned out 15 billion buttons, 200 million metres of zippers, 5 billion metres of fabric and 3 billon pairs of socks. The cities and towns of Guangdong, Zhejiang and Jiangsu provinces, the wealthiest regions of China, teemed with hundreds and thousands of migrant workers drawn from the 1.3 billion-strong population of the country. And it wasn't only the numbers with a line of zeros tacked on to the end that were noteworthy but also those that began with a mere decimal point.

It was in the markets and warehouses of these towns that the world came to hunt for a bargain and usually found one. From tea cups to artificial flowers and key chains to stuffed toys, the 'made in China' prices of products manufactured here were world-beaters, a fraction of what consumers around the globe would finally pay to the Wal-Mart and IKEA outlets where they bought their coffee cups and toasters.

The embodiment of these mind-bending statistics, big and small, was a county-level town in Zhejiang province called Yiwu. Although passed over by most popular guide books on China, Yiwu was home to a sight every bit as awe-inspiring as Beijing's Forbidden City or Xian's terracotta warriors: Yiwu International Trade City—the largest wholesale market in the world.

Spread over 2.6 million square metres, Yiwu's market boasted 50,000 stalls selling 400,000 categories of products, and it stood as testament to the fact that almost anything, from African art to statues of Ganesha, could be made in China, and cheaper.

I visited the town in early 2006 on a reporting assignment for the *Hindu*, the newspaper I was working for by then. The reality of both the number and diversity of products actually on display in the market hit me with an almost physical impact. Walking through floor after floor, jampacked with a measureless smorgasbord of bric-a-brac, made me feel tipsy, as if I had just knocked back two glasses of wine in quick succession.

Each floor of the mega mall-like market was divided up into sections, dedicated to a single broad category of product. In the 'Hardware Tools and Fitting' section, for example, you could find car jacks and cheese graters; thigh exercisers and pruning shears. 'Fabric Plush Toys,' on the other hand, revealed an ocean of hanging toys, inflatable rafts, kites, balloons, rattlesnake-sound-making eggs, superman outfits, cabbage patch dolls, Snoopies and everywhere: Santa Claus.

By 2006 some 70 per cent of the world's Christmas ornaments were estimated to originate in China, a country that was still officially atheist. That Christmas was increasingly 'made in China' was evident in Yiwu. Entire groves of artificial trees, tribes of angels and squadrons of reindeer were available for sale. But it was Santa who was the undoubted star of the show. Santas playing the electric guitar, the trumpet, the violin and the bongo abounded, as did Santas on motorcycles, attached to parachutes and swinging golf clubs.

But while the town did seem partial to Santa, it was by no means mono-religious in outlook. Commerce was agnostic. Thus, framed, illuminated verses from the Koran sat right next to scrolls depicting rotund Ganeshas and luridly-blue Krishnas.

One stall owner who stocked portraits of the Virgin Mary, Saraswati and Ganesha explained to me that these were all manufactured only a few kilometres away from the market, in Yiwu itself. A standard-sized scroll with a religious icon was for sale at from a dollar to a dollar and a half, but if bought in bulk the owner said she could reduce the price by more than half.

The stall was part of the 'Tourism Crafts' section, a floor of baubles that could potentially stock every gift shop on earth. 'African carvings' that were made in Henan, decorative bottles of 'champagne' made in Guangzhou and Ganesha paintings made in Yiwu.

Yiwu's government estimated that 8000 foreign merchants lived in the city all year round. Another 200,000 visited for short-term shopping sprees, buying up 400,000 containers full of products for re-sale to over two hundred countries across the globe. Nearly 60 per cent of all products sold in Yiwu's market were exported out of the country. By early 2006, some seven hundred foreign companies had set up representative offices in the town, including most of the world's top retailers like Wal-Mart, Carrefour and IKEA.

But it wasn't only or even primarily the big names that sourced products from Yiwu's market. I visited at around ten in the morning on a Tuesday and the International Trade City was already thrumming with thousands of individual buyers from all over the world. Within the space of an hour I had talked with traders from New Caledonia, Dubai, Pindi, Mumbai, Istanbul and Milan.

Indians and Pakistanis were particularly visible. I met Jayesh, a buyer from Mumbai, who said he had been coming to Yiwu for three years. He usually made four trips a year to the town, buying container loads of garment accessories each time. A fancy button that would cost Rs. 1.50 in India could be bought for a third less in Yiwu, he said. But it wasn't just the cheaper prices that brought him back again and again to the market, he emphasized. Rather, it was the sheer variety of the products that had him hooked.

'There's no way you could find this kind of variety in India,' he said, pointing at a shop whose walls were cracking open from the effort of trying to hold in the tens of thousands of multi-coloured and patterned buttons it displayed.

Jayesh went on to tell me that he owned a small shop in Mumbai's Dadar neighbourhood. 'I also used to have my own manufacturing unit,' he added proudly. Then suddenly crestfallen, he continued, 'But I had to close it after a few years. Just too many labour problems in India. If you employ five workers, they form a union and their productivity is very low. Indians only really understand the *danda* (the stick). You need to whack people to make them work, like animals. What we need is a government like these Chinese. No unions, no nonsense. Just work hard. Look at what China has achieved. Look at this market.'

This was a common enough view amongst the Indian middle classes and I had heard it before. But I still felt chilled at the undisguised nastiness of Jayesh's views; his open approval of Chinese authoritarianism, his unconcealed contempt for Indian workers.

Then I paused for a moment and tried to imagine Jayesh's life as a small shop owner in Mumbai. This was a city where the vast majority of the over sixteen million people who somehow cram themselves into the metropolis have no access to basic municipal amenities. No running water, sporadic and often stolen electricity, no toilets and no space.

Two-thirds of the city's population had one room only to call home and according to the 1990 census the average numbers of persons who lived in this one room was 4.7.[1] Almost seven million people were officially categorized as slum dwellers in Mumbai, tens of thousands lived over open sewers and several hundred thousand were homeless, living on footpaths.

As for millions of his fellow city residents, daily life for Jayesh must have been a constant low-level struggle: eking water out of his bathroom tap, paying though his nose for a battery-operated inverter for the many hours that there was no electricity every day, fighting his way through the heaving streets of a city with one of the highest densities of population in the world.

I looked at Yiwu, a relatively small county-level town, through his eyes: the broad roads, the clean buildings, taps out of which streams of water flowed on demand, a market without need of private generators to keep the lights on and most of all the glory

---

[1]See Suketu Mehta, *Maximum City: Bombay Lost and Found*, Penguin, 2004, particularly chapter 3.

of space, where one could stretch out both arms and not touch another human being.

I still didn't like his views and nor did I agree with the reasoning behind them, but I couldn't condemn him for them either.

A little later in the morning I wandered into an exhibition hall, also part of the gigantic space of the International Trade City. A few grainy pictures dotted the walls. They were of a small commodities market that had started up in Yiwu in 1984, the unlikely precursor to the flashy new mall that I was standing in.

The pictures showed rows of shacks with corrugated iron roofs, a few bicycles leaning unsteadily against them. Hollow-cheeked men were holding limp chickens by the neck. The market seemed to be selling mostly food produce.

The pictures had the sepia-tinted air of an age when people dressed up to have their photograph taken and hadn't yet learned to smile at the camera. The fact that they had been taken not so long ago strained the imagination.

Walking around Yiwu's bustling shops it was even more difficult to grasp that until the early 1980s commerce itself was outlawed in the town, as in the rest of China. For most of the Maoist period, selling anything for a profit was a crime that could land the perpetrator in jail. Peasants were not permitted to sell their produce for money. Instead they lived in 'people's communes', where they were allocated a ration of food grain according to the kind and amount of work they did.

These chokes on trade must have rankled in Yiwu more so than in other parts of the country given that the city was in Zhejiang province, home to the most entrepreneurial of Chinese people. Zhejiang folk were the equivalent of Sindhis and Marwaris in India. Making a buck was in their blood. Even at the height of the Cultural Revolution stories abounded of people in Wenzhou city, a few hours from Yiwu, trying to sell dumplings to their Red Guard tormentors. Underground factories, illegal peddling, informal financing and other prohibited economic activities were thus never fully stamped out in the region.

The exhibition I was looking at informed me that there had been a traditional culture of trading in Yiwu dating back to 'exchanging brown sugar for chicken feathers'. This rather mysterious statement was without further elaboration but questioning of local officials produced an explanation. *Qiao tang huan jimao*, literally 'exchanging brown sugar for chicken feathers', referred to a bartering system prevalent in the area in pre-communist times, wherein peasants would come in from the countryside with chickens and barter the birds' feathers, which were used as fertilizer, for brown sugar and other commodities.

Following Deng Xiaoping's economic reforms of the late 1970s, the Yiwu government once again gave its people permission to *qiao tang huan jimao,* the local euphemism for trade. In 1982 the government formulated its 'four permissions', according to which peasants were granted permission to engage in trade, permission to sell rural products in urban areas, permission to sell goods transported over a long distance and permission for trading through multiple channels.

It struck me that in China virtually all important government policies, local and central, were preceded by a number. My favourite was the 'two whatevers', which was shorthand for 'resolutely upholding whatever policy decisions Chairman Mao made and unswervingly following whatever instructions Chairman Mao gave'. In addition there were Deng Xiaoping's 'four modernizations', Jiang Zemin's 'three represents' and Hu Jintao's 'eight honours and disgraces'.

It was interesting, this Chinese penchant for numbers—for reducing complex policies with far-reaching consequences to crisp bullet point-like catechisms, easy for people to remember and repeat; efficient for propaganda and distracting from the details of the content itself.

In any case the 'four permissions' proved to be transformative of Yiwu's fortunes. From a collection of stalls selling chickens and vegetables along with a few combs and razor blades in 1984, Yiwu's market was conducting business amounting to several billion dollars a couple of decades down the line.

The town had also developed a substantial manufacturing base and local factories helped to keep the market shelves stocked with supplies.

In 2004, sock-making enterprises in Yiwu alone exported a jaw-dropping three billion pairs of socks. I visited the town's top sock-maker, Lanswe Langsha Knitting Company Ltd, whose factories churned out over one million socks a day. According to their corporate brochure, the company had experienced a 500,000 per cent growth in assets in the eleven years between 1995, when it was founded, and 2006.

As I waited to meet Aven Wang, the assistant manager of Langsha's import and export department, I looked at the posters on the walls of the company showroom. Langsha had created 'Ten Firsts', one claimed. I began to read:

LANGSHA

1. First to be China's Well-known Trademark, as No. 1 brand for socks in China
2. First to be the King of socks in China
3. First to advertise on China Central Television
4. First to put forward Concept of Intangible Asset (Brand-ization)
5. First to bring up the sock culture and build up sock model team

My reading was cut short by the arrival of Aven, who gave me a quick tour of one of the factories. Amid the metallic hum and hiss of machines spitting out socks in varying stages of completion, factory workers were only visible intermittently. On average one worker was needed to tend twenty machines, Aven told me. In total, Langsha owned some 6000 sock-making machines.

The company's annual revenue in 2006 was around $100 million, but its founder, Weng Rongjin, had humble beginnings. Weng had begun his career in the 1980s as a small-time trader, buying socks from Guangzhou and selling them in Yiwu's market. All over Zhejiang I encountered analogous stories of individuals who had transformed the tiniest of back-room assembly operations started up in the '80s into world market-capturing manufacturing enterprises by the late '90s.

Perhaps nowhere had more people gone from penury to plenty than in Wenzhou, a city a few hours drive south of Yiwu and possibly the single most entrepreneurial place in all of China. Eighty per cent of the world's metallic-shell lighters were produced there and another 80 per cent of its zippers. The tens of thousands of workers, often as young as sixteen, in Wenzhou factory assembly lines also made 25 per cent of China's shoes, 80 per cent of the country's spectacles, 60 per cent of its razors and 65 per cent of its electricity transformers. Ninety-five per cent of Wenzhou's produce was exported.

I visited Rifeng Lighter Co Ltd, where the company's 52-year-old founder-owner, Huang Fa Jing, chain-smoked his way through telling me a story almost as common in Wenzhou as metallic-shell lighters. In 1984 Huang had found himself ignominiously unemployed when he was laid off as a technician from a machinery manufacturing plant. He then embarked on a series of entrepreneurial adventures which saw him setting up first an electrical appliances workshop with a total investment of $2500, followed by a spectacle-manufacturing outfit.

Finally in 1990, in partnership with his brother-in-law, he founded Rifeng lighters. At the time there were over 2000 family-owned lighter manufacturers in Wenzhou. Fifteen years later, following waves of consolidation, there were less than 500. Rifeng was among the most successful of these, with a workforce of over

400 and an annual production capacity of ten million lighters. The company exported 90 per cent of what it manufactured and earned $5 million in revenues in 2005 from its exports.

A few kilometres away, at the Kangnai shoe factory, the company's Vice President, Zhou Jinmiao, had a similar tale to tell of the firm's founder, Zheng Xiu Kang. Zheng had resigned from his job, also in a machinery factory, as soon as Deng Xiaoping began to reform the economy in the late 1970s. In 1980 he set up a tiny, two-person, shoe-making workshop in a room in his home where he and his wife made shoes by hand and then took out on the streets to sell.

By 2006, Kangnai made eight million pairs of shoes a year and had 2500 own-brand retail stores across China. The company employed close to 5000 workers and exported 10 per cent of what it manufactured to over thirty countries.

It occurred to me that it must have been a stroke of luck to be unemployed in the early 1980s. Those unable to find a job in a state-owned-enterprise or laid off from one, were given the permission, revolutionary at the time, of forming a *getihu*—a single body unit. They were in other words classified as 'self-employed' and allowed to start up small private businesses.[2]

In 1981 China's State Council issued a regulation enabling the *getihu* to employ as many as seven workers. The reason for this particular number was the fact that Marx had identified the threshold for the exploitative capitalist firm as comprising more than eight people. The purpose of the new State Council regulation was primarily to facilitate the absorption of the growing numbers of unemployed in urban areas.

By the late 1970s some seven million educated city folk who had been sent to the countryside for re-education during the Cultural Revolution had started to make their way back to the cities. On returning they were assigned jobs in work units but in

[2]James Kynge, *China Shakes the World: The Rise of a Hungry Nation,* Weidenfeld & Nicolson, 2006, pp. 14-18.

the process those with fewer educational qualifications were either squeezed out of jobs or unable to find work in the first place. Between 1979 and 1987 Wenzhou alone registered 190,000 businesses with less than eight employees.[3] It was from the ranks of these jobless that the future magnates of China's private industry emerged. But to achieve success they first needed to grow beyond the limit of the eight-employee firm. A range of creative solutions were devised, ones that enabled these larger enterprises to maintain a façade of collective or socialist ownership and avoid the constraints imposed on private firms.

Thus emerged a series of 'red hat' or *hongmaozi* enterprises; firms that wore a 'red hat' to disguise their private entrepreneur boss's capitalist head.[4] These 'red hats' posed as collectives often by affiliating themselves with an established collective or state unit and paying a fee for the use of that collective's name, stationery and bank accounts.

What I realized was that much of China's economic reform process was not a top-down affair steered by the wise helmsman Deng Xiaoping, as was often the picture in the popular imagination, but rather a messy, bottom-up affair in which unauthorized experimentation was crucial. Acts of creative disobedience and active subterfuge from below were as much a force in shaping China's economic growth as were central government directives from above.[5]

In India a common argument to explain China's seemingly smooth march to prosperity in comparison to India's own halting steps towards economic reform is that as a dictatorship the CCP had supreme control. It thus only needed to issue an edict from the

[3]See Will Hutton, *The Writing on the Wall: China and the West in the New Century*, Little, Brown, 2006, p. 107.

[4]Ross Garnaut & Ligang Song (Ed): *China's Third Economic Transformation: The Rise of the Private Economy*, RoutledgeCurzon, 2004.

[5]Yaling Liu, 'Reform from Below: The Private Economy and Local Politics in the Rural Industrialization of Wenzhou', *China Quarterly*, No. 130, 1992.

corridors of power in Beijing and immediately disciplined cadres all across the country would busy themselves implementing the said regulation with zeal, or so it was thought.

The reality was closer to the sentiment expressed in the ancient Chinese proverb, 'The mountains are high and the emperor is far away.' By the time I moved to China, Beijing routinely admitted to the difficulties in getting its edicts implemented. From measures to cut pollution and save energy to orders to close down illegal private coal mines, the central government was constantly struggling to have its orders obeyed in the provinces.

China's polity was simultaneously top-down and decentralized. It was a system where without the will at the top, change at the bottom was difficult to effect. However, change at the top did not automatically spell change at the bottom either. The provinces had their own vested interests to protect, entrenched ways of operating and pet projects to promote. Their goals and the manner in which they sought to achieve them were thus often in variance with those of the centre and if Beijing's diktats were found too inconvenient, they were simply ignored.

By the twenty-first century this loss of control on the part of the centre was decidedly detrimental to Beijing's efforts to rein in the worst of the excesses it had itself unleashed by incrementally ceding control to the provinces. But in the early days of the reform process, the willingness of local officials to collude with entrepreneurs and to disobey the centre was a key factor in the country's economic success.

For example, the private enterprises in Wenzhou could never have taken off without access to lines of credit. But banks were not allowed to lend to private companies until the late 1990s. Local officials thus turned a blind eye to the emergence of a shadow banking network and so called 'money houses', informal banks which posed as collectives.

While in Wenzhou, I met with Xie Hao, Deputy Secretary General of the city municipal government. The official's eyes twinkled as he emphasized Wenzhou's exceptionalism. 'Wenzhou has a special history, special culture and special location.'

Indeed Wenzhou was the beneficiary of a combination of bad topography and incomprehensible linguistics. The city was surrounded by mountains and water and the lack of arable land had forced the local people to depend on trade rather than farming. Geographically remote, the city's peculiar dialect wasn't understood even by people from nearby towns, so that it had always been isolated from the rest of China. 'We are far away from the central government and so have had more room for manoeuvre. And we have always been very practical, not ideological,' concluded Xie.

Wenzhou's officials were part of a uniquely Chinese breed of entrepreneurial bureaucrats; a contradiction in terms in most parts of the world, but a common enough category in China. The 'red hat' enterprises and 'money houses' of the 1980s could never have operated without the acquiescence and collusion of these officials.

What motivated them to take such risks? In part it was a lack of other options. Given Zhejiang's proximity to Taiwan, a potential conflict zone, Mao had decided not to base large state-invested projects in the area. This created a vacuum for the city's entrepreneurial people to thrive in. In the absence of large state-owned enterprises that could be used as vehicles for investment and creating infrastructure, TVEs (town and village enterprises) and their 'red hat' affiliates were the only available route to economic development. Local officials realized that these firms were needed to create jobs and generate taxes.

That they presented officials with ample means to private enrichment couldn't have hurt either. More often than not the officials were themselves direct shareholders in the enterprises they protected.

Deng Xiaoping had made it clear that there was no communist virtue in poverty and that to get rich was in fact a glorious goal. This enabled the pursuit of 'getting rich' to be the touchstone of local government policy rather than adherence to central government diktats that continued to be burdened by the ideological constraints of communism. 'Make practice the sole criterion of truth,' said Deng, and many local officials decided to do just that.

The result was an incongruous mix of ideological cocktails where communist cadres pursued capitalist profit justified in the name of socialist goals. Deng's great achievement was thus to facilitate the theoretical ambiguity within which this murky mix of politics and business thrived, unleashing energies that would enable China to lift millions out of dire poverty. Some of these millions would even go on to become millionaires.

The embodiment of these trends was the village of Huaxi, officially China's richest village, located in Jiangsu, the province that along with Zhejiang and Shanghai made up the Yangtse river delta.

I arranged a reporting trip to the village in late January 2007, a month after Huaxi had celebrated the forty-fifth anniversary of its founding. I had researched the village in considerable depth before the trip and was prepared to be wowed by its riches.

In 2006, Huaxi's enterprises collectively earned 40 billion yuan ($5 billion) in sales. The average per capita income of the villagers was known to be some $10,000 a year, almost fifty times that of the average Chinese village. I had read that every one of Huaxi's 2000 villagers lived in a large, 500 to 600-square-metre home, owned at least a couple of cars and had assets worth a million yuan ($125,000).

Yet nothing quite prepared me for what I was to see. As I drove into the 'village' row after row of two-storey mansions with shingled roofs, stucco walls and the occasional mock-Tudor turret reared up on both sides of the road. It was a picture-perfect slice of American suburbia, except only a few metres to the south of this idyll, the smokestacks of steel works belched out black vaporous clouds.

To the village's north a detailed replica of the Great Wall of China rubbed shoulders with the 'Sydney Opera House' and other world-famous monuments, in a kitsch amusement park the village committee had built a few years ago. The central part of the village was dominated by a 148-tonne bronze bell, the largest in the world. It had cost the village 40 million yuan ($7.9 million) to have it made in Wuhan and transported to Huaxi. It served little purpose other than proving the fact that if Huaxi wanted it, Huaxi could afford it.

The entire village was peppered with large signs proclaiming 'Huaxi, number 1 richest village under heaven.'

Huaxi folk were obviously no ordinary peasants. They were successful industrialists who traded with countries across the world from India to Spain and who owned factories in places as far-flung as Vietnam and Mexico. But to add to the already complex plot, Huaxi villagers were no ordinary industrialists either.

All the land in the village was communally owned and the majority of the needs of the villagers were communally met. In a throwback to Maoist times and in contraposition to the trend in contemporary China, Huaxi villagers were provided with free health care and education by the village commune in addition to pensions and an allowance of some 3000 yuan ($370) a year for food.

In short, Huaxi defied categorization.

At the helm of the village was an 80-year-old former party secretary, Wu Renbao, who was credited with more or less single-handedly having steered Huaxi's people out of rags and into Rolls-Royces.

I had arrived in Huaxi on a weekday evening and was told I could meet with Wu only the next morning. A guest house had been arranged for me to stay the night in, an official with the village's publicity department told me. He had a young lackey, Wu Lei, drive me there.

Wu Lei, who was in his early twenties, had recently married and moved into his own two-storey, 600-square-metre home. He gripped the steering wheel of his somewhat dusty Toyota with masculine firmness but the nail on the little finger of his right hand was long and oval shaped, obviously laboured over with an emery board or nail file.

I had noticed this feminine accoutrement on men in India and it wasn't uncommon in Beijing either. The usual explanation was that a long fingernail signalled the person's disassociation from manual labour. I asked Wu Lei why he had grown out his nail.

He looked hard at his pinky finger before shrugging his shoulders. 'I don't know?' he said. Then he stuck his nail into his ear and mimed scraping out the insides. 'I guess it's easier to clean my ear,' he chuckled.

My guest house 'room' turned out to be a suite of enormous proportions including a sitting room, a bedroom, a study and a bathroom that could have accommodated a football game. Every room, including the loo, came appointed with a flat screen TV. Grecian pillars framed a swanky jacuzzi in the bathroom and every surface in the suite had liberal coatings of gilt. It was a rococo fest that would have warmed Louis the XIV's heart.

The next morning, I met Wu Renbao. He came dressed in simple peasant clothes, flannel trousers and jacket, at odds with the flashy surroundings of the gleaming pagoda-style hotel in which the interview took place. He was accompanied by his New Zealand-returned niece, who acted as interpreter since Wu preferred to speak in the local dialect.

With a folksy manner and easy smile that revealed worn-down, stained teeth, Wu had the appearance of a kindly uncle, but when he spoke, a sharp intelligence shone in his eyes.

Wu had been Huaxi village's Communist Party secretary from its founding in 1961 until 2003, making him perhaps the longest standing party secretary of any village in China. This feat was made even more impressive by the fact that Wu had successfully managed to keep a machine parts factory running in the village even during the Cultural Revolution, a time when people were disgraced, imprisoned and beaten for far less egregious 'capitalist' offences.

Wu cackled in glee when he recalled what he termed his 'secret factory'. 'Whenever county officials came to visit the village, I would quickly send away the workers to the fields and then once the officials had left they would return to the factory to work,' he said. The factory had purpose-built high walls and a single, unimposing entrance, Wu explained, and it was thus able to avoid detection. As a result of the money the village made from the factory it was able to avoid the worst deprivations of the period.

After the onset of economic reforms, Wu once again bucked the nationwide trend and instead of dividing up village land and handing it over to individual households for farming, he decided to keep the land communal. His focus, however, was away from agriculture and towards developing industry.

'I have always been a good communist,' said Wu, 'because I have always made it my goal to work for the people and make everyone rich.' He added, 'I believe in practice, not theory, and in learning what's best for my village from facts rather than theoretical formulations.' Echoes of Deng were rarely far from Wu's words.

Over the years several Chinese commentators had pointed out that Wu's disarming charm hid a canny and even ruthless politician who was obviously better connected than his rustic appearance revealed.[6] Despite repeatedly flouting central party directives Wu never lost his job and Huaxi's enterprises were able to grow quickly and strongly through the 1980s, even as private enterprises in other parts of the country struggled to get access to credit.

When asked to explain how he was able to retain his position through the ups and downs of China's tumultuous history, Wu was dismissive and only said, 'I have never been afraid to lose my job.'

Under Wu's watchful eye, an umbrella company for Huaxi's village enterprises, the Huaxi Group, was established in 1994 and by 2007 it boasted over sixty companies, mostly dealing in textiles

---

[6]'It Takes Brains and Guts', *China Daily* (Hong Kong Edition), 19 August 2003 (http://www.chinadaily.com.cn/en/doc/2003-08/19/content_256229. htm).

and iron and steel. In 1999, the Huaxi Group became the first village enterprise to list itself on a stock exchange.

Following the listing all Huaxi villagers were compelled to buy into the company's shares, which could then be used to buy more houses and cars from the village committee.

The concept of 'ownership' in Huaxi was complex. Villagers earned a small salary in cash from the company they worked for, but the majority of their wealth came from a substantial bonus and the dividends from their stock. However, 80 per cent of their bonus was compulsorily reinvested in the commune. Thus despite being millionaires on paper, the villagers were in fact only allowed to receive a total of 30,000 yuan ($3700) a year in cash, including salary and dividends. In the event of their leaving the village, all their paper assets would be forgone, as would their villas and cars.

Wu said the secret of Huaxi's success lay in his agnosticism towards different ideological 'isms'. 'What is capitalism? What is communism? The only "ism" I believe in is making people rich,' he laughed. Then more seriously, 'Everything has its good points and bad points. Our villagers get dividends from shares, that's capitalist. They also get free health care and education, which is communist. Moreover, they get a salary and bonus, which is socialist. We just take the best and reject the worst of everything.'

But Wu missed out another 'ism', one that he had also been accused of—feudalism. Huaxi was in many ways a Wu family fiefdom. When Wu retired in 2003, his fourth son, Wu Xie'en, took over the reins as party leader. The village's top posts were littered with Wu's relatives.

The former party secretary's eyes glinted cold for a quick moment when asked to respond to these charges. 'Power in Huaxi is not with the Wu family,' he snapped. 'Power is with the family that has served Huaxi village for more than forty years. If there were more families like us, all of China would be rich,' he concluded.

Then he looked at me keenly and pointing a finger in my direction said, 'I can guarantee that every single person in this village is richer than you.' This was an indisputable, if unhappy, fact and I nodded glumly in assent.

'If you can find me any other village in the world that is richer than ours, I will give you $10 million,' Wu said as a parting shot before he shuffled off for his next appointment.

Later, I was taken to see Wu's home. While all the other villagers in Huaxi had built and moved into modern American-suburban-style houses, Wu continued to live in an old apartment built in the 1980s. The 80-year-old spoke of little but money. Rich, richer, richest were some of the commonest words in his vocabulary. Yet he dressed simply and lived humbly.

'I am only here to serve the people,' Wu had said to me, for once quoting Mao rather than Deng.

In all this development, what was the role of corruption? As in India, corruption in China was a fact of life. In both nations it was the honest official rather than the corrupt one that gave people pause for thought. The Transparency International Corruption Perception Index of 2006 ranked the countries neck to neck with China marginally better off at 72nd place out of a total of 163 surveyed countries, while India bagged the 74th place.[7]

The only difference between the two, I liked to joke, was that in China officials were corrupt but they delivered; in India they were simply corrupt.

According to China's National Audit Office, local officials 'misspent or embezzled' almost $700 million of funds intended for the building of roads in 2005 alone, siphoning off more than $200 million supposed to compensate farmers for land acquired for highway projects.[8]

---

[7] http://www.transparency.org/policy_research/surveys_indices/cpi/2006

[8] '$700m misused in road projects on '05', *China Daily*, 26 March 2007 (http://www.chinadaily.com.cn/china/2007-03/26/content_836808.htm). According to China's National Audit Office, a total of $21.49 billion was spent on China's top thirty-four road-building schemes in 2005 of which $700 million was discovered to have been misused.

But although officials in China were more than likely to skim off the top or even dig deep into funds intended to construct a road, at the end of the day the road was built.[9]

Friends in Beijing who were journalists from western countries would often express disgust at the levels of corruption in China. As evidence for the claim that corruption was only getting worse one journalist mentioned a report by Chinese scholar Sun Yan according to which the number of arrests of senior cadre members, the vast majority on corruption charges, had quadrupled between 1992 and 2001.[10]

I was certainly amazed at the information but not in the manner in which my friend intended. What surprised me was that so many high-ranking officials had been identified, tried and punished for their behaviour, used as I was to the powerful in India happily continuing their political or bureaucratic careers regardless of all manner of corruption charges levelled against them.

The economic success of Zhejiang and Jiangsu provinces was certainly accompanied by a fair share of law breaking, bribing and much corruption. Nonetheless, that the region's entrepreneurs and entrepreneurial officials were dynamic and creative was also evident.

Could this success be replicated south of the Chinese border, in India? What was holding back Gujarat and Maharashtra with their Jains, Marwaris and Sindhis—communities that were every bit as entrepreneurial and dynamic as people from Zhejiang or Jiangsu—from achieving the same?

---

[9]Writing in the *Financial Times* Arthur Kroeber of the *China Economic Quarterly* points out that corruption in China has generally been of the 'lubricating rather than the destructive kind', resembling more the corruption that characterized late nineteenth-century America which was a concomitant of rapid economic growth, than the 'kleptocratic, zero-sum corruption' seen in many African countries. See Arthur Kroeber, 'The Underestimated Party State', *Financial Times*, 26 February 2007.

[10]Sun Yan, *Corruption and Market in Contemporary China*, Cornell University Press, 2004.

Seeking answers I travelled to Shaoxing, a small city an hour's drive from Zhejiang's capital Hangzhou that, like Yiwu, few outside of China had heard of. The city was the nerve centre of the textile world connected by crisscrossing flows of fibre, yarn, and fabrics to markets stretching from India to the Middle East, Europe, the United States and Australia.

It was in Shaoxing's Textile City—the world's largest textile market, spread over 2.8 million square metres of space crammed with 12,000 shops—that the who's who of the global textile industry converged to shop. And when they did, the middlemen or indenting agents that they hired to secure samples and place orders were, more often than not, Indian.

It was thus in little-heard-of Shaoxing rather than the gleaming metropolis of Shanghai or capital Beijing that one of the largest Indian communities in China was to be found. According to the city's public security bureau, in 2006, 1670 Indians were registered with the authorities as permanently residing in the city and two hundred Indian trading companies had been issued with business licences. But informal estimates suggested the actual numbers of Indians who lived and worked in Shaoxing may have been closer to 10,000. The majority of these formed a floating population of traders who spent substantial parts of the year in the city on short-term business visas which they repeatedly renewed in Hong Kong.

In 2006 the trade volume between India and Shaoxing was worth $145 million. But for the Indian traders there, most of whom were Sindhi, India was only one of many markets hungry for China's cheap and ready textiles.

My visit to the city was arranged with the help of Kishore Badlani, the founder of a Shaoxing-based trading company and Vice President of the Shaoxing Indian Business Association (SIBA). Mr Badlani's personal geography revealed just how globalized this group of traders was.

Born in Ulhasnagar, on the outskirts of Mumbai, Kishore, or Kebby as he liked to be called, had followed the textile trade to Ho

Chi Minh City in Vietnam. Following the Asian financial crisis his Vietnam business went bust and he moved to Seoul in Korea before finally arriving in Shaoxing in 2000.

'We have always followed the market,' explained Raju Gianchandani, originally a Jodhpuri, who moved to Shaoxing in 1999 from Korea and was one of the first of this Indian community of textile traders to have made their home in China. 'Earlier most of us were in Dubai or Korea but as China came up and became the factory of the world, it made sense to move here. Prices were cheaper here and because the market was still new, there were opportunities for everyone,' he explained.

I was having dinner with eight SIBA members at a restaurant called Lemon Grass, one of five Indian restaurants in Shaoxing. The traders were unanimous in their complaints about Chinese food. They swapped food-related horror stories involving 'hundred-year-old-eggs' and chicken feet. Indian restaurants like Lemon Grass, which was owned by Kebby as a side business, were life savers but finding 'good food' was still tough, they said.

Yet, despite the moaning, none of them had any plans of moving away from Shaoxing. 'No doubt I miss India, and it's also coming up well now,' said Raju, tucking into a plate full of daal and zeera aloo, 'but still China is way ahead for textiles.'

He went on to talk at length about how Chinese labour was not only cheap but also more skilful and disciplined than its Indian counterpart.[11] Everyone agreed that China's flexible labour laws which allowed for ease in hiring and firing and the lack of strong workers unions in the country gave businesses there an edge over Indian enterprises.

The traders here were only elaborating what Jayesh, the buyer from Mumbai I had bumped into in Yiwu, had said.

---

[11]According to a Morgan Stanley report the output for Chinese workers in the apparel sector is 35 shirts per worker in an eight-hour shift compared to 20 shirts in India. See Chetan Ahya and Andy Xie, *India and China: A Special Economic Analysis*, Morgan Stanley Research, 2004, p. 22.

Like Jayesh, they spoke of Chinese 'discipline' and 'no-nonsense' attitude in tones of open admiration. Did any of them feel nervous about the future, given the contradictions generated by China's continuing one-party political system, I asked. They looked blank. I explained that in the absence of genuine participatory mechanisms the disaffection amongst large groups of Chinese society created fundamental instabilities that many commentators felt could hurt continued economic growth. Did they agree?

'I don't know about that,' responded Raju, 'but their infrastructure is also really good.' Seemingly unaware of the non sequitur he went on to explain that European and American textile buyers preferred China to competitors like India because of the dependability of the country's entire supply chain from ordering to shipping. Delivery times and costs were crucial variables in the textile trade and China's superb infrastructure ensured speed and cost efficiency.

Flexible labour policies combined with modern technology and factories had already led to spectacular gains in productivity in China. The supporting infrastructure necessary to facilitate and capitalize on this productivity was the other key element that the Chinese were busy putting in place, with considerable success.

There was perhaps nothing that engendered as much China-envy south of the Himalayas as the country's multi-laned, smooth highways. At the start of the 1990s India's highway infrastructure was actually ahead of China's in terms of total route kilometres as well as route km/head of population.[12] Fifteen years later, while India's expressways continued to languish in potholed chaos, China boasted a world-class highway network of some 41,000 kilometres, second only to that of the United States in size.

Chinese planners had in fact learnt their lessons from the United States. They were aware that the US interstate system was

---

[12]Clel Harral, Jit Sondhi and Guang Zhe Chen, *Highway and Railway Development in India and China, 1992-2002*, World Bank, 2006.

estimated to have reduced the costs of producing goods and services by over $1 trillion in the first forty years of its operation since 1956.[13] China was determined to do the same.

According to the Chinese Transport Planning and Research Institute, 24,000 kilometres of new highways were built between 2001 and 2005 averaging a staggering 4800 kilometres a year. This was roughly equal to the total expressway length of Canada and Germany combined, the two countries that ranked third and fourth in the world in terms of expressways. In India such figures might cause more than a few eyes to pop right out, but in China, 41,000 kilometres of gleaming freeways were still not considered sufficient.

Another 24,000 kilometres were slated for construction till 2010, the target being to have a network stretching some 65,000 kilometres by then and reaching a length of 85,000 kilometres by 2020.

China's National Expressway Network (NEN), or *gaosu gonglu*, had been designed to connect the country's landlocked and relatively impoverished interior with prosperous coastal provinces like Zhejiang along the eastern seaboard. Highways had thus been used to stitch the country together with asphalt and concrete, binding the more remote areas closer to the centre while at the same time addressing concerns of the urban-rural and interior-coast income divides.

Travel in China had been transformed by the NEN. In the early 1990s a journey of a hundred kilometres used to mean a day's travel in most parts of China. By 2006 it usually took an hour or two at most. In many places new expressways had opened up vast new markets. Another consequence of highway development was a dramatic improvement in food security.

In Beijing, even up to the late 1990s, the primary vegetable available in the winter was cabbage, so that the city's streets were famously piled high with the vegetable throughout the long cold

---

[13]James Kynge, *China Shakes the World: The Rise of a Hungry Nation*, Weidenfeld & Nicolson, 2006, p. 31.

period. By the time I moved there, the cabbages had disappeared from the capital's streets and instead shops were stocked with the choicest of fruits and vegetables trucked in from China's warmer southern areas.

Just-in-time delivery had become possible allowing manufacturers and distributors to hold smaller inventories and respond more quickly to changing market tastes. By 2006, Wal-Mart relied on a single major distribution centre in Guangdong province for supplying stores throughout China, something that would have been unthinkable without the recent expansion of the NEN.

In parallel to the frenzied construction of roads, China was also in the midst of a great railway boom.[14] According to China's Ministry of Railways, in 2006 alone, 155 billion yuan ($19.7bn) was invested in railway construction allowing 912 km of new lines to be completed, 1016 km of lines to be double-tracked, and 1609 km of new lines to begin construction.[15]

China was also busy speeding up its trains. The country already boasted the fastest train in the world, the Maglev, which connected Shanghai's Pudong International airport to the city at a

---

[14]See Clel Harral, Jit Sondhi and Guang Zhe Chen, *Highway and Railway Development in India and China, 1992-2002*, World Bank, 2006. The report points out that in the early 1990s India's railway infrastructure was actually ahead of China's in terms of total route kilometre and route kilometre per head of population. Over the next ten years, however, China's rail network outstripped India's on virtually every parameter. Between 1992 and 2002 while India's overall rail network route kilometre grew by only one per cent, double track by 10 per cent and electrified lines by 48 per cent, the corresponding figures for China were 24 per cent, 69 per cent and 50 per cent. The report points out that investment in the railways in China during this decade was estimated at $85 billion, compared to $17.3 billion in India.

[15]'China Invests 155b Yuan in Railway Construction in 2006', *China Daily*, 1 January 2007 (http://www.chinadaily.com.cn/bizchina/2007-01/01/content_772996.htm).

maximum speed of 450 km per hour. In addition it had plans for a high-speed 1320 km Beijing-Shanghai rail link, a route that when complete would cut the travelling time by train between the two cities from twelve hours to five.

Of course such concerted infrastructure building came at a cost, both social and environmental. Most notably the building spree had displaced millions of people, most of them poor farmers who often received scant or no compensation, had little recourse to the legal system and were unable to exercise a vote to shape the direction of polices that impacted their well being.

China's expanding roads also brought with them a concomitant boom in car ownership, leading to serious environmental challenges in a country that was already plagued by pollution. China was home to sixteen of the world's twenty most polluted cities, according to the World Bank. The health costs related with outdoor air pollution in urban China in 2003 amounted to between 157 billion yuan ($21 bn) and 520 billion yuan ($69 bn)—depending on the method of calculation used—or between 1.2 and 3.8 per cent of GDP.[16]

Having grown up in Delhi I thought I had a high tolerance for pollution, but the relentless year-round fug that hung over Beijing had begun to wear down even my India-fortified immunity to bad air.

It was thus months, for example, before I realized that on a clear day the city's western Fragrant Hills were plainly visible from a height, in our neighbourhood. It was a magical moment to wake up one day, look out of the window and behold mountains where until now there had only been half-built skyscrapers. Unfortunately such a day came around at best once a month and the frequency of these days did not increase over the years, even as the number of cars on the roads rocketed.

---

[16]World Bank & SEPA, 2007, *Cost of Pollution in China: Economic Estimates of Physical Damages.*

By May 2007 the city was host to over three million cars and was adding another 1000 to the already gridlocked streets on a daily basis.

Although industrial activity and the relentless construction in Chinese cities were partly to blame for their dirty air, automobiles accounted for a substantial percentage of the pollution.

Were these costs worth it? The answer depended on whom you asked. Dislocated and under-compensated farmers were likely to respond differently to local manufacturers. People with severe respiratory disorders and lung disease might not quite see eye to eye with car salesmen.

Much would also depend on the choices China made going forward. Adopting environmentally friendly technologies and developing a stronger legal system were both essential, although it was less than clear how or even whether China would be able to commit to these given the limitations of its political structure.

Overall, however, I believed China's infrastructure construction to have been crucial to its success in lifting the majority of its population out of poverty and in helping to speed up the economy with associated trickle-down benefits for even those sections of society usually thought to have been left out of the boom.

As a result, absolute poverty of the kind where children with distended bellies and flies in their eyes play on open gutters while their parents scavenge for scraps of food was surprisingly and hearteningly difficult to find in China. I was aware that the rich and well-located region of the Yangtze river delta was the wrong place to look, but even in remote and ostensibly dirt-poor provinces like Qinghai, Gansu and Ningxia, I was to find that poverty in China had acquired a relative rather than absolute quality.

In Ningxia, for example, a remote northern region that was under siege from an ever expanding desert, my purpose in visiting was to report on the province's fight against desertification. Over the years village after village in Ningxia had disappeared under the encroaching tentacles of sand, locking the area into a vicious circle of drought and poverty.

I went to the Ozymandian Su Bu Jing township in the province's north-west, a collection of largely deserted sand-covered hamlets. Following two decades of depopulation, Su Bu Jing's name had quietly stopped appearing on maps in 2003.

I met 60-year-old Qiao Gui Yin, one of the hundred or so people left in Shuang Jing Zi, one of the villages that used to fall under the erstwhile township administration. Qiao's face was furrowed and his voice was unsteady in the manner of the very old.

For half an hour he talked non-stop about how poor his village was. It had been fifteen years since any of the village's young men had been able to find a bride willing to move to a hopeless and doomed village like Shuang Jing Zi, he said.

His own son had left the village and gone to work in Yinchuan, the provincial capital. Had he been to Yinchuan himself, I asked? 'Oh yes!' Qiao replied, his face lighting up for the first time. 'It's a wonderful, modern city, much better than Beijing.' Had he been to Beijing I asked? 'No, no!' Qiao responded. 'Just seen it on TV.'

'You have a TV?' I asked in surprise. 'Of course I do,' he brushed my question aside as if it were insignificant.

I went on to discover that Qiao had a TV, a DVD player, a motorbike and electric fans for the hot, dusty summer. In India he would have been classified as middle class.

The landscape between Shaoxing and the closest airport at Hangzhou was lined with bathroom-tiled chateaux replete with the kind of blue plexiglass windows that had beset my BBI apartment building. These were enormous affairs, often four storeys high, with villa-style roofs and ornate entrances. In them lived the peasant millionaires that the area teemed with.

The six-lane highway my taxi was gliding along cut right through them, like a broad butter knife. I put away the magazine I had been flicking through, my eyes easily tired in the moving car. It was a weekly called *Shaoxing Magazine Consumption*, written in Chinese but the headlines of the articles had also been translated into Chinglish. 'Popularity in 2007; The Cowboy Is Also Dissolute', read the title of a piece on the growing popularity of cowboy-inspired clothing in 2007. 'The Summit of the Hypersensitivity Disease in Spring Coming Again,' stated another, about a story on pollen allergies.

Magazine stowed safely away, I began to think some more about Chinese entrepreneurship. There must be more to it than what could be explained by good roads and flexible labour policies. In the 1980s, when the seeds for the later success of the majority of Zhejiang and Jiangsu firms were first sown, neither roads nor policy were supportive of local entrepreneurial endeavours. Yet person after person in the towns and cities of these provinces took huge risks, raising money from friends and family and gambling all on the off chance of success.

'That's because in China people don't think they get another chance in life. If you get an opportunity grab it, tightly, it may be the only one you ever get,' explained my friend Edward a few weeks later. We were sitting in a trendy courtyard-style bar tucked away in a Beijing *hutong*, sipping Mojitos and discussing my recent trips to the Yangtze river delta.

Edward was in his mid-thirties, with a slim body and narrow face that were somewhat overwhelmed by his large, owlish glasses. Originally from Wuhan, he had lived in Beijing for years, running his own, moderately successful advertising and event management company. I had first met him in late 2004, when CII hired him to help out with the advertising and logistics for an exhibition of Indian industry they had been organizing in Beijing.

Edward had lately taken to spending all his free time playing the stock market online, an increasingly popular pastime amongst China's middle class. 'It's like gambling,' he admitted, 'but then you know we Chinese are famous gamblers.' I nodded in agreement, having recently been to Macau. The tiny enclave had sent shockwaves across the gambling world when in 2006 it overtook the Las Vegas strip on gambling revenues.

'For us Chinese there is only the now,' Edward smiled and

drained his glass. Then he smacked his lips once and repeated, 'You get one shot, you take it, whatever the risk, because later everything might have changed.'

The upshot of what Edward seemed to be saying was that Chinese society suffered from a fundamental lack of trust in the future. Like all generalizations it was a statement that perhaps claimed too much too easily, but like all good generalizations it also contained a core of truth.

Given the repeated hairpin bends of China's recent history, his explanation made sense. Over the last several decades the ground beneath Chinese people's feet had turned to quicksand time and time again, a trend epitomized by Mao's famous 'hundred flowers' move.

In 1957 the Chairman was so confident the achievements of the communist revolution were secure that he called for a 'hundred flowers to bloom', seeking out differences of opinion that would form the basis of a communist civil society. For weeks open debates on the merits of his policies were permitted and criticism was solicited. This brief period of freedom was followed by a brutal crackdown in which 300,000 intellectuals were branded counter-revolutionaries and imprisoned or exiled to labour camps.[17] The 'hundred flowers' proved to have been a mere ruse used by Mao to smoke out dissenters.

In contrast, I perceived an underlying stability to society in India, which in the absence of a genuine revolution had been protected from the violent hiccoughs of China's past. There were those who had nothing and there were those who had everything and by and large these two categories remained separate. The privileged had not experienced sudden, cataclysmic deprivation and nor had the poor been given the opportunities to strike it rich on any significant scale.

---

[17]Jonathan Spence, *The Search for Modern China* (second edition), W.W. Norton & Company, 1999, pp. 539-543.

Yet despite these differences, entrepreneurship was certainly flourishing in India as well. A fact that hit home when one morning a few days after my story on Yiwu's market had appeared in the *Hindu*, I opened my email and found the following message from a reader.

Dear Madam,
I am regular reader of your articles on China. A few days back, I read your article about the market in YIWU in Southern Chinese Zhejiang Province.

I am the inventor of 'Disposable Armpit Perspiration Pad' bearing Indian Patent no.181248. The product is similar to sanitary napkins/baby diapers. This can be manufactured by existing machinery used for the production of sanitary napkins with slight modification in the Dies.

Can you help me in locating a reputed, reliable and honest supplier in China who can supply me in bulk quantities?

Please find attached drawings of the product.
I am also prepared to go over to China, if required.
Thanking you

S.V.
PERUMTHANNI,
TRIVANDRUM

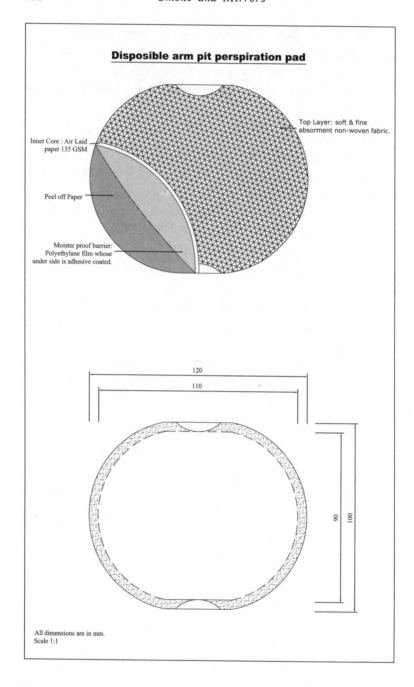

Disposible arm pit perspiration pad

Top Layer: soft & fine
absorment non-woven fabric.

Inner Core : Air Laid
paper 135 GSM

Peel off Paper

Moister proof barrier:
Polyethylane film whose
under side is adhesive coated.

120

110

90

100

All dimensions are in mm.
Scale 1:1

Opiate of the Masses

Edward had suggested that the Chinese appetite for risk sprang from the common perception that 'you only get one shot in life'. Whatever the validity of his explanation, this was a notion that was deeply antithetical to Hindu philosophy with its emphasis on karma and rebirth. Similar concepts, however, existed in Buddhism and China was a Buddhist country or at least it had been before the communists turned religion into a bad word.

Over time it became increasingly clear to me that the relationship most Chinese shared with religion was a difficult one to unpack, particularly from an Indian perspective.

I came from a country where religion did not dominate life as much as form the basic substratum, upon which life was acted out. In India, religion was not something one either chose to believe in or not, it was rather part of the warp of the unconscious assumptions that comprised what passed for common sense. It was a country where you were almost more likely to be thought of in need of a shrink if you claimed not to believe in God than if you admitted to intimate chats with Him on a daily basis.

The world I grew up in was one where you awoke to statues of Ganeshas miraculously drinking milk; where people outside the finance ministry genuflected to monkeys who had just emerged unmolested from the ministry building sated after a morning romp destroying files and government furniture; where thieves across the city made hay harvesting goodies uninterrupted from homes in which entire families sat in front of the TV screen in rapture, blind and deaf to anything save the latest episode of their favourite mythological epic—the Ramayana.

The lack of a constant and visible religiosity in China was thus something that struck me hard, particularly in my first couple of years in the country. The Beijingers I met seemed far too pragmatic, almost too adult, to be overly fussed by religion and its strictures. There was no nipping out of office for a quick prayer, no fasting in honour of a favoured god on Mondays or Tuesdays or even Thursdays, no restrictions on food—root vegetables, garlic and onion all being permissible.

The festivals they celebrated were largely secular—May 1, Labour Day; October 1, National Day; March 8, Women's Day; and so on. Even the most significant of all festivals, the lunar Chinese New Year, had no obvious religious content. It was marked primarily by families gathering to eat special foods and letting off an arsenal of firecrackers.

Used as I was to holidays and religion being almost synonymous—Diwali, Holi, Janmashtmi, Christmas, Easter, Guru Nanak's birthday, Eid twice a year, Ganesha Puja, Dussehra, etc., etc.—this was a whole new world.

'India? Yes. Very good! Birthplace of Buddhism,'—was the common response of many Chinese I met to my nationality. It was a response that in the manner of its delivery more often than not diminished India by confining it to the single dimension of religion.

At the Centre for India Studies at Peking University, for example, the country's premier Indology research centre, courses were taught on Indian languages and Indian religions, period. Neither the Indian economy nor the country's role in international relations was thought worthy of addressing. Indian history and culture were reduced to and subsumed under religion.

In framing its discourse on India in religious terms, China was only following a pattern long prevalent in the West. But China was of the East. Animism, folk religions, Taoism and Buddhism had long, fable-laden tentacles stretching deep into the past here. The condescension towards Indian religiosity that I often encountered in the country was thus a surprise, as was the lack of overt spirituality or religious belief within China itself.

Of course, despite the multi-layered religious history of the Chinese civilization, contemporary China was communist and an entire generation of Chinese had been indoctrinated to equate religion with primitive superstition. Communist modernity had little patience with the opiate of the masses.

During the Cultural Revolution temples and places of worship across the country had been attacked, deities defaced and innumerable cultural treasures wantonly destroyed. Monks had been publicly paraded in the street and flogged. Those who avoided this fate were left in penury as temples were closed down and converted to secular uses like granaries, schools and government departments.

It was the Communist Party that people were taught and expected to believe in rather than God. By the time I moved to China the belief structures had once again changed and the new God lived in banks and ATM machines.

'I don't believe in socialism and capitalism and communism,' Wu Renjie of Huaxi village had said to me. 'I don't believe in Buddhism or Taoism or any ism at all.'

He had paused for effect before delivering the denouement: 'I only believe in money.'

Wu's was a common enough punch line. I had heard it expressed in China repeatedly.

Given China's past this focus on the material was perhaps only natural. The ability to make money had been a hard-won right and was new enough not to be taken for granted. India was a poor country and its rat-and-monkey worshipping society was thus not one that the Chinese with their burning hunger for prosperity and modernity necessarily looked up to.

But condescension was a folly that could cut in two directions. For many Indians the term 'atheist' was akin to an insult. 'Is it true that these Chinese are atheists?' I was asked time and again by businessmen from India whom I met in the course of my work with CII. The tone of horror imbuing the question was unmistakable.

On one occasion I was having lunch with a delegation from one of India's leading cement manufacturing companies hosted by a Chinese firm interested in a potential tie-up with them. As usual, the meal was progressing unhappily. The hosts had been stunned when informed that the majority of the guests were vegetarian. They recovered only to order a menu that consisted largely of seafood and vegetables lightly garnished with minced pork.

The guests were able to eat virtually nothing that was on offer and kept asking me in Hindi to order them some plain rice. I tried to explain to them that the hosts would lose much face if they had to resort to feeding their guests mere rice.

As the lunch wound down the leader of the Indian delegation inevitably asked me, complete with the standard tone of horror, if it was really true that all Chinese were atheists. I answered saying that this was untrue. The delegate looked relieved. I added quickly that it *was* true that the country was no longer as religious as it had once been, prior to the communist revolution. 'What a pity,' he replied making 'tsk tsk' sounds and shaking his head from side to side.

Feeling peevish and tired I decided to challenge him rather than keep my opinions to myself, as was usually best on these occasions. 'Why is it a pity?' I asked. 'I'm not religious and there's nothing wrong with that.'

The delegate looked concerned. 'What do you mean you're not

religious? How can that be?' he replied. 'You are an "Aiyar", a Hindu.'

'Yes, perhaps I am culturally, but I don't believe in God,' I said, increasingly ticked off.

'*Aisi batein nahin kahtein beta*,' the delegate scolded in response—'You mustn't say such things, child.'

China's departure from Indian-style religiosity was a relatively recent phenomenon and as I learnt to look beyond first impressions I realized that while the country's religious roots might have been slashed at by the communists, they were in the process of tenaciously growing back.

The longer I spent in China the more obvious it became to me that alongside pervasive money worship, a subtle but palpable resurgence of interest in the spiritual was also emerging. Buddhist icons in taxis, religious chants emanating from shop interiors, prayer beads fashioned into bracelets on the wrist of a subway commuter: the signs were all around me.

When Chen Xiaoxu, a famous actress-turned-successful-businesswoman, appeared in all the leading local media smiling serenely but barely recognizable with a tonsured head, it was a confirmation of this trend. The 42-year-old celebrity, who had been a devout Buddhist for several years, had decided to renounce the world and become a monk. In doing so she had given up a fortune valued at some $25 million.

'For quite a long time, I devoted all my energy to amassing a fortune. Now, I've found that a bigger fortune has not given real joy and happiness to me and my family,' she was quoted as saying in explanation of her decision.[1]

Chen took the plunge in February of 2007 by which time a more general and widespread religious renaissance was rippling

---

[1]'Search for Inner Peace', *People's Daily* Online, 13 March 2007 (http://english.people.com.cn/200703/13/eng20070313_356973.html). Chen died a few months after her conversion. She was found to have been suffering from breast cancer.

across the country with gathering force. Once defaced temples were being expensively renovated, once reviled monks were finding seats in the national parliament and a once suppressed religiosity was finding release in urban and rural areas alike.

One more of the 'achievements' of the communist revolution was coming undone, opening up one more contradiction for the CCP to straddle. Not only was a communist party presiding over the emergence of one of the world's most unequal societies, but an atheist party was actively encouraging a religious revival.

In April of 2006 the Chinese government organized what it billed as the first World Buddhist Forum in Hangzhou, an officially sponsored meeting of Buddhist leaders from around the world. The Dalai Lama was predictably not invited but the event was given headline coverage for days in the official media.

At the forum a series of senior party leaders talked of the role that Buddhism could play in promoting a 'prosperous and harmonious world', echoing a pet political catchphrase of China's President Hu Jintao, under whom the drive to build a 'harmonious society' had become the centrepiece of the government's agenda.

But even more than Buddhism it was the traditional philosophy of the sage Confucius that found increasing resonance in Mr Hu's political homilies. 'Confucius said, harmony is something to be cherished,' he stated in a keynote address to senior party cadres in early 2005. From then on Confucian values such as unity, morality, and respect for authority were a constant in the President's public exhortations.

In 2006 Mr Hu went as far as promulgating a formulation called the *Ba Rong Ba Chi*, or 'eight honours and disgraces', a morality checklist of sorts, much of which could be traced to Confucian thought. The eight honours extolled conservative virtues like obedience, hard work, and plain living while eschewing chaos and the pursuit of profit at the expense of others.

There was little mistaking the fact that only three decades after Red Guards had been encouraged to rampage across the country shouting chants of 'Criticize Confucius', the sage was back in favour with the authorities.

By 2007, the year I began to write this book, barely a day went by without the local media carrying a story that paid homage to the philosopher. I discovered that a county in China's central Henan province had instituted a new criterion by which to assess promotions for local officials.[2] These had little to do with typical assessment guidelines like meeting family planning quotas or creating jobs.

Instead officials in Changyuan County would be judged on the basis of their filial piety record or the degree to which they were assessed as being caring towards their parents. The county had announced plans to send teams of people to interview the families and friends of officials to ascertain how they measured up on this most Confucian of values. 'Officials should possess traditional values like filial piety, which is the foundation of a successful career,' an article quoted the local party boss as saying. This was the same party that under Mao had encouraged children to turn on their parents for the smallest of infractions.

The reasons for this volte-face were obvious. From a revolutionary force, the CCP in the twenty-first century had grown into a status quo power. The only clear purpose underlying its increasingly contradictory policies was to continue to stay in power. In achieving this purpose social stability was perceived to be of paramount importance.

A stable, obedient society that dutifully took orders from a wise and paternalistic leadership, in short a society that followed the hierarchical and stable precepts of Confucianism, was thus an ideal that had emerged for the CCP. Such a society would allow it to claim the legitimacy to rule, untrammelled by the dissent and disaffection that confronted the party in reality.

As the contradictions between a party that formally espoused egalitarian socialist ends for the betterment of workers and peasants

---

[2]Xinhua, 'Filial Piety Plays a Part in Promotions', *China Daily*, 9 April 2007.

while in practice facilitating an unequal and often rapaciously capitalist system bubbled over, the country was wracked with protests and riots.

Yawning inequalities, vanishing provisions for education and health care, unpaid wages and pensions and rampant official corruption were combining to create disenchantment across large sections of Chinese society, in particular among the peasants and workers that were the mainstay of the CCP.

For the party this turn of events was deeply worrying, carrying as it did the seeds of a grassroots people's movement the power of which the CCP knew all to well. Religion, the party was thus coming to realize, may be an opiate, but opiates soothe tensions and calm frayed nerves. In teaching people to be content with their lot, the anti-revolutionary thrust of traditional philosophies like Confucianism and Buddhism had a distinct appeal for the country's leadership.

Moreover, beyond its own self-interest, the party was also aware of a genuine moral vacuum that was hollowing out the ethical foundations of Chinese society, leading to an unbalanced, single-minded focus on money. The worry was that this obsession with profit excused corruption and venality while devaluing trust and honesty.

Freed to find prosperity after decades of unnatural restrictions, a culture of getting rich quick had indeed pervaded contemporary China, spawning greed, envy and obsession with wealth. China's new rich styled themselves as *tu di*, or 'dirt emperors', and lived lives saturated with luxury sedans, ostentatious villas, beautiful mistresses and sumptuous meals that could cost thousands of dollars a pop. This was the lifestyle that increasing numbers of youngsters aspired to.

Under Mao the communists had worked hard towards the destruction of religion, aiming to transform a nation of Buddhists and Taoists into one of non-believers. Replacing religion as the moral foundation of society was the ideology of communism, which despite its antipathy to the spiritual, served a similar social function to that of religion. It provided the nation with a moral compass and welded society together in common belief.

Following the economic reforms of the past few decades, belief in communist ideology had waned, leaving behind a vast moral emptiness. Money worship might have substituted Mao worship but morality and Mammon were not always a comfortable fit.

The prioritization of money over morality was exemplified by a host of scandals that began to rock Chinese society in which the lives of tens of thousands of innocents were put at risk in the pursuit of profit, with a callousness that could only be described as evil.

One of the most tragic episodes emblematic of this trend took place in the mid-1990s in China's central Henan province, when a government-organized blood-buying programme resulted in the contamination with HIV of the entire province's blood supply.

Hospitals in Henan at the time were suffering from a blood shortage. Local officials thus set up a large number of blood collection centres where they paid donors, mostly impoverished farmers, around $6 per bottle of blood. To maximize profits, they took to separating red blood cells from the plasma and then re-infusing the donors with pooled red blood cells so that they could donate blood more frequently. At some point HIV-contaminated blood entered this bank of pooled blood and before long the virus began to spread.

Up to a million villagers in the province became infected with HIV as a consequence, according to local AIDS activists, although the official government figure is much lower at 30,000. Given its complicity in the scandal, the local government carried out a harsh campaign to keep information about the spread of AIDS and its own role in it from getting out, arresting activists and censoring media.

Once the story came to light, thanks in large part to investigations by journalist Pierre Haski of the French newspaper

Liberation,[3] China's central government tried to make a clean breast of the affair. Today the local government claims to provide all HIV patients with free anti-retroviral drugs and free education for the tens of thousands children left orphaned by AIDS deaths. But AIDS activists say that despite cosmetic improvements real justice for the infected peasants remains elusive. Many of the low-level officials who ran the blood sale schemes in the '90s and made money off it have not only never been brought to book but are now in powerful senior positions.

The Henan blood scandal was far from an isolated incident. Over the years I lived in Beijing, fresh immoralities involving fake medicines, fake baby milk powder, contaminated food and botched surgical procedures by unlicensed practitioners surfaced with predictable regularity.[4]

For many Chinese these were proof of an underlying imbalance in society. There was a rip in the ethical fabric of the country and perhaps inevitably people were once again turning to religion in the hope that it might help stitch up this tear.

Thus while the official number of Chinese who were categorized as 'religious' according to government figures was a hundred million, a number that had remained unchanged for years, a survey conducted by professors from Shanghai's East China Normal University between 2005 and 2007[5] concluded the real number was at least three times more at three hundred million. The survey also found that 62 per cent of respondents who described themselves as religious were of the post-Cultural Revolution generation, aged 16-39, and that a substantial percentage came from the wealthy, economically developed coastal areas.

I was increasingly intrigued by this new passion for the

---

[3]Pierre Haski, *Le Sang de la Chine*, Grasset, 2005.

[4]Walt Bogdanich and Jake Hooker, 'From China to Panama: A Trail of Poisoned Medicine', *New York Times*, 6 May 2007.

[5]Wu Jiao, 'Religious Believers Thrice the Estimate', *China Daily*, 7 February 2007.

spiritual amongst what I had come to consider as an almost peculiarly pragmatic and materialistic people. I decided thus to travel to the heartland of Chinese Buddhism—Henan.

The very same province where official venality had descended into extreme moral corruption as evidenced by the AIDS atrocity, was also the birthplace of Chinese Buddhism. In Henan's Luoyang city, Baimasi or the White Horse temple was the first Buddhist monastery to have been built in China, almost 2000 years ago in A.D. 68.

Baimasi was moreover the embodiment of a seminal episode in Sino-Indian ties having been built to house two Indian monks, Dharmaraksa and Kasyapa Matanga, who were responsible for the first of what would turn into a flood of Chinese translations of a Buddhist sutra.

Buddhism's journey from the dusty plains of northern India across the formidable Himalayan barrier and into central China had exerted a profound civilizational and cultural influence on the erstwhile Middle Kingdom and helped foster a broad range of contacts material and intellectual, secular and sacred between China and India that lasted well into the eleventh century.[6]

These were links long forgotten in India and only superficially retained in the Chinese consciousness but visiting Baimasi in person was a sharp reminder to me of how Chindia was neither as new nor perhaps even as bogus a concept as I had sometimes assumed and argued.

It was late in April of 2006 and unseasonably cold when I drove up to the temple. It looked ordinary enough. The grey, tiled roofs of its pagodas turned gently upwards and the bronze statues of Bodhisattvas glinted bright in the shafts of sunlight that pierced through the otherwise gloomy interiors.

I met with the temple's abbot, Yin Le, surprisingly young at

---

[6]See Amartya Sen, *The Argumentative Indian: Writings on Indian Culture, History and Identity*, Penguin, 2005. See in particular chapter eight: China and India.

forty-one, and with an infectious smile which he flashed often as
he gave me a tour. He took me to the burial mounds of Dharmaraksa
and Kasyapa Matanga, serene spots, swept clean, within the temple's
grounds. According to Buddhist tradition monks were not permitted
to be buried inside a temple complex, the abbot told me, but the
two Indian monks' contribution to Buddhism in China had been
deemed so great that an exception had been made for them.

He added thoughtfully, 'So many hundreds of years ago when
distances were great and the means of communication few, our
countries still had such close contacts. Now we have so many
planes and computers but we hardly know each other any more.
It's a strange state of affairs.'

Plumes of incense twirled over us and for a moment it was as
if I were sucked back in time by the smoke to A.D. 64, when the
Eastern Han dynasty emperor, Mingdi, had a dream.

The emperor dreamt of a deity flying over his palace, a vision
that greatly agitated him. The next day he asked his ministers for
an interpretation of the dream and was told that he had probably
had a vision of the Buddha. Mingdi then immediately dispatched
a delegation of eighteen trusted officials to India to find out more
about Buddhism. When his ambassadors returned from their trip,
they brought with them a forty-two-chapter-long sutra, an image of
Gautama Buddha and two eminent Indian monks, all on white
horses.

A year on, the emperor ordered the construction of the White
Horse temple in commemoration of the horses that had borne the
Buddhist relics to Luoyang and to house the two Indian monks
whose graves I stood looking at, hundreds of years later.

Yin Le began to tell me about an Indian-style stupa, the first
of its kind in China, that was soon going to be built on a plot of
land to the west of the main temple. He took me to the building
site. A commemorative plaque rose up from the dug-up earth. I
had arrived only a few days after the groundbreaking ceremony for
the project had taken place.

The construction of the stupa was being funded by the Indian government to underscore the long history of Sino-Indian friendship. The proposal had first been mooted during Vajpayee's trip to China in 2003. The Indian Prime Minister had visited Baimasi on a scheduled half-hour stop but the abbot told me that he had in fact stayed almost two hours.

I could well imagine Vajpayee overstaying his allotted time at the temple. There was a magnetic pull to it that I felt as well. In the past I had dismissed the almost compulsory recitation of the 'ancient bridge of Buddhism' by Indian and Chinese leaders as a convenient side-stepping of the far less edifying reality of the present state of bilateral ties. But the temple evoked a powerful sense of history and for the first time I felt as though the antique threads that had bound the country I was born in and the country I had come to live in counted for something, even in the twenty-first century.

As we walked away from the stupa site and towards the abbot's living quarters, we passed a series of small pagodas and shrines. A shiny, large image of the laughing Buddha caught my attention. Somehow the elegantly angular, tranquil Buddha sporting a top knot, as we knew him in India, had in China translated into a bald, fat and jolly being.

Yin Le noticed my interest. 'This Buddha stands for tolerance and he is fat because you need to have a big stomach to tolerate all the evil in the world,' he said and smiled broadly. The abbot had much to smile about.

Like other temples across China, Baimasi was in the midst of a renaissance. Yin Le recounted how only five monks had been left at the temple during the Cultural Revolution, scrabbling to subsist on some eleven acres of poor quality land. By the time of my visit, the temple owned over 130 acres of prime land and housed 120 monks. Millions of dollars, much of it government money, had just been spent on spiffing up its various buildings. Moreover, although the temple charged tourists $5 for an entry ticket it was exempt from paying taxes.

Around 2000 people visited the temple every day, the abbot said, and the number of regular devotees was shooting up. At weekend prayer meetings more people showed up than there was space to accommodate them. 'This is a prosperous time in China and so people are satisfied with their material lives. But they are coming to realize that money alone isn't enough and they are searching for that missing something to give their lives meaning,' he explained.

Then, looking over his shoulder at the party official who was trailing behind us quickly added, 'And of course, the government allows us full freedom now.'

My visit to Baimasi had been organized through Luoyang's local foreign affairs office (FAO), in compliance with the reporting rules that governed the activities of foreign journalists in the country at the time.

Although more often ignored than obeyed, these rules required foreign correspondents registered in Beijing to seek the permission of provincial government offices before applying for interviews and meetings when travelling outside of the capital. The rules were scrapped in early 2007, but when I visited Baimasi they were still in force and the abbot had insisted on my alerting the FAO as a precondition to meeting with me.

The unhappy result was that the abbot and I were chaperoned throughout the meeting by a fleshy, belching local party official who had obviously arrived straight from a long, boozy lunch.

For most of the afternoon he followed a few steps behind us with a bored sullenness. Occasionally he would interrupt Yin Le and 'correct' him. When the abbot explained his take on the upsurge in religious interest across the country, the FAO official piped in, 'Buddhism builds a harmonious society.' 'Yes,' Yin Le then repeated slowly, 'It builds a harmonious society.' Earlier, when the abbot told me the temple had some 2000 visitors per day, the FAO official snapped '4000.' Once again, Yin Le acquiesced, but his bright smile was no longer in evidence.

It was becoming increasingly clear that ultimately the real boss in the temple wasn't the abbot but the drunken party official.

Despite all the rhetoric about religious freedoms the CCP continued to set strict parameters within which this 'freedom' could be practised. Heads of temples, mosques and churches were hand-picked by the party. All places of worship had to be registered with the government. And freedom of religion was allowed only as long as the believers continued to accept the Politburo rather than a religious leader as their supreme authority.

Thus Catholics for whom the Pope rather than Hu Jintao elicited true devotion were subject to tight controls and ties between Beijing and the Vatican had been severed since 1951. 'House church' Protestantism, which involved informal gatherings by believers in private homes or other places outside of authorized churches, was similarly vulnerable to crackdowns, its leaders arrested and imprisoned, often without trial or access to lawyers on the dubious grounds of their having 'endangered national security'.

No religious group had been as viciously decimated, however, as the quasi-Buddhist Falun Gong sect which had flourished in the mid-1990s, developing a devoted following of tens of millions within a few years. Alarmed at the emergence of a disciplined and well-organized grouping of people outside the umbrella of the CCP the government came down on the sect with ruthless intensity, imprisoning and allegedly torturing members by the thousands.

By the time I moved to China the Falun Gong had few visible traces left within the mainland. Merely typing the words into a Google search engine could cause the entire search function to become disabled.

The party's new-found 'respect' for religion was thus a much qualified phenomenon. For the CCP religion had become a useful tool for the control of a disgruntled population and the perpetuation of its own rule. But the formula for what was an acceptable level of devotion was clear: loyalty to party and country, which were conflated, came first, loyalty to a religion a distinct second. People were thus free to believe, but just not too much; they were encouraged to attend to their spiritual needs but only as long as these were tempered by the materialistic.

No other place symbolized this strange mixture of the sacred and secular as much as a monastery some two hours drive from Luoyang, set high up in the misty Song Mountains. This was a monastery that had exercised a peculiar fascination across the centuries. Shrouded in swirls of myth and mystery the temple's fame had long crossed Chinese borders, thanks to Hollywood and Jet Li.

It was to this monastery that I headed next to see for myself the famous Shaolin temple and its kung fu monks. In the popular imagination Shaolin was synonymous with the rigid discipline and deep spirituality of the cryptic Zen Buddhism practised at the temple. But I had read enough about the temple's latest endeavours to be aware that the Shaolin I was going to see was more akin to a well-oiled corporation than an ascetic order of monks.

It was raining quite hard as I arrived at the temple but there was a fleet of tourist buses parked outside the grounds. Shaolin entertained a million visitors in 2005, I learnt later, all of whom paid 100 yuan—$12—to gain entry.

The monastery's buildings were surprisingly new, mostly dating back to the eighteenth and nineteenth centuries. Expensive facelifts in the 1990s only added to their flashiness, but the trees in the grounds were gnarled with age, some a thousand years or more old. They were the only surviving witnesses to stand testimony to the temple's centuries old history as it was repeatedly razed to the ground, rocked by civil strife, mauled by invaders and played with by capricious emperors.

As I peered around from under an umbrella, I was brought face-to-face with the Indian roots of what I had always thought of as a quintessentially Chinese institution, one more reminder of the real depth of the historic linkages that had fettered the two countries together.

I found myself staring at a large dull bronze statue that occupied pride of place in one of the main pagodas. Even through the driving rain it was impossible not to notice the statue's distinctively Indian features.

The bronze was in fact a likeness of Bodhidharma, an Indian monk who founded the Chan or Zen school of Buddhism circa A.D. 517, and who is credited with having developed the unique Shaolin-style of kung fu that had made the temple famous the world over. The temple itself had originally been built in A.D. 496 in honour of another Indian monk called Bada, or Batuo in Chinese.

Bodhidharma, or Damo as he was known in China, was the subject of numerous legends. He was believed to have meditated non-stop in a cave near the temple for nine years. The discomfort from long periods of inactivity led the monk to punctuate his meditation sessions with periodic bouts of physical exercise, or so the story went. He thus gradually developed a set of eighteen routines that combined his previous knowledge of yoga (Mohan I realized, was not quite the pioneer I had credited him as being) with new moves of his own creation. It was these eighteen movements that went on to form the basis of Shaolin-style kung fu.[7]

---

[7]Martial arts weren't all that Bodhidharma was credited with. He was also associated with another practice even more inextricably entwined with the Chinese identity: tea-drinking. The story went thus: one day some time during his nine-year-long meditation in the cave, Bodhidharma momentarily lost his concentration and fell asleep. This lapse enraged him so that he tore off his eyelids in self-disgust, an action meant to prevent any future recurrence of the crime, it being difficult to sleep in the absence of eyelids. Tea enters at this point in the legend, since two tea bushes were said to spring up at the very spot where the monk's discarded eyelids fell. Bodhidharma then plucked a few of the leaves from the bushes and dropped them into boiling water to discover that after drinking water thus enhanced, he found himself to be more alert. Tea-drinking was introduced to China.

'We have Indian roots,' admitted Shi Yongxin, Shaolin's abbot, during an interview. The double chin that underlined his round face wobbled as he continued, 'But over the centuries our style of worship has mixed with Taoism and Confucianism and what we practise today is quite far away from our original roots.'

What Shaolin seemed to 'practise today' was indeed quite far away from anything I had seen in India or elsewhere, beginning with the fact that the temple's abbot liked to call himself the CEO of the monastery.

Shi, who had been Shaolin's abbot since 1987, was clothed in the yellow robes of a monk, with a weighty rosary draped around his neck. But the bulge of a mobile phone was unmistakable through the folds of his robes as he handed me his business card at the start of the interview, complete with the temple's website address.

It was clear that in Shaolin, Buddhism was big business and its CEO was unapologetic for the temple's blatant commercialism.

'In the past, monks relied on farming to make a living. Today we have to rely on tourism,' he said chattily. 'Advertising and publicity have always been integral to Buddhism because how else can we diffuse Buddhist philosophy into society at large? China has been a commercial country for over 2000 years. What we are doing is nothing new.'

But in fact under Shi's guidance Shaolin had notched up a series of firsts including the setting up of China's first temple-based website in 1996 when few in the mainland had even heard of the internet. In 1997 the abbot hired lawyers to fight trademark violations, in order to protect the Shaolin 'brand' which had been much exploited and used to sell everything from colas to bicycles.

Shi then went on to dispatch hitherto secluded monks to perform martial arts all over the world and encouraged others to learn foreign languages and go abroad to study for MBAs and PhDs.

Around half of the temple's two hundred monks spoke a foreign language, Shi revealed with undisguised pride. English, Korean and Japanese were the most popular but a few had even begun to learn Farsi. 'As we speak at least a dozen monks from our monastery are studying abroad for degrees in Singapore, Sri Lanka, England and America,' he said, counting off the countries on the extended fingers of his hand.

The abbot's latest commercial venture was the production of an international, televised martial arts contest, the winner of which would then star in a series of movies the temple was investing in, through one of its commercial spin-offs called Shaolin Temple Culture Communications Co Ltd.

'Shaolin has been the subject of so many films but none of them portray the real spirit of our temple,' said Shi by way of explanation. He claimed the reason for the temple's foray into movie making had to do with revealing the spiritual side of Buddhism rather than the boom-bang of martial arts that Hollywood depictions of the monastery usually focused on.

But in the temple itself this spirituality was tough to come by. That morning I had spent a few minutes chatting with a gaggle of brown-robed, wide-eyed novice monks in their mid-teens. They had confessed in a gasp of nervous laughter their scant interest in Buddhism. 'I am here to learn martial arts,' said one of them, a 17-year-old. 'I'm not sure I'll want to stay here all my life.'

Apprentice monks in Shaolin had to choose at eighteen whether or not to stay on at the temple as confirmed monks, Shi explained. Those who stayed were divided into two groups: monks with a yen for performance and kung fu, and those of a more spiritual bent who wished to focus on theology and meditation.

In the early afternoon I was taken to watch a kung fu performance featuring young apprentice monks, two of whom looked no older than five or six years old. The room smelt dank and sweaty but the young monks were impressively supple as they went through their gravity-defying set pieces.

I was able to have a quick chat with one of the older boys, Shi Yen Jie, who had been in Shaolin since the age of twelve. He was now twenty-two. Shi Yen Jie like the overwhelming majority of apprentice monks had chosen to join the kung fu performance stream. He said he enjoys being a monk because of 'the travel'. I was a bit taken aback by his answer until I discovered he had already performed in England, Italy, Switzerland and the United States. 'I haven't been to India yet,' he added. 'Do you think it's worth visiting?'

On average the monk spent some five or six hours a day practising kung fu. Meditation time was usually an hour but it depended on his performance schedule, he said.

Shaolin's commercialism meshed well with the Chinese leadership's vision of religion and both the temple and its abbot had benefited from this convergence. The monastery was easily one of the richest in the country and Shi himself was a party pet, regularly hailed as an exemplary Buddhist leader in the official media.

The abbot was also a deputy to the National People's Congress, China's rubber-stamp parliament. Equally comfortable quoting Mao and the Buddha, Shi was proof of the fact that despite the official spin to the contrary, religion continued to play second fiddle to politics.

Thus barely a week went by without the abbot giving interviews on Buddhism and a 'harmonious society'. Our interview was no exception. 'Buddhism can relieve the strain and stress among people and gives them strength to face adversity, thus enhancing social accord,' Shi explained. 'Chinese culture values the concept of harmony, which is quite similar to Buddhist doctrine.'

I was quickly becoming sick of any form of the word 'harmony' or *he xie*.

When it was time to say goodbye, Shi asked me to recommend an Indian sculptor to him. He wanted to commission another bronze of Bodhidharma but didn't think a Chinese artist would be up to rendering an Indian face with accuracy. 'Please make some inquiries and email me,' he said, folding his hands in a farewell namaste.

Henan may have been the birthplace of Buddhism, but as the ample number of 'Muslim restaurants'[8] in Luoyang and other cities in the province indicated, a substantial portion of the province's religious tapestry included Islam.

Muslims in China in fact constituted a substantial minority and numbered between twenty and thirty million, although accurate data was almost impossible to come by. While the country's religious revival was largely focused on 'indigenous' Chinese traditions like Buddhism and Confucianism, Islam too had begun to garner greater attention from the faithful.

The two main groups of Muslims in China were the Hui and Uighurs. The latter were a much persecuted lot of Turkic ethnicity. For Beijing Uighur Islam was intertwined with ethnic separatism in the western province of Xinjiang, where most of them lived and as a result the practise of religion in the region was tightly controlled.

Hui Muslims, on the other hand, enjoyed greater leeway. Numbering about ten million in total the Hui were descendants of Middle Eastern traders and their converts who first travelled to China along the silk route during the Tang dynasty (A.D. 618-906).

Centuries of isolation meant that they had blended in with the majority Confucian and Buddhist population. As a result, although officially classified as a distinct ethnic community, the Hui were physically indistinguishable from the Han. The primary way of telling the two communities apart was the absence of pork from the diet of Hui Muslims, a meat that for the Han was a primary staple.

I had always considered myself to be culturally Muslim in part, having come from a country that had benefited from centuries of

---

[8]These were restaurants where all meat on offer was halal and no pork was served.

Islamic rule. I had grown up in Delhi, the seat of the Mughal Empire, and had lived in Nizamuddin, in the shade of the emperor Humayun's tomb. The language I spoke was sweetened by the Urdu in it. In school I learnt to dance Kathak. At home we ate halwa and kheer as treats.

My first 'best friend' at age four was Sadia Moinuddin and sometimes on the weekend I would squeeze on to a scooter along with her and her father, brother and burkha-clad mother. We would ride into the clatter and warmth of Old Delhi and visit with her relatives in small drawing rooms dominated by large posters of Mecca.

Years later, a few weeks before I was to head to the London School of Economics, I sat in my mother's home in Nizamuddin chatting with Soren Schonberg, a Danish friend from Oxford who was visiting at the time. We found ourselves talking about the culture or people we believed to be the most alien or 'other' to us. Soren began first and to my surprise (this was before 9/11) he picked the Middle East, which to me was almost reassuringly familiar in the texture of its foods, the rhythm of its languages and the strong brown beauty of the faces of its peoples.

Soren went on to ask me for my pick. I paused in consideration for barely a moment before answering, 'The Chinese.'

Six years later, having lived in China for four of those, I decided to take a closer look at developments in Chinese Islam. It was to Ningxia Hui Autonomous Region, the northern province flanked by the Gobi desert, that I headed to find out more. Ningxia was one of the poorest areas in China. It was also home to 1.8 million Hui Muslims who comprised 35 per cent of the province's total population.

On my first day in the province I drove in and around the provincial capital Yinchuan with Ma Xiao, Vice President of the Islamic Association of Ningxia, a jowly, bespectacled middle-aged man who sported a snazzily crocheted skull cap. We visited mosques, attended Koran classes, interviewed imams and met with some local government bigwigs.

The physical presence of Islam in the city was ubiquitous with the reaching minarets and crescent moons of mosques punctuating the skyline with constancy. As with Buddhist temples, mosques that had been destroyed during the Cultural Revolution were being restored and new mosques were going up as well.

Ma Xiao revealed the province to have some 700 officially licensed imams and more than 3000 mosques. And what about unlicensed ones, I asked? He shifted in his seat uncomfortably before replying, 'Yes, who knows how many of those there are.'

One indication of Ningxia's Hui Muslim population's renewed interest in Islam Ma continued was an explosion of youngsters studying Arabic. There were currently over 5000 Manla, or young Islamic disciples studying Arabic and Islamic doctrine part-time, in the province, he said. Even the Ningxia Economic Institute had begun to offer three to four year-long Arabic courses and Ningxia University had opened an Arabic language department.

The mosques we visited had also all begun to offer free Arabic classes for anyone who was interested. At Yinchuan's Xi Guan mosque, for example, over three hundred students had started to study the language since courses began in 2004. What was intriguing was that a full third of these language learners were women.

I sat in on one of the classes at the back of a room packed with women between the ages of thirty and seventy. Over the top of a sea of white headscarves the teacher was barely visible as she led the class in Arabic chants from the Koran.

Afterwards I talked to a few of the women. They seemed eager to chat and surrounded me in a crush. Some fingered my clothes. Others asked about Indian Muslims. Were they like Pakistanis?

A 40-year-old housewife with heavily kohl-lined eyes, unusual in China, was the most vocal. 'Earlier we were too busy just making a living. Now that we are richer we have more time to focus on the spiritual,' she said, echoing a sentiment I had repeatedly heard at Buddhist temples. She continued, 'By learning Arabic I can read the Koran in the original, which is my duty as a Muslim.'

Added Ma Fen Zhen, who at seventy was the oldest student in the class, 'When I was a girl most of us women were illiterate. We knew nothing about the world. Taking these classes gives us so much knowledge about how to conduct ourselves as good Muslims and the right values with which to bring up our families.'

This feminist twist to Islam in Ningxia was an example of the uniquely Chinese characteristics that set the practice of the religion amongst Hui apart from other Muslims. A hundred miles east of Yinchuan, in the small town of Ling Wu, I met Yang Yu Hong, one of two female imams at the Tai Zi mosque.

Young, pretty and feisty, Yang had received her title of imam from the Islamic Association four years ago. She was one of approximately two hundred certified women imams or *nu ahong* in the province. Yang stoutly denied that there was anything un-Islamic about the concept of female imams. 'There are many things that are easier for women to talk about with other women. And everyone, man or woman, has a duty to study and understand the religion.'

But this tradition of *nu ahong* in China was less revolutionary than it first appeared. While the women were granted the title of imam they remained unqualified to lead men in prayers. Their role was more that of a teacher and their students were exclusively female.

Ma from the Islamic Association was distinctly derisive of the whole concept. 'Women imams?' he laughed dismissively when I asked him about the practice. 'The *nu ahong* are respected women whom the community looks up to but of course they do not have the same religious powers as men.'

'Men and women are equal,' insisted Yang Yu Hong a little anxiously, when I asked her whether she felt it unfair that male imams could lead females in prayer but not the other way round. 'It's just that our roles are different.'

It transpired that the support base for this Hui 'tradition' of female imams was stronger in the CCP with its communist ideology of gender equality than amongst the Hui themselves. As with the Buddhist temples the party was a constant, if invisible, presence in the mosques. Proselytizing remained strictly forbidden. Children below eighteen were not permitted to receive religious instruction at all. All imams had to be licensed by a government approved body and all mosques registered with the State.

But despite these continuing political controls, Islam in Ningxia was gaining in popularity and as was usually the case in China there was an economic rationale driving the phenomenon.

'Other provinces have ports and natural resources. In Ningxia we have Muslims,' said Chen Zhigang, the Han Deputy Director General of Ningxia's Investment Promotion Bureau in a matter-of fact way when I caught up with him towards the end of my three-day visit. 'Muslims are in fact our competitive advantage.'

To exploit this 'competitive advantage' the Ningxia government had organized for the first time a massive Halal Food Exhibition that coincided with my stay in the province. Chen said the aim of the exhibition was to help establish connections between the food industries of Ningxia and the Middle East. He claimed contracts of 10 billion yuan ($1.25 bn) were expected to be signed during the four-day-long event.

The exhibition was only one manifestation of a broader trend. As the oil-rich Middle East became an increasingly important trading partner for China, the country's Hui population with their Arabic language skills and cultural affinity to Islamic countries were coming to be seen by the authorities as a valuable economic resource.

One of Ningxia's largest exports to other parts of China was thus the Arabic interpreters much in demand in certain cities. An article in the *People's Daily* claimed there were over 2000 such interpreters from Ningxia in Yiwu alone. The average salary for these interpreters was 3000 yuan ($375) a month, equal to the annual income of most households in the poorer parts of Ningxia.[9]

---

[9]Xinhua, 'More People from China's Major Muslim Region Work with Arabic', *People's Daily* Online, 1 February 2006 (http://english.people.com.cn/200602/01/eng20060201_239692.html).

Job opportunities as much as piety thus went some way in explaining the huge new demand for Arabic language skills.

The links between commerce and religion were, however, neither simple nor one-directional. One consequence of the increasing trade with the Middle East was the exposure of the hitherto cloistered Hui to more orthodox Islam as it was practised in Arab states. As a result a new conformity to scripture within the Hui community was emerging.

In the past the Hui were amongst the least orthodox Muslims in the world. Many smoked and drank, few grew beards and Hui women rarely wore veils.

But ever since business imperatives ended their isolation and began to take them abroad, stricter ideas of Islam had crept into the Hui community. Mosques in Ningxia had thus started to receive worshippers five times a day and more Hui women had taken to wearing headscarves. Skull caps for men, once a rarity, were also in wide evidence.

According to Ma over 8000 Muslims from China went on *Haj* to Mecca in 2005. In addition, hundreds of Hui students had begun to study in Muslim countries like Pakistan, Syria and Saudi Arabia.

Luo Zhan, the head Imam of Xi Guan mosque, spoke of these new developments approvingly. 'After we began to interact with Muslims from other countries we realized what a big gap there was between their level of understanding about Islam and ours,' he said. Luo went on to explain that even a decade ago being Muslim for most Hui simply meant landing up at the mosque for big festivals like Eid. 'Most people did not take Islam as something fundamental to their everyday life. This is finally changing,' he concluded with satisfaction.

In several of the conversations I had with people at the mosques a strong identification with the wider problems of the Islamic world was evident. 'It's American policy that has given all of us Muslims a bad reputation,' said Yang, Tai Zi mosque's *nu ahong*, aquiver with indignation. 'We are a peace-loving religion,' she went on and the fifty-odd women in the classroom nodded in assent. 'Yet, look at what lies they spread about us,' Yang finished bitterly, to increasingly loud murmurs of support.

Economic considerations had persuaded the Chinese government to relax restrictions and even to actively support the development of connections between the Hui and the larger Islamic world. But this was a policy that could easily backfire. In the short three-day period I spent in Ningxia it became evident that the growth of orthodoxy amongst the Hui could cause serious tensions with the Han.

'Earlier the Hui were just like us except they didn't eat pork. Now they think they are very special. They think of themselves as foreigners,' one Han government official in Ningxia complained. Already, confrontations between the two communities were common enough, often sparked by minor incidents.

In 2004, for example, large parts of Henan province were placed under martial law after fighting between Hui and Han that spread to include thousands of people and left dozens dead. The fighting began when a Hui man bumped into a Han girl with his vehicle and refused to pay compensation.[10]

Latent tensions were further exacerbated by government policy which provided potentially restive minority communities like the Hui a variety of sops. For example, the Hui were exempt from China's one-child policy (unless they worked for the government, in which case the policy applied) and special quotas were reserved for them at universities and government departments.

The Hui themselves pointed to their impoverished reality as proof that the job quotas only benefited a tiny minority of their community. The majority continued to have few job options other

---

[10]Jehangir Pocha, 'Ethnic Tensions Smolder in China', *In These Times*, 28 December 2004.

than as shop and restaurant owners of speciality 'Muslim' food.
But such logic did little to prevent Han resentment against the
Hui's 'special' privileges from rising, particularly in a backward,
desert-swept province like Ningxia where competition for jobs was
always intense.

Ma and I had been chaperoned by a local FAO official, a
surprisingly genial and helpful elderly man called Liu. Mercifully
uninterested in feeding me propaganda, Liu neither interrupted nor
'corrected' Ma, unlike his Luoyang counterpart, and was to all
appearances a knowledgeable and agreeable guide to the province.

However, on the second day of the trip, when Ma was no
longer with us, Liu proved less circumspect. Cautiously at first but
with gathering enthusiasm he spoke of what he called the 'real' Hui
situation in Ningxia.

'The Hui have a bad reputation amongst the Han because
they are dishonest. Han drivers are even too scared to go into a
Hui area.' 'Why?' I queried, puzzled by the assertion. 'Because
if the driver even accidentally grazes a Hui person on the streets,
the whole community will gang up and beat the driver, maybe even
to death,' Liu continued with seriousness, oblivious to the
irony that in the 2004 Henan incident exactly the opposite had
happened.

Liu's last words on the matter pointed to communal tensions
that were graver than I had imagined or gathered from reading the
local media. 'Frankly, the main job of every government official in
Ningxia these days is simply to keep the peace with the Hui,' he
said, leaving me with much to chew on.

It was clear that the party's attempt to use religion to create an
ideal 'harmonious society' could easily boomerang. Religion the
world over was a force capable of dividing as much as uniting,
something we in India knew only too painfully. Moreover, although
it was hoped religion's opiate would act more like a soothing salve
for society's dissatisfactions, it was equally possible that religion
could become the channel through which a frustrated populace

vented their discontentment with a party from which they felt increasingly alienated.

In temples, mosques and churches an alternative to the party leadership and an alternative to the party as a focus of people's loyalty existed; options that were lacking for Chinese in the secular world. The CCP, well aware of these dangers, worked hard towards ensuring that religious practice and leadership remained subservient to the state. Through a mix of repression and cooption it was largely successful in this goal, but the sustainability of such a strategy in the long term was questionable.

It was doubtful to me that in the absence of substantial policy measures aimed at redressing the inequalities of access and opportunity that had come to afflict China, religion could somehow magically provide the basis for social stability. Even in highly spiritual India, the poor and disaffected regularly voted with their feet, throwing out government after government in the hope of improving their lot in the here and now, rather than simply accepting their marginalized condition as karma. Conflating religion, including the Buddhist-Hindu variant, with passivity was simply wrongheaded.

A few months after I returned to Beijing from Ningxia I spent my first Christmas in China. Usually, Julio and I spent the holiday in Spain with his family. Christmas in Beijing was to provide me with perhaps the most offbeat 'religious' experience I encountered in all my time in China.

Despite being an unbeliever I loved the ritual and celebration associated with religious festivals and I tried to make it a point of attending Christmas Eve midnight mass wherever in the world I happened to be on the night. I had thus joined a range of masses from the sublime at Tewkesbury Abbey in Gloucestershire to the minimalist in one of New Delhi's Catholic churches.

In Beijing, we decided to attend mass at the city's oldest Catholic church located to the southwest of Tiananmen Square at Xuanwumen. The taxi we flagged down to take us there on

Christmas Eve smelt faintly of garlic. The driver appeared in a bad mood and cursed loudly at the cars he veered sharply to overtake.

'So, it's Christmas tonight,' I said breezily, hoping to distract him from his foul temper. A stony silence followed. 'Are you a Christian?' I persevered. No answer. 'A Buddhist?' I asked a tad desperately. The driver turned around to look me straight in the eye for a second before swivelling back to face the road. 'I believe only in money,' he said sullenly, his tone signalling the end of the conversation.

It was a blisteringly cold night, windswept and damp, and it had taken some courage to venture out. But as we sat in the enforced silence of the garlicky cab I comforted myself with the thought of the warm church we would soon be arriving at, gently heated by the fullness of a congregation out in strength. Just how full this could mean was something my imagination spectacularly failed to grasp.

The first signs that something unusual was afoot came almost a kilometre before we pulled up by the church. A long, thick queue of mostly young, fashionably dressed Beijingers snaked out of the church entrance, the whipping wind playing havoc with the salon-styled hair of those lining up. I looked at my watch. It was only around eleven. We had thought it wise to leave early on the off chance the church would be too crowded to find a seat in later.

We alighted from the taxi and tried walking into the church, only to be brusquely told to get in line. As we trudged to the back of the queue, we noticed that on occasion some of those lining up would step out into the shadows of the leafless trees that lined the road. Whispered conversations followed by some kind of furtive exchange then took place. It was all very mystifying. ·

I stood in the queue while Julio went off to investigate. He arrived fifteen minutes later along with two young boys who flashed 'organizer' badges and handed us special 'passes' that would enable us to enter without the queuing. 'You are genuine Christians and this night is for you,' one of the boys said solemnly. 'Not like these people here for whom this is just a game.'

I looked sharply àt Julio and from his guilty refusal to meet my eye deduced that he had sold us to these earnest young church-helpers as devout believers in Christ. My desire to catch a glimpse of what was going on inside overrode any pangs of conscience, however, and I merely smiled agreeably at the young boys and accepted the pass they offered without further ado.

They walked us to the front of the church and on the way explained that the furtive transactions we had noticed were an exchange of money for one of the 'passes' that we had just received. 'It's disgusting,' said the solemn boy. The passes, we learnt, were a tactic devised by the church to ensure that regular parishioners, numbering around 3000, were able to gain access on the night, while the novelty seekers were kept at bay.

The plan was an obvious failure. The church was leaking people with well over 5000 individuals packed inside the building and the grounds. Those queuing up outside must have numbered another two or three thousand.

Just past the church entrance giant flat screen LCD displays adorned the building's facade, providing a view for the hundreds who had been able to squeeze into the grounds but remained unable actually to push their way inside. Everywhere, giggly, gangly couples hung on to each other's arms, chattering excitedly, stealing quick kisses.

Midnight mass, it seemed, was the ultimate date for Beijing's hipsters. A few minutes before the mass was scheduled to start, a loud shout went up and the crowds within the church went wild, fingertips waving in the air, girls jumping on to their boyfriend's shoulders to get a better view.

Outside the LCD displays revealed the cause of the excitement. Santa Claus had arrived complete with red suit and white beard and was throwing candy into the congregation, much like a rock star might dispense personal items to feverish fans.

We managed somehow to shove our way into the church. I found myself separated from Julio, surrounded by strangers who were taller and bigger crushing in on me from all sides. A little whorl of panic began to rise up inside my throat and then suddenly the scene calmed, like the ebbing of a large wave. The mass had begun.

There were no LCD screens inside the church and all I could see were the backs of the heads of those in front of me. But in the sudden silence the voice of the priest leading mass rang out strong and clear. His words were in Chinese but the intonation was wholly foreign, ancient and Latin-like.

The majority of those gathered inside the church appeared to know when and how to respond to the evening's proceedings, answering the priest with chants of 'Amen' at all the appropriate points. When the riff of the first hymn of the evening, 'Silent Night', filled the church, I began to make my way back into the grounds outside. It had become difficult to breathe within the building itself.

Julio was out on the lawns, sweating, even though the temperature must have been close to ten below zero. I walked up to him and he held out his arms for me. We stood there embracing for a few seconds, only one of hundreds of young couples in similar repose, gazing at the singing congregation inside, on LCD screens.

Later that night I lay awake for hours, unable to sleep. Images swirled around in my head like snowflakes. 'I am Shaolin's CEO', 'Harmonious society', 'Muslims are our competitive advantage', the words echoed on a loop as I tossed and turned. Faces merged and morphed into each other: Yin Le's smile, Shi Yongxin's wobbling double chin, Hui traders at the Halal Food Exhibition and Santa handing out candy at midnight mass.

As I had suspected from my early days in the country, China's relationship with religion was indeed a tough one to deconstruct. The ubiquitous coupling of the commercial and spiritual, political and sacred made it hard to put a finger on what was really going on. But a few months later I finally came across a different kind of religiosity, one that struck a more familiar chord.

CHAPTER TEN

Shangrila

The air was strawberry-fresh and I breathed in great mouthfuls partly for the pleasure of it but also because I was out of shape. By the time I had climbed up the little hill behind the cluster of wooden homes that made up Hamugu village I was tired enough to need to sit down for a few minutes. Not so my 8-year-old companion Lopsang, who had kept up his non-stop chatter all the way to the top and showed no signs of ceasing.

'What did the Dalai Lama say when you met him?' he asked. 'Was Dharamsala beautiful like Hamugu village?' 'Can you help me get a passport?'

Later I sat eating lunch with his family. The food was unadorned: steamed bread, eggs and Yak butter tea. Lopsang's energy was unflagging and the little monk-in-training ran around the dingy room while we ate, pointing out odds and ends he said had come from India. 'Do you want to see an Indian film?' he asked excitedly, as the idea struck him.

I agreed, expecting the usual song-threaded Bollywood concoction. The boy rummaged around in a drawer and produced a DVD which he inserted into a player. I arranged myself comfortably on a chair in readiness for the pelvic-thrusting dance sequences that were the norm in Hindi cinema and was taken aback by the unsteadily shot opening scene that followed. Six Tibetan Buddhist monks in full ceremonial attire blowing mightily into ornate copper long horns filled the screen.

Slowly it dawned on me that this was a burnt DVD copy of a home-made film shot in Dharamsala, the seat of the Tibetan government-in-exile. We watched the film for a few minutes in silence. Then the boy's father asked where in India I came from. New Delhi, I replied. 'How far away is that from the capital of India?' he asked. I explained that Delhi was the capital. When he spoke again, a minute or so later, the father looked confused. 'You mean Dharamsala isn't the capital?'

It was early in the summer and I was spending a few days in north-western Yunnan talking to locals about a series of proposed dams on the Yangtse river that if built would not only necessitate the relocation of some 100,000 people but would also swallow up one of the country's most renowned natural landscapes—the Tiger Leaping Gorge.

I had based myself in the town of Zhongdian, a two-hour drive north of the gorge. It was to be my first brush with Tibetan China. Although officially part of Yunnan province, Zhongdian bordered the Tibet Autonomous Region (TAR) and the majority of its population comprised ethnic Tibetans. The Dalai Lama claimed the area to be part of greater Tibet, a region he accused the Chinese government of having divided across different provinces of which the TAR was only one, so as to be able to impose its rule more easily.

The Chinese countered that these were merely the politically motivated ravings of a 'splittist'.

Zhongdian had officially been renamed Shangrila in 2002, as a marketing ploy intended to lure in dollar- and yuan-rich tourists, eager to find the kind of unsullied natural beauty associated with the name.[1] If the packed flight in from Kunming, Yunnan's capital, was any indication, the strategy had proved on target.

From the moment I emerged from the town's tiny (but shiny new) airport there was a familiar flavour to the air. I sniffed spices and butter lamps, incense and flowers. Brilliantly coloured prayer flags sent thousands of wishes fluttering up to the heavens, attached to every conceivable grounded object from electricity poles to tree trunks. It was indicative of the kind of visceral religiosity that I associated more with India than China.

The faces of the people were browner. Their jewellery was of the type I grew up buying from the stalls in Delhi's Janpath. Shop-fronts sported a script that I couldn't read, but felt I should be able to.[2]

The first thing I did after checking into a hotel was to call Lin, a local contact whose number had been given to me by the friend of a friend who had spent some time in this part of the world the previous summer. I had talked with Lin the day before flying out from Beijing and had told him I needed his help in arranging for a driver and translator. I also wanted more generally to pick his brains for interesting places to visit or people to interview while I was in the region.

Lin told me to wait for him at the entrance to the old town, a wonderfully atmospheric collection of cobbled streets and wooden homes. I waited, a little tense, unsure of what to do with myself in this unknown place that I had only a few days to learn about.

I had no idea what Lin looked like and so smiled brightly at every male who approached the corner I stood at. I grinned at a

---

[1]The idea of a 'Shangrila' first captured the western imagination following a 1933 James Hilton novel, *Lost Horizon*, which described a mountaintop paradise where people lived in harmony revelling in learning and profound inner peace.

[2]I later discovered that the Tibetan script is based on Devnagari which also forms the basis for Hindi.

moon-faced monk in a Northface jacket. Next it was a gimpy old
man with a gold tooth. Both smiled back, the latter's tooth flashed
bright in the gathering twilight.

Finally, a muscular motorbike vroomed up to the curb and an
equally well-built, leather-booted, jean-clad Lin dismounted and
turned to greet me. He shook off his helmet to reveal thick, long,
black hair held off his face in a ponytail and smiled a deep, wide,
dimpled, smile. Lin was a dish. He was also to prove remarkably
friendly and helpful.

As he led the way into the old town and across a large square
towards the bar that was our destination, he counted off the
number of his relatives who lived in India: cousin, uncle, another
cousin. This was a phenomenon that would recur with regularity
over the next few days.

'She's from India,' people would point at me in loud whispers.
'My niece is in India.' 'My brother studied in India.' 'Oh Madhuri
Dixit!' 'I can cook Indian food.' 'Namaste!' 'Can you help me get
an Indian visa?' Ripples of excitement seemed to spread everywhere
I went. The longing with which the people I talked to imbued the
word 'India' was unusual to me. This is what I imagined Americans
must feel like in many parts of the world.

As we sat sipping tea and slurping up noodles Lin, who I
discovered worked as a guide in an adventure tourism company,
gave a friend a call and asked him to join us. The friend spoke
excellent English having studied in India for many years, Lin
informed me.

It took Gonpo, the English-speaking friend, only a few minutes
to show up. 'Namaste,' he smiled as he took a seat next to us and
handed me his name card. Like Lin, Gonpo worked in a travel
agency, but given his fluent English he catered mainly to western
tourists.

'In any case I don't want anything to do with Chinese clients,'
he spat. I was surprised at the venom with which he invested the
word 'Chinese', until I learnt that unlike Lin who had been born
locally in Zhongdian, Gonpo had grown up in Lhasa.

Ethnic Tibetans in the provinces of Sichuan, Gansu, Qinghai and Yunnan had been largely sheltered from the worst brutalities of the State against their culture and religion. More successfully assimilated into the mainstream than their fellow Tibetans in the TAR, people like Lin had grown up speaking Chinese rather than Tibetan as a first language.

They were also the material beneficiaries of governmental efforts to create infrastructure, boost tourism and raise incomes. Zhongdian was an example.

After being re-christened 'Shangrila', the number of visitors to the town began to shoot up. The majority of the tourists were Han Chinese, including many young, eastern avatars of western hippies—hooked on the exotic fantasy that Tibet had always represented. Thus, as was often the case in China, the desire to make a profit proved more potent than any ideological consideration and efforts to preserve the local Tibetan culture had actually been stepped up, or so Lin claimed.

The town authorities had ordered that Tibetan-style homes were to be preserved and rebuilt. All shops and hotels had moreover been made to trade-in Chinese character signs for new ones that included the Tibetan script.

Gonpo snorted loudly at this point in Lin's narrative. He laughed cynically as he recounted examples of the garbled Tibetan that had gone up on some store fronts, much like the 'Chinglish' that afflicted Beijing. A sign that should have read 'Beauty Centre' instead proclaimed, 'Leprosy Centre'. A restaurant that wanted to invite potential customers to 'Eat Yak Meat Here' ended up menacing them by claiming that 'Yak Eats You Here'.

The 'Chibetan' may be funny, said Gonpo, watching me smile as I took notes, but it also pointed to a depressing reality where many Tibetans in Yunnan were pathetically rusty or simply incompetent when it came to using their own script. 'Even this Lin here,' continued Gonpo pointing to his friend across the table, 'can barely write Tibetan any more.' Lin countered the criticism with an air of good-humoured resignation. 'It's just the way it is,' he said.

Gonpo glowered at him before continuing. 'The Chinese think they can buy and bribe us into loyalty but they never can. For a Tibetan our only loyalty is to the Dalai Lama.' In China, these were dangerous sentiments to be expressing. The party may have been loosening its once total control on what citizens could or could not think, but this limited liberalism emphatically did not extend to any signs that could be construed as political separatism.

In the TAR, Gonpo went on, Tibetans lived a life under siege. Expressions of cultural and especially religious identity were looked upon with suspicion and once under suspicion a Tibetan in China was under the ever present threat of arrest and torture. In the past, protests against Chinese rule had been put down with ferocity. No one was spared, said Gonpo, monks and nuns were beaten, many killed, others crippled or maimed for life.

The mood around the table had turned grave. Lin's usually bright eyes looked shadowed.

I asked Gonpo about India. How had he made his way across? Why had he returned?

'I went,' replied Gonpo, 'to see the Dalai Lama. It is the duty of every Tibetan to see him once in their life.'

Gonpo had made the journey to India on foot, stealing first into Nepal and then crossing over into India. This was a trek I was told that was somewhat of a rite of passage for young Tibetans, especially men, in China. Like Gonpo they would make it to India, stay for a few years, learn English, renew their spiritual links with those amongst their community in permanent exile and finally return to China to their families.

'I came back because this is my home, not India,' said Gonpo. Job prospects for English-speaking Tibetans like him were also far brighter in China than in India. In Zhongdian he made a decent living, well-heeled western travellers being willing to pay top dollar for guided tours of the rugged reaches of Shangrila.

And although grateful for the shelter and opportunities that India had provided for his community, life wasn't easy for Tibetans in India he said. Brutalized by the Chinese, in India they were simply looked down on, reduced ironically to 'Chinks'.

I remembered back to my college days at St Stephen's in Delhi. During my three years as a philosophy student there, my friends and I often used to visit a Tibetan settlement not far away from the college, nicknamed Chang Town after the Tibetan barley beer, for a lunch of momos and noodles.

There was always on these occasions a sense of entering unknown and somehow dangerous territory. The boys would warn the girls not to make eye contact with the 'Chinks'. 'If you get into a fight with a Chink, you're dead.'

During the meal people would joke about whether the meat we were eating was dog.

It wasn't only the Tibetans who were subject to this unselfconscious bigotry, but Indians from the North-East as well. The Sikkimese, Manipuris and Nagas all found themselves painted with the broad brush of 'Chinkiness' and subsequently formed a ghetto-like community on the college campus. A Naga friend once told me how it was difficult for her and her friends to gain admittance into popular nightclubs. 'They think that "Chinks" are trouble; that we like to fight and do drugs. That we steal and that our women are prostitutes,' she had said.

I believed Gonpo when he claimed it hadn't been easy for him in India.

The next day I was away from Zhongdian visiting Tiger Leaping Gorge and investigating the big dam story.

The formal announcement for the plan to construct a dam on the gorge had been made in 2003. The project, which had a planned generating capacity of 20 million kilowatts of power once finished, was a joint venture between the provincial government and a subsidiary of the China Huaneng Group—one of the largest state-owned enterprises in the power sector, headed by the son of former Prime Minister Li Peng.

Pre-project planning and activity had been on for the last few years, including geological surveys and the measuring of the homes and land of those that would need to be relocated. Environmental and social impact assessments were reportedly in the process of being carried out.

The basic problem was that all of this was being done in total secrecy. The social impact assessment, for example, was supposed to involve the participation of the people whose lives would be affected by the dam. In reality, however, none of the farmers who would be forced to move if the dam were to be built had been given any information regarding compensation or the scheduling for the dam.

Several of the farmers in the area I spoke to during the day said they hadn't even heard of the proposal to build the dam and were cheerily confident that they would never have to leave their ancestral homes.

I thought of the over forty-year-old controversy over the big dams on the Narmada river in India.[3] Middle-class city folk had over the years become inured to newspaper headlines arguing the effects of the dam on displaced peoples. Often tribals, usually poor and marginalized, the tens of thousands of dam-affected peoples in India had been uprooted with little or no compensation and woefully inadequate rehabilitation.

In China, the lot of those displaced by dams was similar although on rehabilitation the country probably scored higher than India. What was absent in China were the Medha Patkars and

---

[3]The Narmada Dam project, which involves the construction of a series of dams on the Narmada River, was conceived of as far back as the 1940s but first took form in 1979 with the purpose of generating hydroelectricity and improving irrigation. Since its inception the project has been dogged by controversy and has met organized opposition from the Narmada Bachao Andolan (Save Narmada Movement) whose leader Medha Patkar has come to symbolize the plight of the people displaced by the dams. The construction of the dams is an ongoing process as is the fight to ensure adequate compensation and rehabilitation for those affected.

Arundhati Roys and genuine debate on the social and environmental costs of big dam projects.

In 2006, the country already had over 85,000 dams, some 46 per cent of the world's total. Experts put the number of those displaced by these dams at a staggering sixteen million. Yet the local newspapers only carried happy stories about well-resettled villagers grateful to the government for having given them glossy new homes. Once in a while a story on embezzlement of relocation funds would emerge but this would invariably be followed by glowing reports of the stern action the government had taken to deal with the guilty parties.

Overall I believed the poor in China to be better off than those in India. Yet, the powerlessness of dam-affected people drove home a different point. In India, a vote did not always translate into a voice, but when it did it could be a powerful source of protection for those who were otherwise weak. In China, on the other hand, although on average the government performed a better job of providing services and opportunities for its poor, there was no recourse for the marginalized when the government itself turned tyrannical.

I returned tired to Zhongdian that night. The day had been emotionally draining. I called Lin to ask if he had managed to find me a driver and interpreter for the next day. He had located a good driver, Lin replied, but not an interpreter. It was high season and English-speaking locals were much in demand. The driver, a Tibetan called Dorji, could speak Chinese and I should be fine even without a translator, Lin assured me.

'Dorji'll take you around to a few villages and wherever else you want, but it's a pity about the bad timing,' he continued. Confused, I asked him what he meant. 'Oh, don't you know?' Lin queried. 'The Panchen Lama will visit Zhongdian tomorrow for the first time. The villages will be empty. Everyone will be going to seek his blessings.'

The Panchen Lama was the second-most important religious

figure in Tibet and in his eleventh reincarnation had emerged as the object of a tug of war between the Dalai Lama and the Chinese government.

Following the death of the tenth Panchen Lama in 1989 two different boys were declared to be his next reincarnation.

The Dalai Lama's nominee, Gedhun Choekyi Nyima, disappeared in 1995 at the age of six and was believed to have been under continuous house arrest since then, prompting some international human rights watchdogs to call him the world's youngest political prisoner. In the meantime the officially atheist Chinese government declared their own candidate, Gyaltsen Norbu, as the 'real' Panchen.

Norbu was kept away from the Panchen's traditional seat in Tibet's Shigatse city and was largely confined to Beijing, where he spent his childhood receiving an 'education'. He was rarely seen in public and had only just made his debut on the world stage a month earlier in April, at Hangzhou's World Buddhist Forum.

At the forum the 16-year-old had delivered a terse speech praising the Chinese government for providing a 'favourable environment' for Buddhist belief.

Now he was in Zhongdian for his first public appearance in this Tibetan majority area.

'Are you going to go see the Panchen?' I asked Lin. 'Well, we all know he's not the real one,' he replied, 'But I think I might just go and take a look anyway.'

The next morning I awoke to a hotel awash with armed Public Security Bureau personnel. They were all part of the Panchen's entourage, some of whom were staying at the same hotel as me. Dorji called while I was eating breakfast. He had been turned away from the hotel's entrance. No cars were being allowed in and the entire stretch of road aligning the hotel had been cordoned off.

He asked me to meet him at a spot off the main road, a ten-minute walk away. I agreed and hurriedly finished off the remains of my breakfast before heading out. Outside I stopped dead in my tracks. It was a bright, cloudless day and I could see several kilometres into the distance but not far enough to see the end of the queues of people who were trudging along in single file past the hotel entrance and further east.

I joined the crowds for a few minutes before turning off to meet Dorji at the appointed spot. The driver's face was sunburnt and lined but he had kind eyes and a gentle voice. 'The Panchen is blessing people all day long at a temple across that hill,' Dorji said to me in lieu of a greeting, pointing east into the horizon.

'No cars are allowed along the route so people have to walk at least four kilometres to get there.' 'That's a lot of people I just saw making the trip,' I replied. 'Well, the queue began to form before sunrise,' said Dorji 'and I don't think it will stop till late in the evening.' 'Don't you want to go?' I asked.

'I have a job to do,' he responded. 'Besides, he's not the real Panchen.' 'And all these people, do they believe he is the real Panchen?' I asked. 'No! No! Of course not. But they're curious and even if he isn't "real", he is the only Panchen they're ever likely to meet!'

Lin's predictions had been right. Most of the villages we visited that day were empty, their inhabitants off to be blessed by the Panchen. Only in Hamugu did we find some signs of life when we bumped into young Lopsang and his family, who invited us to have lunch with them.

Lopsang was a monk-in-training at the Songzanlin monastery, the largest Tibetan Buddhist monastery in Yunnan, some five kilometres from the centre of town. Like almost everyone else in Zhongdian, Lopsang had various relatives who were either currently in India or had been at some point in the past. He was desperate to go himself and asked countless questions about distances and airlines; passports and ticket prices.

It was highly unlikely Lopsang would ever be able to obtain a passport and his only real chance of making it to India would be on foot, through Nepal, along the same route that Gonpo had travelled. But who was I to tell him that?

After we finished our lunch and watched a bit of the 'Hindi' movie, Lopsang asked if I could give him a lift to the monastery. A visit to Songzanlin was already on our agenda and we agreed. On the way Dorji told me that the monastery's abbot had spent several years in India in Dharamsala prior to having taken up his position at Songzanlin. 'You can try and interview him,' Dorji urged. 'It'll be a good story for you.'

Like other temples across China, Songzanlin had been badly damaged during the Cultural Revolution. It had since been meticulously restored and housed both freshly painted murals and over eight hundred monks. An entrance ticket cost almost four dollars and platoons of tourists covered every inch of the temple, lighting huge wads of incense in offerings, their faces obscured by the bluish wafting smoke.

Dorji led me to the room where the abbot spent part of his day receiving and blessing visitors. There was a queue outside and on Dorji's instructions I joined it. The line moved quickly, each audience seeker getting barely a few seconds alone with the abbot. I found myself being ushered into the room before I had quite figured out what I would say.

The abbot was seated in a corner and beckoned for me to approach. I went up to him and kneeled as he blessed me. The abbot looked into my face and asked where I was from. This was the opening I had been looking for.

'I'm from India,' I said. 'It's an honour meeting you.'

'I've heard that you have in fact spent time in my country. How long were you there for?' I continued.

By now I had become accustomed to the very fact of my being Indian leading to instant celebrity status and I expected the abbot to respond at the minimum with warmth. Instead he looked strained, his mouth drawn into a thin, straight, line. 'You're mistaken,' he said. 'I have never been to India.'

There was little for me to do in the awkward silence that followed except to leave and make way for the next in line.

When I told Dorji of the abbot's denial, he looked disappointed. Then he said. 'I guess he has to be careful. It's easy here for people to get into trouble.'

The driver's words echoed in my head when I read about a 17-year-old Tibetan nun being shot dead by Chinese soldiers while crossing over into Nepal in September, a few months later.[4]

The next morning I returned to Beijing to write up my story on the planned dam, but my thoughts were filled with Tibet. It was late May and the Chinese newspapers were full of triumphant stories about the new railway to Lhasa nearing completion. The first ever train from Beijing to the TAR's capital was scheduled to leave on 1 July. I was determined to get on it.

---

[4]See Jano Gibson, 'Murder in the Mountains', *Sydney Morning Herald*, 12 October 2006; Leonard Doyle, 'China Tries to Gag Climbers Who Saw Tibet Killings', *Independent*, 11 October 2006; The Campaign for Innocent Victims In Conflict or CIVIC blog: http://action.civicworldwide.org/blog/comments.jsp?blog_entry_KEY=21828&t=

CHAPTER ELEVEN

Roof of the World

The train rolled out of Beijing West Railway station at 9:30 p.m. on 1 July, illuminated by the flash of scores of cameras trying to capture the image for posterity. Outside on the platform, TV cameramen chased after the T 27 Lhasa-bound express filming manically all the way until even the tail-end of the train faded away into the dark night. In turn, within the train compartments, 850-odd tourists, journalists and government officials jostled with each other to get their cameras in position, snapping away at the very photographers who were busy photographing them.

Forty-eight hours later, when it pulled up in Lhasa having snaked its way across 4000 kilometres, this train would create history. For many of the passengers it would be the kind of journey to regale grandchildren with for years to come. For the journalists on board, however, there was little need to wait for grandchildren given that we had editors around the world in impatient expectation of daily stories filed from the train itself.

Tibet had been the embodiment of an exotic fantasy for centuries. A Buddhist Shangrila, mysterious and remote, locked away within high mountains from the frenetic modernity of the outside world. But the Qinghai-Tibet railway, the completion of which had taken place a year ahead of schedule, would unlock the gate to the roof of the world and had unsurprisingly unleashed with it a torrent of admiration and criticism.

It was the world's longest and highest highland railway; an engineering marvel that the Chinese government claimed would bring about an economic renaissance in a region that had thus far remained poor and underdeveloped.

But lined up against the government's claims were an array of critics ranging from international human rights organizations to Richard Gere. The alarm was being raised regarding the destructive potential of the railway for Tibet's pristine environment and unique culture. The Dalai Lama had highlighted the increased ease with which troops could now be deployed in the TAR increasing Beijing's military hold over the region.

Beijing's assertions of the economic opportunities the railway would create were disingenuous, the critics argued. The railway would only facilitate the more efficient exploitation of Tibet's rich mineral resources, which would then be carted off on trains to benefit industries in other parts of China, they charged. The railway, the Dalai Lama and his supporters feared, would also speed up the allegedly deliberate 'Hanification' of the TAR by easing the way for an influx of Han Chinese migrants into the region.

It was the kind of story that was honey to journalists, combining controversy and drama with the romance of a great, long cross-country train journey.

The Chinese foreign ministry had reserved forty tickets for foreign journalists on the first train from Beijing and had held a lottery to select the 'winners' amongst the scores of scribes who had applied. In reality it was less of a lottery and more of a carefully considered vetting process in which geographical spread was one of the main deciding criteria. As one of only three Indian journalists in China, compared to the dozens of Americans or French reporters who covered the country, my chances of getting on were quite high.

And so I found myself on board the T 27 as it pulled away from the Beijing West railway station, snapping away with my camera along with everyone else. The train itself was in regular Chinese style divided into three classes: soft sleeper, hard sleeper and soft seats. Journalists, of whom there were some 150 on board, were housed in hard sleeper—six to a compartment—akin to the Indian three-tier. The tickets had cost us $100.

I had the right-hand side middle bunk of my cabin which I shared with reporters from the *Washington Post, USA Today, Le Figaro* and the German Press Agency.

The first evening on board I walked up and down the length of the train a few times, looking around and taking notes. Hu Jintao's eight honours and disgraces intermittently adorned the carriages. All signs were in Chinese, Tibetan and Chinglish. 'No occupation while in stop', admonished the plaques outside the loos, unfortunately militaristic in tone for a train the government spin doctors were trying their best to rid of occupation-related connotations.

All the carriages were interconnected giving free access to the passengers. The first few compartments beyond mine were filled with journalists busy plugging laptops into the few available power sockets. Walking past them took me to the soft sleeper class cabins, where tickets cost around $50 more than the hard sleepers. These were outfitted with TV screens and were shared by groups of four.

Many of the cabin doors were open and inside people were chatting away animatedly. As I walked past, several of the groups waved for me to come in and join. I sat down in one cabin with a 60-year-old grandmother and a 40-year-old biomedical engineer. We shared sunflower seeds and a cup of green tea. The grandmother, a retired government official, said it had always been her dream to visit Tibet. She had saved up her small pension for months to be able to afford this ticket. She was a Buddhist and believed she would find the kind of 'pure' spirituality in Lhasa's monasteries impossible to come by in the commercialized temples that were standard in China.

This was a sentiment I heard echoed repeatedly throughout the journey, the first time being the very next morning when I met Li Dan, a 27-year-old teacher from Jilin University who was travelling along with two colleagues. They were all Buddhists, Li Dan explained bright eyed, during an early morning conversation at the washbasin while I sleepily squeezed out toothpaste on to an awaiting brush. Buddhism in Tibet was special, unsullied, she went on.

Did she feel it would retain its purity in the face of the tourist onslaught the train was likely to lead to, I asked. She looked nonplussed before muttering, 'I'm not sure,' and then added, 'But the train is a great achievement.'

For weeks the Chinese media had been filled with paeans to the achievement the train represented. It was being called a 'magical road to heaven' that would bring to Tibet unimagined wealth and good fortune. 'The Qinghai-Lhasa railway is the realization of a 100-year-old Chinese dream,' the P.A. system on the train announced every few hours. It was clear that to disagree would be considered treasonous.

The mood on board was consequently self-congratulatory. 'We Chinese can achieve anything,' a China Central Television journalist boasted to me conversationally as we walked together to the dining compartment later in the morning.

Half-way through the first day on board, the Vice Director of the Ministry of Railways, Zhu Zheng Sheng, held a press conference. He spent most of it talking about the technical hurdles that had been overcome to make 'this dream come true'.

It was pretty impressive stuff.

Over 100,000 workers had been needed to lay the tracks and other related infrastructure since work on the railway started in 2001. The altitudes at which they had worked were so high that crew members had to be outfitted with extra oxygen supplies strapped to their backs. The fact that no one had died of altitude sickness during the construction process, Zhu said, was 'a miracle'.

Indeed when the railway project was first conceived of, the international consensus had been that it was simply unviable. The climate was too cold and oxygen-starved, the terrain too harsh and frosty. Yet only five years after the start of construction and $4 billion later, here we were—a day and a half away from the brand-new, 3600-metre-high Lhasa train station.

The 'magical, miraculous' part of the railway was the Qinghai-Tibet stretch that we would hit on day two. Starting from Golmud in Qinghai it was 1142 kilometres long, the majority of it located over 4000 metres above sea level.

More than 500 kilometres of this stretch barrelled through a sea of permafrost reaching across the Tibetan plateau towards the Himalayas, posing the most formidable of all the various daunting engineering challenges the railway had thrown up. Above the permafrost was a layer of ice that melted and refroze daily with the rising and setting of the sun, so that any track laid here was likely to be unstable and sink.

Zhu said that Chinese engineers had solved the problem by developing a technique which enabled them to permanently freeze the top level of ice and thus prevent it from following its daily pattern of melting and refreezing. Coolants were pumped into the earth ensuring that the ground near tunnels and pillars remained frozen.

After the press conference we trooped back to our cabins for lunch, which like all meals on the train consisted of watery vegetables and unidentifiable boiled meat. Suspecting that this would be the case I had brought a stash of Snickers chocolate bars along for the trip but found to my horror that these had already been ravaged when I wasn't paying attention by Jean Jacques Mevel, the chocoholic correspondent for *Le Figaro*.

Jean Jacques was defiantly unapologetic, although he did land up at our courtyard in Beijing several weeks later with peace offerings of the choicest Cote d'Or.

In the afternoon, I pulled out my laptop, scrunching up

uncomfortably in the middle bunk, to type up my report for the day. Outside a succession of Chinese cities rolled by as the train wound its way through the polluted dustbowls of Hebei and Shaanxi provinces and then west to the home of the Gobi desert—Gansu. The journey's most stunning scenery was reserved for day two when the Golmud-Lhasa stretch would take us through two mountain ranges, the Kunlun and the Tangula. The highest point on the trip was the 5072-metre-high Tangula pass.

Oxygen could get pretty thin at heights like that and the train had well-advertised remedies in place. Every bunk had a special oxygen outlet installed and attendants demonstrated how to use these in case passengers felt the need. Use involved looping some pretty nasty-looking tubes around the ears and then sticking them directly into the nostrils. Additional oxygen would also be pumped through the train from a central air-conditioning-like system along the Golmud-Lhasa stretch.

After finishing my story, I once again walked the by now familiar length of the train, waving to the grandmother and biomedical engineer en route, until I found myself in the hard seat compartment. The ticket for a hard seat was cheap, at just under $50, but Beijing to Lhasa was a long way to be travelling without anywhere to stretch out for a nap.

Regardless of the discomforts, the compartment was packed and buzzing with chatter. Much of the conversation revolved around the potential for getting altitude sickness. Everyone seemed to swear by a medicine called *Hong Jing Tian*, a Tibetan concoction which ostensibly unblocked the user's 'Qi' with wholesome results. Menaced by images of cerebral edema, I became an instant convert and started off on a six-day course of Qi unblocking, borrowed from a fellow journalist who was carrying extra supplies.

I spotted a group of youngsters my cabin-mate from *USA Today* had told me about. They were Tibetan students at the Police Academy in Beijing. One of the hazards of so many journalists travelling together was that we were all interviewing the same people for our various stories.

The students seemed happy enough to chat, however, despite having been subjected to a series of interrogations through the day. They said they were excited to be on the train. It used to take them a week to get home but now the journey time was cut to just over two days.

One of the boys qualified this general enthusiasm saying that he was concerned about the environmental damage the train might cause; the others murmured assent. Then another added that he worried about the loss of jobs for Tibetans that an influx of better educated Han Chinese moving to Lhasa may spell.

There was an uncomfortable pause before a girl in the group quickly spoke—'But there are many benefits to the train too. We can now go back and see our families much more often and the train will also make it easier for Tibetans to get a good education outside of Tibet.'

That night I found it hard to sleep. We would be arriving at Golmud early in the morning and I was gripped by the fear that I would sleep through the stop and miss it. It was just as well I slept lightly. The train pulled up at Golmud station at 5:30 a.m., an hour ahead of schedule. Within minutes the station platform was crawling with bleary-eyed passengers, fumbling for their cameras. This station marked the start of the new Qinghai-Tibet railway. Until now we had merely been travelling along long extant tracks.

Only a few years ago the *Lonely Planet* guidebook had described Golmud as a 'forlorn outpost at the oblivion end of China'. No more. Golmud, like all other cities across China, was in the middle of a construction boom, in part brought on by the anticipation of the flocks of tourists the train to Lhasa would bring. Even from the station platform massive power lines and hulking concrete structures were visible.

Golmud was situated in the centre of Qinghai, a province which at 700,000 square kilometres was somewhat larger than France but with a population of only five million. I had first read about the town, as well as the journey from there to Lhasa, in

Vikram Seth's 1982 travelogue, *From Heaven Lake*.[1] He had described Golmud as a military outpost with a 'free market in mostly bruised vegetables, a movie theatre, a bank, a bookstore'.

More recently I had read accounts of a Golmud that was home to four-star hotels and a giant 'two-storey high TV screen blaring out advertisements for cosmetics and electrical goods'.[2]

The train stopped at the station for only fifteen minutes and it was impossible for me to sneak out and have a look around. I had to content myself imagining the town through the eyes of others who had written about it.

Back on the train I looked out the window and thought back to Vikram Seth's journey on an unheated truck from Golmud to Lhasa. Fighting altitude sickness for most of the way it had taken him and his companions the best part of a week along largely non-existent roads to make that trip. Twenty-four years later it would take me just over twelve hours riding in the temperature-controlled environs of the 'magical road to heaven', breathing in the extra oxygen that began to be pumped in through the train from Golmud on. The train was not, however, pressurized in the manner of aircraft, despite some news reports having erroneously reported that it would be.

After hours of passing through grimy, polluted Chinese cities the landscape I was now looking at was a feast for hungry eyes. The valley broadened and grasslands rolled outwards for as far as the eye could see. There was a collective gasp on board as a fifty-strong herd of Tibetan antelope or chiru ran alongside the railway tracks for a few minutes. I spotted wild donkeys and horses in the distance and the hulking shapes of yaks were framed dramatically by craggy mountains.

---

[1] Vikram Seth, *From Heaven Lake: Travels through Sinkiang and Tibet*, Penguin, 1983, p. 81.

[2] Jonathan Watts, 'The Railway across the Roof of the World', *Guardian*, 20 September 2005.

'Look outside,' commanded the recording on the P.A system, 'You may see the Great Asiatic Ass.'

We were passing through Kekexili, a 45,000-square-kilometre area at the foot of the Kunlun range of mountains that marked the northern edge of the Qinghai-Tibet plateau. This was the natural habitat of the Tibetan antelope. Much had been made by both the railway's critics and supporters of these animals. Detractors claimed the train would spell the death knell for the sensitive animals, already endangered by poaching for their fur—a prized material for expensive shawls.

The Chinese government countered these allegations with their much trumpeted 'wildlife passageways,' mostly trestle bridges, thirty-three of which had been incorporated into the railway's design at key points along the route. The passageways had been built at places where the antelopes were believed to cross during their seasonal migration to grazing grounds and the authorities assured that they would be enough to prevent railway-related chiru accidents.

Past Kekexili, the bald bleakness of the Kunlun range was forbidding as we cut our way across it. 'The Qinghai-Lhasa express has awakened this sleepy wasteland,' the P.A. system opined.

The train climbed steadily but gently as it sped south. At the border between Qinghai and Tibet we passed the much awaited highest point of the journey as we crossed the Tangula range almost without my having noticed. But while the climb itself lacked the drama I had anticipated, the extreme altitude caused drama of its own. Anxious shouts went up all along the journalist-occupied cabins as laptops and i-Pods suddenly failed to work. Pens exploded and packets of chips burst open.

I was rather worried about my unexpectedly dysfunctional laptop given that I was meant to file a story the moment we landed in Lhasa. No one seemed to know if the effect of the altitude on electronic equipment was only temporary or final. To distract myself I walked down to the soft sleeper area and chatted for a while with my biomedical engineer friend, John, an ethnic Chinese who had lived in the United States for over twenty years.

He had a slight headache from the lack of oxygen but was nonetheless charged with the anticipation of our imminent arrival in Tibet. 'Growing up we were taught in school what a backward and primitive place Tibet is,' John said. 'I guess the Chinese will now finally be able to see for themselves if Tibet really is all that different.'

As John's comment indicated, the Han attitude to the more far-flung areas of China's territory was in general less than polite. During his travels across Xinjiang and Tibet Vikram Seth had recorded conversations with Han who were going to live in some of these areas. The migrants he met inevitably complained about having been sent to work in the 'barbarous limbo' of 'New Zealand'.

New Zealand in Chinese was Xin Xi Lan, a name the Han used as an acronym for being consigned to work in Xin-jiang, Xi-zang (Tibet) or Lan-zhou (the capital of Gansu).[3]

While much had changed in the quarter of a century since Seth's journey in terms of the infrastructure of travel, almost nothing had changed when it came to Han attitudes to Tibetans. This was an outlook I had first encountered at the BBI when talking with my students. They often recommended that I visit Tibet (without ever having been themselves) because Tibetans wore colourful 'native' outfits and always greeted visitors with impromptu renditions of folk song and dance.

'Maybe Tibet is not very developed but you will still enjoy the Tibetan singing and dancing,' one of the English Broadcasting majors had said.

Over the years this characterization of Tibetans became wearyingly familiar to me. The Han seemed to view them and indeed the bulk of the other fifty-odd ethnic minorities in China,

---

[3]Vikram Seth, ibid., pp. 39, 107.

solely through the prism of their quaint folk customs. It was as if the minorities were exotic birds.

Thus while a peacock was to be admired and protected for its beauty and colour, other than serving as a tourist attraction it could hardly be expected to contribute seriously to modern society or economic development. And so it was thought of the minorities.

Our last stop before Lhasa was Nagqu, a desolate little town high up on the windswept eastern plateau of Tibet. A handful of local herdsmen were at the station, smiling toothlessly and gazing at us train passengers in wordless wonder. One of them was dressed in an oversized suit and cowboy hat finished off with a heavy string of turquoise and ivory beads. His friends wore *chubas*—long sleeved sheepskin coats. The Han tourists went into picture-snapping overdrive.

It was only a brief stop and soon we were off again to our final destination: Lhasa. As we neared the Tibetan capital the formerly barren landscape was transformed into a carpet of green and yellow. Fields of wheat and rapeseed glinted in the reflection of distant glaciers.

Chinese flags began to make an appearance, firmly affixed atop every passing home, even those of humble herdsmen, an unambiguous statement of sovereignty.

The minutes before we arrived at the train station bang on time at 9:00 p.m. were frenetic. Tourists seeking souvenirs from the trip made a mad dash through the carriageways trying to collect the autographs of every passenger on board.

We alighted onto a spanking new train station: the first passengers ever to have arrived in Tibet from Beijing by train. Almost immediately a wave of Tibetan women engulfed us, wrapping white silk scarves over our shoulders in traditional welcome.

It was a lot to absorb, especially since despite having ingested copious quantities of *Hong Jing Tian* I had developed a persistent headache. I was also anxious to get to the hotel and send off my story. From Nagqu on, I had been relieved to find, my laptop had begun to work again.

It took around twenty minutes before a group of us foreign journalists were able to make a getaway on a mini-bus. I was tired and hungry and when my first glimpse of Lhasa city was of a neon-bright, phallus-like tower stretching up into the sky from atop a hill, I couldn't help but wonder if the altitude was inducing hallucinations.

But then the bus turned a corner and the white-and-ochre grandeur of the Potala Palace swam into view. This was the Lhasa of my imagination. Despite being juxtaposed with the bilious TV tower, the palace was an awe-inspiring sight, even more so the next morning when it was encircled in a swirl of prayer-wheel-turning pilgrims.

Gnarled old women prostrated themselves again and again on the ground as they circumambulated the Potala, a practice I learned was a daily routine for many Lhasa residents. Some were supported by younger children, others had brought along pet dogs for the walk. The tinkle of silver jewellery mingled with the whirling of prayer wheels.

As in Zhongdian, I was struck by how much closer to India I found the overt displays of religious ritual common amongst Tibetans, than to the China that Tibet was today a part of.

Inside the Potala's grounds an interview with Qiangba Gesang, the Palace Director, had been arranged for us.

Qiangba was upfront about his apprehensions regarding the impact of the train on the Potala. The palace restricted visitors to a total of 1800 persons a day, he told us. Tourists were charged 100 Yuan ($12) while pilgrims—mostly nomads and farmers from around the TAR—a token 1 Yuan ($0.12) as entry fee. But the influx of tourists that the railway was expected to bring had caused the palace management to plan on admitting an additional 500 visitors per day.

Qiangba's main concern was that the mud-and-wood structures of the thirteen-storey palace would collapse under the weight of armies of tourists. 'More tourists will be good for Lhasa but not for the palace,' he concluded.

The Potala was the winter residence of the Dalai Lamas and housed the throne where the current Dalai Lama, Tenzin Gyatso, had sat to rule over Tibet before he fled to India in 1959. A continuing ban on the public display of his image, however, meant that not a single photograph of him adorned the rooms of his own former residence.

A journalist asked Qiangba his opinion of these restrictions. In response the Palace Director's jovial expression tightened and he replied tersely, 'We do whatever the government decides.'

In recent times Beijing had begun partially to loosen the strict controls it once imposed on religious worship in Tibet. Concern for China's international image coupled with greater confidence in the centre's ability to isolate and suppress dissent in the region meant that the opening up of spaces for prayer and pilgrimage was increasingly permitted as long as certain rules, such as an absence of any public veneration of the Dalai Lama, were adhered to.

The Potala, which had been given an injection of several million dollars for renovation, was packed with pilgrims. Many of them looked at me with curiosity as I walked around, slightly dizzy with the lack of oxygen and the effort of climbing up the steep stairs along the palace.

A bent-over old lady on the arm of her daughter came up to me and touched my face, gently. She spoke to her daughter in Tibetan who then asked me in Chinese if I were from India. When I replied that I was, there was a charge of excitement reminiscent of my time in Zhongdian and soon I was surrounded by half-a-dozen people with relatives in Dharamsala or Delhi.

At one point even Qiangba took me aside and confided that his older brother had been to India. Some of his relatives continued to live there. 'Have you been?' I asked. 'No,' came the reply, 'I'd like to, but it's complicated.'

After the brightness of the summer day outside, the rooms inside the palace were cool and soothing, lined with dark wood and silk brocades. The smell of yak butter lamps hung heavy in the air.

I chatted for a while with a friendly 27-year-old monk who spoke some English, called Norbu, one of around eighty monks who lived in the Potala. I told him I had come up on the train from Beijing and asked what he made of all the claims and counter-claims about the impact of the new railway.

'Most Tibetans are poorly educated,' Norbu said. He felt that even if the train kick-started the local economy and created more jobs, these were likely to go to migrants from elsewhere in China who were better educated.

Norbu was only echoing one of the main concerns that critics of the railway had long voiced: that the benefits accruing from the railway would not go to Tibetans as much as to Han migrants who enjoyed access to lines of credit and were better equipped educationally to exploit any new opportunities that emerged.

The hotel that we were being put up in, for example, was owned by a businessman from Sichuan province. A quick survey of the shop owners along Lhasa's main shopping street revealed the majority of these to be from outside of Tibet as well.

But like the Police Academy students I had met on board the train, Norbu also admitted that the railway would ease the way for young Tibetans who wanted a quality education elsewhere in China. 'It has its good points,' he said, before switching to an animated monologue on the proceedings of the soccer World Cup that was being played in Germany at the time.

Norbu, it transpired, was a Brazil fan. 'Ronaldo!' he beamed. As he waved goodbye with his right hand, he made a thumbs up sign with his left. 'Ronaldinho!' was the last thing I heard him say.

I walked down the stairs leading to the bottom of the palace slowly. Half-way down I came across a few of the journalists from my group together with some of the Chinese foreign ministry officials who were accompanying us. They were sitting down on the steps in silence, necks craning upwards.

Following their gaze I saw a group of Tibetan women working on restoring a section of the Potala's roof. Scraps of white cloud hung low behind them, in what was otherwise a sky of the clearest blue. As the women worked they sang, a high-pitched keening tune, stamping their feet in unison in an intricate dance.

We sat mesmerized for a few minutes until one of the ministry officials spoke. 'They're certainly great singers, but I'm not so sure about them as workers,' he sniggered and then laughed heartily at his own joke.

Later, as we continued the walk down together, an argument between the official in question and a Danish journalist called Jes broke out. Jes wondered out aloud why Tibetan was classified as a Sino-Tibetan language, given the fact that Chinese and Tibetan were completely distinct.

His question was predictably interpreted as a disguised attack on China's sovereignty and caused the official to launch into an indignant monologue covering the well-travelled ground of how Tibet had always and indisputably been part of China's sphere of influence. Jes pointed out that none of this answered his question, leading only to heightened squawks of indignation on the official's part.

As the argument droned on, I wandered ahead with Xiao Yan, an interpreter with the ministry. She seemed upset by Jes' comments as well and I tried to smooth ruffled feathers by explaining that dissent did not necessarily equal attack, at least in a non-Chinese context.

'Jes is just expressing an opinion. Don't take it so personally,' I smiled. 'In countries like India and Denmark people often openly disagree with each other on a topic and that's okay. They can still agree on many other things,' I said.

'I know,' replied Xiao Yan with a toss of her head. 'But in China it's different. We must all think the same thing.'

Later in the afternoon we visited the Jokhang temple, the holiest of all centres of Tibetan Buddhism. The temple had been built almost 1400 years ago although over the centuries it had been repaired and rebuilt several times.

The Jokhang was less imposing than the Potala, and quieter. The ministry had organized an uninspiring gaggle of guides to show us around and after an hour or so of listening to their listless descriptions of the various Buddha statues on display, I left the group and walked out on to the streets.

The Jokhang was located in the centre of Lhasa's old town and knick-knack crammed alleyways spread out all around it. Everywhere Hindi film music launched an aural assault on shoppers. '*Aapka naam kya hai?*' inquired a young boy in Hindi, 'What's your name?' as I made my way past the crush of souvenir stalls. I stopped to talk with him for a few minutes.

He explained he was a tourist guide who had studied in India for several years. He spoke Tibetan, English and Hindi, but no Mandarin Chinese. Business was bad as a result, he complained. The foreign tourists hadn't made it to Lhasa this summer because of the World Cup and he couldn't communicate with Chinese visitors, which pretty much made him unemployed.

He handed me a business card from his wallet and asked me to call if I needed his services at any point. Then before putting the wallet away he quickly flashed a photo of the Dalai Lama. 'His Holiness is always with us in our hearts,' he said. 'You are a journalist. Please write that in your article.'

The centre of Lhasa had a prosperous look. Its pothole-free roads and swanky shops selling fashionable clothes and cutting-edge electronics gave it as posh an air as the glitzy parts of New Delhi or Mumbai.

I marvelled at the thought that this was one of the poorest parts of China. My wonderment was not shared by everyone. Xiao Yan, the interpreter, was unimpressed. 'I'm a bit disappointed by Lhasa,' she said looking around. 'It's so poor.'

According to official figures, Tibet's annual GDP in 2005 reached 25.06 billion yuan ($3.1 billion). Moreover, the last decade had seen average annual growth rates of over 10 per cent. However, as in other parts of China, there continued to be a substantial chasm between the relatively prosperous city folk of Lhasa and the farmers and herdsmen of the vast countryside. Even on the outskirts of Lhasa, branded stores gave way to crumbling shacks with tin roofs. Nonetheless, over the course of the five days I spent in Tibet, abject poverty was as rare a sight as in the rest of China.

The next day we travelled up several hours north of Lhasa to Namtso Lake, which at 4720 meters was breathtaking in every sense of the word. As our group sat eating packed lunches on the shores of the turquoise water, dirty young children came up to us and begged for food.

I handed over my lunch to them, the altitude having robbed me of an appetite. The scruffy young things devoured the oranges and bread that was part of the packet but when it came to the salted eggs, they wrinkled their noses and blithely tossed them into the lake waters. The kids might have been poor but they certainly weren't starving.

A day later, on the return trip to Lhasa from Nagqu, where we had spent a headache-plagued night, a small group of us journalists stopped by a family of yak herders. A few snotty-nosed kids played with baby goats outside a large tent, while a tired-looking middle-aged lady tended to the yaks.

We plied the woman with questions which she did not seem very interested in answering, unsurprising given our unsolicited intrusion into her busy day. But she did tell us she was the mother of seven children.[4] The family comprised fourteen people in total and in the summer they all lived in the single tent we saw before us.

They made their living selling yak milk. They were poor, she said baldly, they subsisted. But parked next to the shabby tent was

---

[4]While the one-child policy does not apply to Tibetans or most other minorities, they are usually officially only allowed to have two children. However, as this particular example demonstrated, official policies in the remote countryside are more often than not ignored.

a battered old car along with a motorcycle, both of which belonged to the family. As I had found in Ningxia, the meaning of subsistence in Tibet had obviously undergone a transformation.

Back in Lhasa large banners boasting of the golden opportunities that the railway would bring festooned the entrance to the city. New hotels encased in scaffolding were going up. Lhasa's first five-star hotel, The Brahamaputra Grand, had opened its doors a month earlier in June. The Grand Hyatt, Intercontinental Group and Banyan Tree resorts were all reportedly scouting around for properties.

Tibet's tourism revenues were likely to double by 2010 as a result of the railway with half a million more tourists a year to pour into the region. I could well believe it.

That evening I dined out, feasting on yak bourguignon which along with yak burgers and yak curry was an example of just how cosmopolitan eating out in Lhasa had already become. The restaurant I ate in was full even at 11:00 p.m.

I flew back to Beijing a few days later at three times the cost of the train journey. During the five-hour flight I was accompanied by what was by now a familiar feeling: confusion. As was almost inevitably the case when I tried to evaluate my reaction to the 'reality' of China, I was only able to arrive at qualified statements full of 'buts' and 'on the other hands'.

That Tibetans themselves felt colonized by Beijing was unquestionable. The forced imposition of Chinese sovereignty was palpable everywhere in the TAR from the triumphant unfurlings of national flags fluttering from the tenements surrounding the Jokhang to the hastily flashed pictures of the Dalai Lama that many Tibetans carried with them at considerable risk to themselves.

Beijing had won few hearts and minds in Tibet. Small wonder given that barring select puppet-like figures like the CCP-chosen Panchen Lama, Tibetans in general continued to be treated by Beijing as suspect—marginalized and excluded from the policy making that would shape their own future.

This was a plight that Tibetans shared to some extent with all Chinese. China's was a one-party authoritarian regime and public participation in shaping policy was limited everywhere. Nonetheless, given the distinct ethnicity and culture of Tibet there was an especially nasty quality to its 'integration' into the mainland, throwing into bold relief the bullying, homogenizing tendencies of the CCP.

On the other hand, that Chinese rule had brought a degree of material prosperity to Tibet was also undeniable. The railway was only one example of a slew of infrastructure projects that Beijing was spending billions of dollars on constructing in the region. The world's highest airport at Ngari was being built there; roads to formerly dirt-poor, remote areas were being developed and telecom, electricity and drinking water supply grids were being extended across the TAR.

In the past four decades China had raised Tibetan literacy and life expectancy rates significantly, although there was much controversy over the exact figures. Controls on cultural and religious practice were also being relaxed. Tourism was being encouraged and even if one agreed that the accruing benefits went largely to Han migrants at least a portion of the benefits did trickle down to Tibetans as well.

China's strategy of connecting Tibet with the rest of the country was certainly in part motivated by the desire to bind the region politically and militarily closer to the centre. But, simultaneously, there was an economic incentive for Tibetans and Tibet in the bargain.

Comparisons with India's North-East which bordered large parts of Tibet and Yunnan were natural. In the seven states that comprised the Indian North-East, New Delhi ruled with a heavy-handedness similar to that of Beijing in its border regions.

And even as India was hogging global headlines as the junior sibling to China's growth story, the north-eastern states continued to languish in poverty. Per capita incomes in this region were well below the Indian national average. The tribal peoples here remained marginalized and secessionist violence wracked the region in a seemingly endless spiral. New Delhi poured money into the security apparatus needed to clamp down on 'separatism' in the region but infrastructure remained seriously underfunded, thus adversely affecting trade and tourism.

Here, there were no equivalents of the railroads or airports China was building in Tibet. Further, the peoples in the North-East were subject to similar kinds of racism and social exclusion in India that Tibetans confronted in China.

New Delhi's failure was two-fold. It had not only failed to win hearts and minds in the North-East but it hadn't even provided the region with the kind of economic opportunities China was busy bribing its troubled border areas with.

However, although China had in many ways handled the integration of the regions on its periphery better than India had, internationally it suffered from far worse press. There were no Steven Segals crusading in indignation on the part of the Bodos or Nagas. India's democracy meant that it was often let off the hook when it came to human rights violations or abuse of citizens by the state in the name of protecting sovereignty.

But to say this does not mean that India's democracy was meaningless either. The North-East might not have figured prominently in the national imagination or policy priority list, but the local governments that ruled these states were genuinely representative.

Moreover, although the various pleas of the local authorities, for example for cross-border infrastructure development, were often overruled by the centre on security grounds, they were allowed to air their views freely. No matter how critical the North-East's elected leaders may have been of New Delhi's intransigence, they did not risk jail, or worse, for being so.

The fact that despite being amongst the poorest of Indians, the North-East's peoples were hardly clamouring to smuggle their way across the border into Tibet or Yunnan was also revealing. A life in China might have opened up greater economic opportunities but the trade-off in terms of civil liberties was obviously a significant deterrent.

India had not provided the Nagas, Mizos and others in the region with the broad roads or tourism dollars that China ensured for its border provinces, but New Delhi did provide something else: cultural freedom.

The kind of homogenizing cultural diktats so common in China were largely absent in the Indian North-East. I thought about that catchphrase from my school days: 'Unity in Diversity.' Despite the propagandist element to this description there was truth there too. Diversity did not frighten New Delhi in the same way it seemed to Beijing, given that the only majority in India was in fact the experience of being a minority. In China this was a concept that was not only alien but almost incomprehensible.

Thus, culturally at least, the North-East's distinctive identity was unthreatened. The religions practised here were not of the dominant Hindu variety but Christianity, Buddhism and folk animism. The languages spoken here included a smorgasbord of local dialects, many from the Tibeto-Burman or Austro-Asiatic linguistic groups rather than the Indo-Aryan or Dravidian groups from which large languages like Hindi or Tamil derived. But for New Delhi, such heterogeneity in itself did not make the region or its peoples suspect.

In short, to be a Christian Naga who spoke no Hindi in India was a happier prospect than being a Tibetan Lama who spoke no Mandarin in China. In China non-conformity made you suspect; in India it was simply the norm.

The two countries were thus like mirror opposites of each other. One provided roads, schools and electricity but stifled diversity, criticism and participation; the other allowed diversity, criticism and participation, yet achieved little in improving livelihoods and providing economic opportunities.

It was all a bit muddling and by the time I arrived in Beijing airport my head was hurting again. This time even *Hong Jing Tian* could offer little relief.

CHAPTER TWELVE

Squaring a Circle and
Coming Full Circle

Back in *Beixinqiao Tou Tiao hutong*, the mahjong-playing gang still gathered outside the *xiao mai bu* long into the sultry summer nights. Old Lady Fang's son would join in these games, his T-shirt rolled up over his ample belly. Every evening when I returned home, no matter how late, the mahjong players would still be out. They would pause for a few seconds as I walked by and then someone would invariably raise his chin lightly in greeting.

'*Hui lai le.* You're back.' he would say, the unvarying greeting with which my neighbours acknowledged my return home. There was a comforting predictability to *hutong* greetings. They indicated that all was well with the neighbourhood and its cadence.

Summer turned into Beijing's all too brief autumn and before long the ominous hint of coal was in the air—the signatory smell of a *hutong* winter. Other signs of the imminent onset of the cold season also appeared: early morning public toilet users swapped their cotton pyjamas for long-sleeved flannel ones.

I thought back to my early days in the neighbourhood when the pyjama-wear favoured by the residents had caused me to raise an occasional eyebrow. For the pyjama, the *hutongs* were a true liberator. No longer kept to the confines of the bedroom, they were worn by residents on the street throughout the day and no one seemed to think it the slightest bit strange.

Once my preliminary bemusement had passed I had come to greatly appreciate this pyjama-friendly attitude, given the hassle it saved every time I needed to pop around to the corner shop, in search of matches or the like. Occasionally I would take one of my cats, Caramel or Tofu, along for the outing. The cats were big favourites of the neighbours and a crowd would usually gather to fuss over them when I carried them along.

One autumn morning as I made my way home from the shop a group of foreign tourists went cycling past on an organized '*hutong* tour'. They smiled benignly as they looked around with curiosity until they spotted me. At this point many of them looked apoplectic with shock and one of them only narrowly avoided falling off his bike.

I had caused similar reactions in some Chinese when I first moved into the neighbourhood, so surprised had the locals been to see an outsider in their midst. But never before had I elicited such a response from fellow foreigners.

Then I looked at myself from their perspective: decked out in matching pyjama top and bottom, cigarette dangling out of the corner of my mouth, cat tucked under my right arm, bathroom slippers slapping on the street as I strolled along. The *hutongs* had domesticated me.

As 2006 slid by and we embraced the start of another new year in China, my fifth, Mr Wu, our landlord, called to arrange a dinner. It had been a while since we had last gone out together, the *siheyuan*'s plumbing having been relatively well behaved in the recent past.

I quickly agreed to dinner but in doing so, had ulterior motives. Without exception, every time that Julio and I had been out to eat with the landlord on previous occasions, Mr Wu had picked up the tab. This did not reflect his generosity as much as it did our lack of skill in the popular Chinese dining contest of 'who can pay the bill first'.

This was a duel the losing of which brought much loss of face to the defeated party and Julio and I had almost no face left given our abysmal record with the Wus. Here, finally, was a chance at redemption.

It was thus that a few days later we found ourselves in a local Sichuan diner with the three Wus, looking with furrowed brows at the dishes that had been ordered. 'And what's that? Lungs by any chance?' I queried, a catch in my throat. 'Oh you're in for a special treat tonight,' grinned Mrs Wu ghoulishly, stirring the steaming vat with a glinting ladle. 'Its not just lungs, but kidneys and liver too, all mixed up in a broth of stock and blood and flavoured with Sichuan chillies.'

For a moment she looked concerned. 'You don't mind chillies, do you?' she asked attentively. In dumb misery I shook my head. In good conscience I could not claim to be chilli-averse. 'That's all right then,' she said relieved and proceeded to ladle out a particularly large helping of grey, quivering meat, plop into my reluctantly extended bowl.

And so the meal went on. Mixed innards were followed by bullfrog on the bone, so that the meat had to be gnawed off and little bits of cartilage spat out. 'It's not very well known but frog meat is in fact the most delicious of all,' Mr Wu told us knowledgably.

Allowing the landlord to choose the restaurant and dishes was part of our strategy. We would lull him into thinking he was the acknowledged host for the night and then after we had all eaten our fill, Julio would excuse himself to go to the loo but head instead for the cashier where he would sneakily pay the bill. When Mr Wu asked for the cheque, we would triumphantly reveal that it had already been taken care of and try not to smirk when his face crumpled in defeat.

All was proceeding according to plan when half-way through the meal Mr Wu swallowed a morsel of frog the wrong way down and went into frightening convulsions, clutching desperately at his throat as he gagged on a piece of amphibian cartilage. Suppressing base thoughts about this being poetic justice visited for the ordeal inflicted by the landlord on my stomach, I gamely pummelled his back. But it was to no avail. Mr Wu broke away and went dashing out of the room. We were prevented from following by the Mrs, who insisted for us not to worry. 'Old Wu is tough,' she said. 'He'll be fine.'

A few minutes later Mr Wu reappeared, a bit red in the face but obviously recovered. Brushing off our solicitous inquiries he once again tucked into the pig lungs on his plate with gusto. Half an hour on, our appetites sated, Julio slipped off as planned to the 'loo' and stealthily made his way to the cashier where he whispered for the bill. 'The bill?' replied the lady puzzled. 'But that was taken care of by the old man you're eating with half an hour ago.'

Vanquished by the wily Mr Wu yet again there was little for us to do save savour the time we had left in the country. We had no definite ideas for the future yet but the months were skipping past. By the time my five-year anniversary in China loomed I had been offered a six-month-long fellowship at Oxford starting from the fall of 2007. I decided to take it. Julio was also getting itchy feet having spent almost six years living in the country. We were physically still in China but a mental distance from it began to grow as we looked ahead to fresh adventures.

Much had changed since I first washed up in Beijing in August of 2002. Many of our friends—journalists and diplomats—had finished up their three- or four-year-long postings and moved away. My students from the BBI had all graduated and several were now studying abroad.

The Olympics were round the corner and the *chai* signs so ubiquitous during my early months in Beijing were almost gone, the buildings having been busted up months ago. From the ashes of Qianmen where I had once chatted with the ninety-year-old Lao Tai Tai, spiffy new shopping complexes were taking shape.

Taxi fares had been raised twice since my early days in the city.

The drive to eliminate Chinglish was having limited effect. A neighbourhood restaurant had erased the translation of a favourite fish as 'crap' and replaced it with the less entertaining but more accurate 'carp'. A popular city landmark, the large neon sign that once boldly flashed out Dongda Hospital for Anus and Intestine Disease, now politely read the Dongda Hospital of Proctology.

Mohan, the yoga teacher, and Yin Yan, his fashionable financial backer, had become parents, their Chindian baby the physical embodiment of a new wave of cross-border engagement. The W.C club at *Ju'er hutong* had long disbanded, although Old Yang the bicycle repairman was still to be seen around sometimes.

I was overpowered by a strong dose of future nostalgia, looking ahead to a time when I would look back on the present with misty eyes.

Five years was a decent slice of time to spend in a country and I had used it relatively well: travelling and asking questions. But as I geared up to draw a curtain across my China-life, I was increasingly being called upon to answer a few questions as well.

'Where was China heading?' people would ask me when I travelled outside the country to Europe or the United States. Was the CCP doomed or would it continue to be a formidable political force in the coming decades? Would China implode in the absence of a democratic revolution? Was its economic growth sustainable without fundamental institutional reform?

In India, the key question was different. From newspaper editors to the maid at home the most common query I encountered was a deceptively simple one: what could India learn from China? What should India be doing that China had already been doing? For China the US remained the ultimate benchmark when it came to its self-assessment of national power and achievement. But for India, it was China that had emerged as a commonly used yardstick to evaluate its own progress.

Back in China the question I faced with greatest frequency was again different, at once the crudest and perhaps most difficult of all to answer. 'Which is better? India or China?' taxi drivers in Beijing had asked me with monotonous regularity. 'Do you prefer India or China,' my students at the BBI had often queried. 'Do you like living in Beijing? Or was it better in Delhi?' my *hutong* neighbours inquired whenever they got the opportunity.

This last question in its various forms was one that I spent much thought grappling with and my answers were as variable as the day the question was posed. Following conversations with Lou Ya and other toilet cleaners in my neighbourhood I would think back to the wretched jamadarnis back home and marvel at the relative dignity of labour that China's lowliest enjoyed.

In my *hutong* the refuse collectors wore gloves when picking up the garbage on their daily rounds. This single, simple article of protective clothing and the barrier it created between bacteria and skin lent them at least a modicum of self-respect. Their children almost always went to school. They may not have been well educated themselves but could usually read and write enough to avoid the worst kind of exploitation.

These were modest gains and not everyone in China could claim even such moderate progress. But were I one of the millions-strong legions of cleaners, sweepers, janitors or nightsoil workers in India, I would probably prefer by some twist of karma to have been born Chinese.

But on other days I felt differently. These were days when I spent hours hunting for a Chinese source amongst the country's think tanks, universities and research institutes for fresh insight or an alternative point of view on an issue for a story I'd be working on. It was always such dishearteningly hard work.

China's was a pragmatic society and over the years I met any number of people blessed with more than usual amounts of a canny, street smart, intelligence. As evidenced by the Zhejiang entrepreneurs, ordinary Chinese were masters of locating the loophole, of finding escape routes, of greasing the right hands and bypassing stifling regulations. If need be they could sell contact lenses to a blind woman and chicken feet to a vegetarian.

But while it may have abounded with consummate salespeople

and irrepressible entrepreneurs, Chinese society remained deeply anti-intellectual. More a product of a political and educational system that discouraged criticism and encouraged group think than any primordial characteristic, this was the aspect of China I personally found most wearying.

It was the absence of a passion for ideas, the lack of delight in argument for its own sake, and the dearth of reasoned but brazen dissent that most often gave me cause for homesickness. When the foreign ministry interpreter Xiao Yan claimed in Tibet that China was different from other countries in that all Chinese must think the same thing, she was consciously overstating her case in the light of Jes' comments. Even so, a nub of truth in what she said remained.

In China, those who disagreed with mainstream, officially sanctioned views outside of the parameters set by mainstream officially sanctioned debate more often than not found themselves branded as dissidents—suspect, hunted, under threat.

Thus a professor who misspoke to a journalist could suddenly be demoted. An editor who pursued a corruption investigation too zealously might find herself fired. A lawyer who simply tried to help his client to the best of his abilities could, were the client of the wrong sort, ironically land in jail himself.

In universities like the BBI the idea was drilled into students' heads that there were right answers and wrong answers. While ambiguity and nuances may have been both sensed and exploited in practice, on a purely intellectual plane there was little space for them.

For an argumentative Indian from a country where heterodoxy was the norm, this enforced homogeneity in Chinese thought and attitude scratched against the natural grain.[1] There were thus occasions when despite all of India's painful shortcomings, I would assert with conviction that it was better to be an Indian than

[1]See Amartya Sen, *The Argumentative Indian: Writings on Indian Culture, History and Identity*, Penguin, 2005.

endure the stifling monotony of what tended to pass as an intellectual life in China.

But then I would return to Delhi for a few days and almost immediately long to be back in Beijing where a woman could ride a bus or even drive a bus without having to tune out the constant staring and whispering of the dozens of sex-starved youth that swarmed around the Indian capital's streets at almost any given time.

Later on the same day, however, I might switch on the TV and catch a session of the Indian parliament, not always the most inspirational of bodies but when looked at with China-habituated eyes, more alluring than usual.

China's economic achievement over the last thirty or so years may have been unparalleled historically, but so was India's political feat. Its democracy was almost unique amongst post-colonial states not simply for its existence but its existence against all odds in a country held together not by geography, language or ethnicity but by an idea. This was an idea that asserted, even celebrated, the possibility of multiple identities. In India you could and were expected to be both many things and one thing simultaneously.

I was thus a Delhite, an English speaker, half a Brahmin, half a Tamilian, a Hindu culturally, an atheist by choice, a Muslim by heritage. But the identity that threaded these multiplicities together was at once the most powerful and most amorphous: I was an Indian.

India's great political achievement was thus in its having developed mechanisms for negotiating large-scale diversity along with the inescapable corollary of frequent and aggressive disagreement. The guiding and perhaps lone consensus that formed the bedrock of that mechanism was that in a democracy you don't really need to agree—except on the ground rules of how you will disagree.[2]

---

[2]See Ramachandra Guha, *India After Gandhi: The History of the World's Largest Democracy*, Macmillan, 2007.

All of which being true still did not help to definitively answer the question, 'If I could choose, would I rather be born Indian or Chinese?'

Perhaps part of my problem was that unlike how students were educated in China into believing there were right and wrong answers I had been encouraged to do precisely the opposite. 'Always problematize,' my earnest, khadi-kurta-clad professor, Sankaran, used to thunder at us during class in my undergraduate days as a philosophy student in Delhi.

But if forced to reply in broad brush strokes I would assert the following: were I to be able to ensure being born even moderately well-off, I would probably plump for India over China.

In India, money allowed you to exist happily enough despite the constant failure of governments to deliver services. Most Delhi households that could afford it had private generators for when the electricity failed and private tube wells in their gardens to ensure the water supply that the municipality couldn't. The police offered little protection from crime and so many households hired private security guards.

Having developed the necessary private channels with which to deal with the lack of public goods one was free in India to enjoy the intellectual pleasures of discussing the nature of 'the idea of India' or to enjoy the heady adrenalin rush of winning a well-argued debate.

These were real pleasures and freedoms and their broader significance was not merely confined to the elite. A tradition of argumentation was fundamental to India's secularism and democratic polity, with wide-ranging implications for all sections of society.

On the other hand, were I to be born poor, I would take my chances in authoritarian China, where despite lacking a vote, the likelihood of my being decently fed, clothed and housed were considerably higher. Most crucially, China would present me with relatively greater opportunities for upward socio-economic mobility. So that even though I may have been born impoverished, there was a better chance I wouldn't die as wretched in China, as in India.

This was not to deny the importance of the vote for India's poor, which undoubtedly endowed them with collective bargaining power. Dislocating large numbers of people to make way for big infrastructure projects, for example, was an uphill task for any Indian government. As a result, the kind of wanton destruction of large swathes of a historic city like Beijing justified by the hosting of a sporting event would be extremely unlikely to occur in India.

In China, on the other hand, not only did the poor lack a vote,[3] but the CCP was also adept at disabling the capacity of disaffected peoples to organize, thus depriving them of the influence of numbers that could pressure government policy through other means.

However, it was also clear that in India the right to vote did not necessarily or even usually translate into better governance. Fear of alienating a vote bank might persuade a local politician to turn a blind eye to illegal encroachment by migrants on city land. But the ensuing slum would lack even the most rudimentary facilities like sewage or water supplies.

Citizens threw out governments in India with predictable regularity. The country's vast poor majority dismissed on average four out of five incumbents, so that what was called the anti-incumbency factor was possibly the most decisive in any Indian election.

While it was often celebrated as a sign of India's robust democracy, what this state of affairs really reflected was a track record of governance that was so abysmal that even in regions where incomes had improved and poverty reduced, people believed this was in spite of and not because of the government.[4]

[3]Forty million peasants have been forced off their land to make way for roads, airports, dams, factories, and other public and private investments, according to *China: the Balance Sheet*, Center for Strategic and International Studies and the Institute of International Economics: Washington, D.C., 2006.

[4]Swaminathan Aiyar, 'A Vote against Misgovernance', *Times of India*, 15 May 2004.

So ultimately despite political representation for the poor in India and the absence of political participation in China, the latter trumped India when it came to the delivery of basic public goods like roads, electricity, drains, water supplies and schools where teachers actually show up.

This counter-intuitive state of affairs was linked to the fact that while in China the CCP derived its legitimacy from delivering growth, in India a government derived its legitimacy simply from its having been voted in. Delivering on its promises was thus less important than the fact of having been elected.

The legitimacy of democracy in many ways absolved Indian governments from the necessity of performing. The CCP could afford no such luxury.

As a result the Chinese government was more responsive to the socio-economic problems confronting it than it was often given credit for, bringing us back to another of the questions frequently posed to me: where was China headed in the new century?

This was a question I wasn't alone in trying to answer. It was one that preoccupied a battery of analysts around the world and the majority consensus, at least in the West, appeared to be that China's uncomfortable blend of authoritarian politics and liberal economics was unsustainable.

Opinion was divided along the lines of what one author[5] recently described as the 'soothing scenario', according to which democracy in its western liberal form was the inevitable and natural outcome of China's economic reforms, and the 'upheaval scenario', according to which the paradoxes of the current regime would lead to its inevitable and imminent collapse.

That contemporary China was rife with contradictions was undeniable. Its ruling party espoused a communist, egalitarian ideology while presiding over the emergence of one of the world's most unequal societies. Social and economic freedoms chafed

---

[5]Jim Mann, *The China Fantasy: How Our Leaders Explain Away Chinese Repression,* Viking, 2007.

against continued political control. The contradictory needs and aspirations of the urban middle class jostled against those of peasants and migrant workers. From architecture to religion, the uneasy coexistence of ancient tradition, enforced modernity and resurgent tradition was apparent for the looking. For swarms of fortune-seeking foreigners from yoga teachers to hotel doormen, China was fast becoming a land of opportunity, yet hundreds of millions of its own impoverished citizens remained ready to risk their lives for any chance of escape abroad.

The new China was a land of dichotomies: chaos and control, change and continuity, wealth and poverty, good and evil coexisted here in a potentially explosive mix.

But based on empirical evidence as opposed to ideological axioms that claimed one or the other inevitable future for China, the CCP, like most ordinary Chinese, was surprisingly adept at negotiating these contradictions. China's government may have been walking a tightrope but the Chinese were famously skilled acrobats.

Rather than inevitable collapse or democratization it thus seemed to me just as likely that China would continue successfully along its present course of economic growth and reform coupled with only minor political change, for the near to mid-future.

Over the course of the last thirty years China's authorities had demonstrated time and again their ability to identify and respond to key problems caused by corruption, income inequalities and environmental degradation.

Recently, a spate of critics have characterized the Chinese party-state as paralysed or unable to effectively function either as the result of the chronic corruption that plagues it or the inconsistencies between its economic and political policies.[6]

---

[6]See Minxin Pei, *China's Trapped Transition, The Limits of Developmental Autocracy*, Harvard University Press, 2006; Will Hutton, *The Writing on the Wall: China and the West in the New Century*, Little, Brown, 2006; Gordon Chang, *The Coming Collapse of China*, Arrow, 2002.

Over the course of my stay in China, however, what struck me time and again wasn't the unresponsive or sclerotic state of the Chinese government but rather its embrace of pragmatism and willingness to experiment with new ideas. This was particularly striking when contrasted with the tired, ideological opposition by India's communist parties to virtually anything innovative from special economic zones to new directions in foreign policy.

In China, the special economic zones strategy, for example, did not spring from *a priori* assumptions about their theoretical goodness or badness. The original SEZs were initiated to act as laboratories, providing a controlled environment within which to experiment boldly with reforms. Once the experiment was deemed successful, SEZs were more widely adopted so that by the time I moved to China virtually every county and district in the country boasted investment zones of some kind.

Pilot projects were thus the preferred way for the CCP to test out reforms from cooperative medical care schemes in the countryside to proposals to abolish the *hukou* system. The focus was usually on trying to establish what worked best in practice before the wholesale adoption of any new policy.

Of course what 'worked best' was defined by certain parameters, the most fundamental of these being the strengthening or at least the preservation of the CCP's power. It was to this end that Beijing had developed a range of tools of governance. These included brutal repression but also more sophisticated methods like the co-option of key constituencies and the isolation of dissent by control of nodes of information dissemination.

But given China's increasing integration into global trade coupled with the spread of new technologies like the internet and mobile telephony,[7] Beijing was also aware that neither brute force

---

[7]According to China's Ministry of Information Industry, by June 2007 the number of mobile phone users in China had reached 501.64 million. The corresponding figure for internet users was 162 million, according to the China Internet Network Information Center.

nor censorship could guarantee the continued reign of the party on their own.

What was found to work best for preserving the CCP's grip on power was delivering economic growth.

The constituency that benefited most directly from this growth also happened to be the one that had been the most potent force for democratization elsewhere in the world: the urban middle class. By tying the prosperity of this group to the continuance of the party at the helm of policy making the CCP had effectively politically neutralized what could have been its most formidable foe.

The students who marched on Tiananmen in 1989 had been replaced by the likes of Cindy, Grace and my other students at the BBI. This was a tribe that was studiously apolitical and fiercely nationalistic. The freedoms they yearned for—to make money, to fall in love, to get double-eye lid surgery—were theirs for the taking.

In May 2004, I spent several hours interviewing a random selection of ten students for a TV story I was putting together to mark the fifteenth anniversary of the Tiananmen protests and killings.

None of those I talked to, many of whom were top academic achievers, could describe in any detail what the issues at stake in 1989 had been. Most, however, insisted that the 'incident' could never be repeated again.

'You see,' explained Leo, a young man who styled himself as a bit of an alternative thinker, 'Students today are more rational than before.' How so, I asked. 'They know the right approach to solving a problem. It doesn't necessarily have to be violent. Gradual reform is always best,' came the reply.

The consensus appeared to be that the students back in 1989 had been mislead by a few ringleaders who had their own interests rather than those of the community in mind when acting to fuel 'trouble' thus 'forcing' the government's hand. Once again, I was confronted with a situation in which my brightest students presented what was in fact official propaganda as self-drawn and carefully considered conclusions of their own.

The CCP's cooption of the class of society my students belonged to was almost complete. As they rarely tired of pointing out, life for them had been getting better and better. In 2001 entrepreneurs were officially allowed to join the Communist Party. In 2007 the government passed a private property bill, primarily aimed at ensuring the rights of the urban middle class, despite substantial public opposition.

The fact is that were China to hold democratic elections tomorrow, the seven hundred million peasants in the country would be more than likely to vote for policy priorities that were different from or even opposed to those that suited the interests of city-based professionals and business people.

The Chinese bourgeoisie thus had in-built resistance to a scenario that would place them on the same political footing as their less educated and rough-edged compatriots from the countryside. The CCP had been successful not only in persuading them that it was in their self-interest to see the one-party state remain in power but that this was a conclusion they had arrived at all on their own.

But the party was also well aware that the support of the urban elite on its own was insufficient to keep it in power in a country where peasants still formed a comfortable majority. It was to peasant support that the CCP owed its rise to power some sixty years ago and as China's centuries-long history had demonstrated time and again, rulers could ignore the countryside only at their own peril.

In the new century several alarm bells were going off, symptoms of rural disenchantment that could spell serious trouble for the CCP in the future.

By 2005 the number of 'mass incidents' (a rather vaguely defined term used by the police to characterize a range of protests, demonstrations and riots) across China totalled 87,000, according to the government's own figures. This was a 600 per cent increase over the previous decade. The overwhelming majority of these incidents took place in the countryside, where illegal land grabs, illegal pollution by factories, unbridled official corruption and reduced social security provisions were leading to bubbling anger which erupted every once in a while, often in violent form.

As though on cue, from 2005 onwards, the formerly GDP-obsessed rhetoric of the party leadership took a sharp left turn with the creation of a 'new socialist countryside' upheld as the primary future goal of governmental efforts.

The idea was that China needed to focus less on indiscriminate growth and more on redistribution of resources and rebalancing of incomes. The following years therefore saw increased governmental spending on basic education and medical care, additional subsidies for farmers, abolition of rural taxes and large injections of funding in rural infrastructure projects.

In 2006, the police reported a 20 per cent drop in mass protests over the previous year.[8]

One rather startling fact was that China's income inequality measured by the gini coefficient—a commonly used statistical measure of inequality where 0 represents perfect equality and 100 perfect inequality—was at 44.7 worse even than that of India's 32.5.[9]

---

[8]The precise statistics for 'mass incidents' remain a source of some controversy since the Chinese government has issued conflicting figures at different times. Also the terms 'mass incident' and 'public order disturbance' are sometimes conflated while at other times used differentially. Thus although the exact figure of a 20 per cent drop in mass incidents reported by the police for 2006 may or may not be accurate, it is safe to say that the police reported a 'drop' for the first time in a decade of steadily rising public protests. See the following link on EastSouthWestNorth (an excellent blog on China) http://zonaeuropa.com/20061115_1.htm for further discussion on the matter of 'mass incident' statistics.

[9]UNDP, *Human Development Report*, 2005.

For the CCP the width of the income gap was embarrassing. It was also potentially the greatest threat to its legitimacy. Hence redressing the gap was zeroed in on as an issue in need of urgent attention.

However, unlike the strategy deployed under Mao, the new leadership aimed not at achieving equality of outcomes but rather equality of opportunity. Education, which had for long played second fiddle to the building of roads and other infrastructure, once again loomed large on the policy agenda.

A programme for nine years of free public education in the poorer inland provinces was launched with the intention of extending it to cover the entire country within a decade. Massive ramping up of higher education was also being undertaken. The number of university graduates quadrupled in the five years since I moved to China.

Similarly, other potential flashpoints like the regional income gap, corruption and environmental pollution were also being addressed.[10]

It could with some truth be argued that Beijing's responses to the challenges confronting it were akin to putting a bandage on a broken arm. Many of the fires the CCP was busy putting out were of its own making, the result of flaws in the basic structures of governance.

But it could also be argued that in addition to slapping on bandages on obvious wounds the leadership was making some attempt to actually mend the arm itself, with one caveat: it was Chinese rather than Western medicine that was being looked to for a cure.

Traditional Chinese medicine (TCM) did not submit to the rigours of the western scientific method. Even so, the Chinese had persisted in using it over the centuries and with scant regard for

---

[10]See Arthur Kroeber, 'The Underestimated Party State', *Financial Times*, 26 February 2007.

western scepticism. The vast majority of Chinese were united in their opinion that TCM was effective.

Back when I was still at the BBI, a student called Flora had wanted to be excused from class for a few days. Her mother was seriously ill, she said. I had heard Flora's mother lived in Canada and asked if she was planning to fly over to join her mom. 'Oh no,' Flora replied. 'They can't treat my mother properly in Canada. She's returning to Beijing to see a Chinese doctor.'

Returning to the issue of political reform, the Chinese leadership asserted that such reform was not only possible but already under way. The pace and the terms of this reform were, however, dictated by Chinese history and culture rather than axiomatically following the liberal western multi-party mould.

In short it was Beijing's assertion that Chinese ailments could best be treated with Chinese medicine.

The West may remain sceptical of the efficacy of these reforms, pointing out all manner of inconsistencies in the model, but China had confounded western predictions time and again. The country had developed its own kind of state-led capitalism and would similarly forge its own brand of one-party 'democracy', or so went the claim.

The cornerstone of the CCP's proposed political reform was the development of the rule of law. The idea was that instead of multi-party democracy a system of checks and balances would be developed within a one-party state, primarily by guaranteeing that the country would be ruled according to law rather than imperial or bureaucratic fiat.

Instead of the vote, people were thus being granted a series of tactical legal 'rights'. These included the right to sue government agencies on certain issues, to private property, to religious freedom and so on.

As a result, although the law was still viewed primarily as an instrument of control, a simultaneous and competing perception of the law as a check on the power of government and guarantor of individual rights was also being promoted.

A consequent gradual rise in legal consciousness was apparent. The movement known locally as 'rights defence' or *wei quan* gathered force, particularly in the aftermath of Sun Zhigang's death in 2003. The massive public outcry that followed the beating to death of the young graphic designer led the government to abolish the anti-vagrancy laws that had allowed the police to arrest Sun simply for not having any residence documents on him.

The *wei quan* movement comprised scholars, lawyers and activists, connected by the internet and united in their attempt to close the gap between the law on paper and its actual efficacy in protecting the rights of citizens.

Over the years the movement had several successes, on occasion forcing the government to reverse unpopular measures and bringing to the attention of the public, grievances that would otherwise have remained unreported and unknown.

The *wei quan* activists did not focus on regime change. Their aim was not to topple the CCP but rather to hold the CCP to its own promises. They took up cudgels against the abuse of power by local officials that more often than not had the central government on their side. Typical issues the rights defence movement was involved with included local conflicts over illegal land grabs, urban development and environmental pollution.

Central to the ability of the movement to have any real impact were the new technologies of the internet and mobile telephony. Examples were abundant.

In late 2003, for instance, the rich wife of a business tycoon driving a BMW killed a poor tractor-borne peasant in the north-eastern city of Harbin. When the rich woman was let off by a court in what came to be known as the 'BMW case' an upswell of public anger resulted in a concerted internet campaign demanding justice which eventually forced the provincial government to order a retrial.[11]

---

[11]In the end the verdict was, however, the same.

By the time of my fifth year in China barely a week went by without reports of internet activism influencing government decisions. Plans to construct a chemical plant in the city of Xiamen were frozen after thousands of residents, afraid of the ensuing pollution, joined in opposition through a flood of mobile phone text messages. Slavery networks involving brick kilns were busted in part after public outcry expressed through the internet forced the authorities into action.

From exposing official negligence in coal mine accidents to the rescue of cats in danger of being served up as dinner, the internet, despite all the attempts by the government to control it, was providing the focal point for the emergence of a nascent civil society.[12]

The *wei quan* movement had clear limits. When it crossed those boundaries the authorities could come down hard. Local officials hounded activists, harassing them and even threatening them with their lives. Lawyers who took up touchy causes were imprisoned themselves.

If a matter was deemed too sensitive, internet chat room managers were ordered to delete discussions on it. Net activists who persisted in publishing information that the leadership claimed to be 'anti-national' or 'anti-party' faced arrest and persecution.[13] The internet itself was subjected to a range of technological

---

[12]For an informative analysis of the political functions of internet-mediated networks see Guobin Yang, 'Activists Beyond Virtual Borders: Internet Mediated Networks and Informational Politics in China', *First Monday*, Volume 11, 2006 (http://firstmonday.org/issues/special11_9/yang/).

[13]Guobin Yang (ibid) argues China's uniqueness originates in its combination of high levels of internet regulation and internet activism. He says that while online-based networks in China differ from those in other countries in that they have 'an informal, episodic, and emergent character ... when critical social issues enter China's internet-mediated networks, they activate the network structure and transform them into advocacy networks'.

controls such as keyword filtering and blocking of 'controversial' websites.

However, rather than old-style blanket repression the CCP's tactics and aims had evolved to cope better with the complexity that new technologies introduced into the government-citizen dynamic. For the authorities the internet presented both a threat and an opportunity. On the one hand it enabled networks that could circumvent and thus break the party's monopoly on information. On the other hand public opinion as expressed in internet chat rooms was also an important feedback mechanism for the CCP, a means to test the pulse and mood of the nation.

The preferred strategy of the leadership was therefore one of selective repression that singled out only those who openly challenge the party-state's authority while leaving the general public alone.

Undoubtedly the Chinese government's concept of political reform begged several questions. To establish the rule of law without an independent judiciary was like trying to square a circle, as was promoting the internet as a tool of public participation while simultaneously expending considerable energy in curbing that very potential.

The CCP's dual-track approach to political reform mixed continuing repression with greater participation, a high-stakes and potentially dangerous strategy. Not only could it fail to achieve substantial progress, it could also backfire on the party.

If after raising certain expectations of reform amongst the public the CCP was unable or unwilling to fulfil them, the eruption of serious friction was a distinct possibility. Since a fundamental overhaul of China's political system remained off the agenda, the edifice upon which society was built remained unstable. The CCP was thus forced into a semi-permanent crisis-response mode.

However, Beijing's achievement was in keeping the tensions simmering rather than bubbling over. And although crystal ball gazing is a hazardous business, I would nonetheless assert that the

CCP will likely be able to keep the flame low enough to avert an explosion for a while to come.

The party was determined to do whatever was needed to stay in power. If this required ceding some of that power by submitting itself (or at least certain parts of it) to select checks and balances, I believed that would be direction the CCP would lean towards.

Maintaining a one-party system subject to the rule of the law was probably a project that would always remain incomplete. Thus rather than squaring the circle, the CCP would at best be able to pull the circle into some kind of amoeba shape in between.

However, India's democracy was far from being a fully actualized ideal either. While the voting component of a democratic polity may have been achieved, the transparency and accountability that were also part of the package remained lacking. Yet, in spite of its manifest flaws, Indian democracy had continued to persist more or less uninterrupted for sixty years.

China's regime could also continue to exist despite the inconsistencies generated as it constructed the half-way house of economic liberalism and one-party rule that critics had long been predicting was unsustainable.

That there were reprehensible aspects to the continued one-party authoritarian rule of the CCP was not something I cared to deny. But I also believed that far from being in immediate danger of collapse the Chinese regime was set to stay for at least a decade, if not longer. It would moreover persist in recognizable form, changing only within the broad political and economic contours that characterized it in the present.

It might well be asked at this juncture, as in fact many did of me, that were my predictions for China to be borne out, what lessons did I think the mainland's recent history and foreseeable future held for India?

Over the last few years the issue of 'lessons learnt' for India from China and vice versa had acquired a fashionable flavour on the international conference circuit. Excited journalists, sage management gurus, eager businessmen and oily politicians were of one when it came to spouting Chindia-scented rhetoric replete with catchphrases that stated the obvious but whose import was less so.

India was good at software, China had hardware, was one such 'insight'. India should learn to invest in infrastructure from China while China should look to India's financial and legal institutions for tips, was another.[14] In short, the consensus seemed to be that India should get the roads and China the democracy.

There was a nice symmetry to these sentiments that captured the way in which India and China did in fact mirror each other's failures and achievements. But even the less perspicacious amongst critics on both sides of the border had little trouble pointing out that if China had democracy perhaps it would not have the roads.

The plain fact was that democracy was often used as an excuse in India to justify bad governance, just as India's democracy was used as an excuse in China to carry on with its (relatively) efficient one-party dictatorship. India was the example of choice in China when it came to pointing out the pitfalls of democracy, while in India those who admired China's achievements simultaneously bemoaned the fact that they could come only at the cost of democracy.

But this was exactly where I felt the argument went awry. Democracy, with its stress on consensus building, may have slowed down the decision-making process in India, but at the same time the institutional foundations it secured for the country should have made it easier rather than more difficult to govern well.

A free media meant that New Delhi enjoyed better feedback mechanisms than Beijing. Solid checks and balances built in through independent institutions such as the Supreme Court and the Election Commission meant that despite its chaotic appearance India was probably better able to withstand sudden shocks than China.

---

[14]See Chetan Ahya and Andy Xie, *India and China: A Special Economic Analysis*, Morgan Stanley Research, 2004.

As the SARS cover-up and ensuing panic had demonstrated, the ability of China to negotiate crises associated with unexpected health or environmental catastrophe was suspect. The CCP had proved to be a consummate juggler but the very fact that it had to keep so many balls up in the air put strains on the system that India was free of.

India's achievement in having constructed a sustainable and functional, albeit far from perfect, democracy was a formidable one. Rather than being abused as an apology for the inability of the government to facilitate socio-economic development it should have been upheld as proof that India was up to challenges tougher than the building of shopping malls and highways.

That even an unrepresentative, authoritarian party wracked with contradictions could have succeeded so well in improving the material lives of its citizens should have been a matter of both shame and hope for India. Shame that on most scores of governance it had been bested by a dictatorship and hope that if a comparably large and poor country could lift itself out of poverty without the legitimacy and institutional stability of a democracy, then the same was certainly achievable for India.

Where the post-reform CCP differed from most other dictatorships that had sprung up in the developing world was that it cared about legitimacy and had made delivering economic growth the cornerstone of that legitimacy.

What India's political parties could truly learn from Beijing's technocrats was thus to look beyond electoral validation to the delivery of growth and public goods as their ultimate, or at least penultimate, goal.

To exhort Indian politicians to act selflessly for the good of the country was hopelessly naïve, but this is where valuable lessons from the CCP could be drawn. The Chinese Communist Party was hardly a disinterested or charitable enterprise, but it seemed to have recognised that nakedly clinging to power would eventually prove self-defeating. If the ultimate goal was to remain in power, more than brute force and short-sighted profiteering were necessary.

Long-term survival required pragmatism, adaptability and above all a public that could link governmental policy with improved prospects for themselves or at minimum the next generation. Were Indian politicians unable or unwilling to 'learn' this from their Chinese counterpart the world's most populous democracy risked being shamed by a one-party dictatorship.

It was up to India to prove to the world that roads and democracy could coexist, even in the developing world. Already the country's economic growth story in the new century was proving wrong the critics who believed democracy inevitably obstructed economic development in low-income countries.

Unfortunately, however, a lot of this new growth was occurring in spite of rather than because of the government. It was the private sector that was creating the global buzz. Business sectors like IT that were putting India on the international map were the same ones that had begun life largely ignored and unregulated by the government.

Were Indian governments to improve their performance in the delivery of basic public goods including education, sanitation, drinking water and electricity, they would create a platform from which economic development could not only really take off but do so in a sustainable and grounded manner.

China's primary edge over India was that when it began its economic reform process it did so from a social base that was more advanced in terms of literacy, life expectancy, gender empowerment and dignity of labour.

Thirty years later, despite some rollbacks in China's social achievements post-reform as well as moderate advances in India's, it was still these same parameters that presented the toughest chasm for India to bridge.

For India to 'catch up' with China, building infrastructure and increasing exports would never be enough. As long as half of all Indian women remained unable even to write their own names, trumpeting India's imminent 'overtaking' of China, as some in the country were wont to do, was balderdash.

*

As I sat in my courtyard writing these words, a curious feeling stole over me, as though time had at once sped up and slowed down. I looked outside. Tofu, the cat, was stalking a dragonfly that hung off a bamboo thicket. Diagonally across, the pomegranate tree was fruitless but defiant. It had survived an insect infestation earlier in the year and lost all its pomegranates but next year I hoped that fruit would hang ripe from its branches again.

In the kitchen I could hear Li Ayi shouting into her mobile phone, giving an unknown someone instructions on how to fry up samosas. I was freshly struck by the marvel of a peasant woman from Anhui province having become conversant with the secrets of Indian gastronomy in Beijing. 'Put lots of chilli in,' she bellowed. 'Hello? Can you hear me? Yes, good! Lots of chilli; Indians like that,' she continued.

Her cooking instructions were interrupted by a competing cry. '*Wan bao, wan bao,*' the deep throated announcement of a newspaper vendor cycling past, joined the aural mosaic that patterned *hutong* life. And I felt sad because this moment could not last for ever, but also happy because it existed at all.

I looked once again into my blinking computer screen and realized that the grand themes evoked by the three questions I had been trying to answer could also be applied on a more modest scale, to matters seemingly pedestrian but of significance to me personally.

There was much that India could learn from China and China from India and the world from both. But what was it that I had learnt on an intimate, micro level from the last five years?

There were so many, many little things that sprang to mind in response. But these were learnings that were often difficult to summarize in words. They were contained rather in gestures or expressions or scents. The hint of grief in the eyes of Mrs Wu as she smiled; the way in which Lao Tai Tai had held her impossibly tiny, once-bound feet away from her body; the ketchupy sweet smell of a McDonald's burger mingling with the sharp odour of the aptly named *chou* or 'stinky' tofu.

Above all, the last five years had taught me that the contradictory can coexist. This had less to do with the CCP and the paradoxes it needed to resolve and more to do with Mr Wu. Our landlord had been a source of deep frustration from his early morning visitations and courtyard sweeping to his near poisoning of us with frog's innards and goodness knows what else.

Yet, he was a decent human being. He had unclogged the W.C., replaced fused light bulbs and mended kitchen leaks with dedicated energy. He had reluctantly agreed that the mango yellow I had chosen to paint the courtyard's interiors with was 'not *that* ugly'. He had gradually desisted from unsolicited visits before 9:00 a.m.

In short when I thought about leaving Beijing, it was his image: a 60-year-old retired railway official, atop a noisy moped, that brought a persistent little lump to the throat.

I had also learnt that even the most alien of places can become beloved. Looking back to my first few months in Beijing when I went about terrified at the prospect of being spoken to in what sounded like guttural barks at the time, the distance between then and now seemed considerably longer than the five years it had actually been.

It was slightly distasteful to me to recall how I had once perceived the Chinese. They had intimidated me with their chopsticks and unfathomable countenance. When was it exactly that their faces softened? That the neighbours' chatter in Mandarin stopped jarring and became instead a soothing backdrop to a life I came to treasure?

What I had learnt then was that it was deeply wrong to be put off by the unknown. Even when something appeared alien and daunting on the surface, familiarity lay closer than imagined. You only needed to turn a corner to find it.

And finally I had re-learnt the lessons my philosophy professors had already taught me back in college: that quick judgements and received wisdom were not to be trusted; that the truth was always difficult and rarely singular.

There were so many moments over the years when I felt tempted either to demonize or glorify what I witnessed. But then these would be followed by other moments when I was suddenly less sure of the moral foundation of the righteous conclusions I had arrived at earlier.

What I realized for certain was that as my professor Sankaran had exhorted me to be, I was reasonably good at 'problematizing' everything, but less good at arriving at firm conclusions. This was perhaps a good thing. Then, on the other hand, perhaps it wasn't.

Epilogue

The relentless nature of changing China had been exciting, but also exhausting. Even if I closed my eyes and stood absolutely still, the country around me continued to buck and rear without pause. Trying to get a real grip on my China life had often felt impossible, like holding on to shifting sands.

I was thus looking forward to some time in Oxford with its unruptured steadiness; its cobblestone streets and old buildings in no danger of being painted with *chai* signs. After the constant movement of China, I was ready for stasis.

But as I went through the laundry list of last-minute chores before I left, I couldn't help feeling a nagging sense of incompleteness; as though something had still not quite joined up.

It took me a few days to work out that this unfinished feeling was in fact the call of the ghost of the BBI. By August of 2007 it had been almost three years since I had been back to visit the college. My students had all graduated but to leave the country without saying goodbye to the place where my China life had begun, felt wrong.

I thus found myself on the subway, that had at last been extended to the college, en route to the BBI, or CCU (China Communications University) as it had been renamed a couple of years ago.

The train that I was riding on was sleek and bullet-shaped. It smelt of plastic. I felt giddy as I got off at the stop, disoriented by the newness of everything. It was my first time to arrive at the college by train.

I had a quick flashback to the other first time I had pulled up at the BBI's gates, five years ago in a small rusty red cab of a variety that had long been retired from the roads. 'Spread window civilization and practice carriage culture' the sign that had hung off the cab's front seat had read.

I laughed out aloud when I remembered my attempts at communicating with the receptionists at the International Building that day and how they had written out Chinese characters in the air for me to read.

The train station was large and airy, filled with the clacking of shoes. Out of the windows on the north side I spied the main entrance to the college. Despite the name change it looked reassuringly familiar. A young guard stood at the entrance framed by the antennae of the satellite dishes that adorned the roof of the administrative building.

When I looked to the other side of the station, however, much had changed. Where there had once been the makeshift stalls of Hebei peasants offering up carrots and potatoes, a Toyota showroom stood instead. I stared at it in surprise before accepting its presence and moving on, walking briskly towards the college gate. I had had much practice dealing with similar moments over the years and I knew that a few less vegetable selling shacks were probably the least of the transformations I would encounter that morning.

As suspected, I found the dining hall where I used to lunch over bowls of steaming noodles metamorphosed into a well-stocked supermarket selling everything from DVDs to cat food. Walking further I discovered the red-brick building where the classes for the foreign language students used to take place, gone, replaced by a giant construction site.

The sports ground, though, looked much the same. There was

still a week of summer vacation left and so it was as empty as it had been during its first few months in existence, when the college authorities had declared it off-limits for students. I was comforted by this anchor of sameness amidst all the froth of change.

The international building was also largely recognizable with its white bathroom tiles and blue windows. But it was now connected through a glass-encased aerial corridor to a new complex of shops and cafes.

I couldn't believe my eyes as they beheld the fancy new area. A coffee shop with real espresso on offer adjoined a bar advertising cocktails. 'In my day hot water from a flask to pour over green tea leaves had sufficed,' I thought, and then immediately felt old and curmudgeonly.

I walked into a beauty salon that was part of the complex. A young boy with peroxide hair looked up lazily. It was obviously a slow day, the campus still not having opened for the new semester. I asked for a hair wash and head massage.

He led me to a comfortably padded seat and began to work shampoo into my hair, gently massaging the scalp. I was tired. Not only from all the walking but emotionally as well. The morning had been a long journey into the past and I had met several ghosts along the way.

I had recalled my first day in class and how bewildered I had been when students began to introduce themselves as 'Better' and 'Anapple'. There were so many memories to smile about: the nail-scrapingly futile weekly meetings with the perspiring Dong Li, the badminton-playing hordes that had taken over the campus during SARS and even the smell of vinegar that had permeated the buildings for weeks thereafter.

The head massage felt wonderful and I relaxed into wondering what had happened to some of the students I'd lost touch with. Where was Gina, for example? The girl who had told me I was beautiful if 'a little black'. Cindy I knew was in L.A. studying journalism. Fat was in Wisconsin studying something I couldn't remember. Byron worked with Reuters in Beijing. Better I had heard was a producer at one of the provincial TV stations.

'Are you a teacher here?' the boy washing my hair asked suddenly, interrupting my meandering thoughts. 'I used to be, five years ago,' I replied. 'I see. And now you've moved on and found a better job?' he smiled. I looked up at him and shrugged my shoulders.

Select Bibliography

Aldrich, Michael, *The Search for a Vanishing Beijing: A Guide to China's Capital through the Ages*, Hong Kong University Press, 2006.

August, Oliver, *Inside the Red Mansion: On the Trail of China's Most Wanted Man*, Houghton Mifflin, 2007.

Becker, Jasper, *The Chinese*, John Murray, 2000.

Blofeld, John, *City of Lingering Splendour: A Frank Account of Old Peking's Exotic Pleasures*, Hutchinson, 1961.

Chang, Gordon G., *The Coming Collapse of China*, Arrow Books, 2002.

Jung Chang and Jon Halliday, *Mao: The Unknown Story*, Random House, 2005.

Jung Chang, *Wild Swans: Three Daughters of China*, Harper Perennial, 1991.

Clissold, Tim, *Mr China*, Constable & Robinson, 2004.

Das, Gurcharan, *India Unbound*, Viking Penguin, 2000.

Economy, Elizabeth, *The River Runs Black: The Environmental Challenge to China's Future*, Cornell University Press, 2004.

Greenfeld, Karl Taro: *China Syndrome: The True Story of the Twenty-First Century's First Great Epidemic*, HarperCollins, 2006.

Guha, Ramachandra, *India after Gandhi: The History of the World's Largest Democracy*, Macmillan, 2007.

Hessler, Peter, *Oracle Bones: A Journey between China's Past and Present*, HarperCollins, 2006.

——,*River Town: Two Years on the Yangtze*, Harper Perennial, 2001.

Hughes, Christopher and Gudrun Wacker (eds): *China and the Internet—Politics of the Digital Leap Forward*, Routledge, 2003.

Hutton, Will, *The Writing on the Wall: China and the West in the 21st Century,* Little, Brown, 2006.

Kynge, James, *China Shakes the World: The Rise of a Hungry Nation,* Weidenfeld and Nicolson, 2006.

Li Zhisui, *The Private Life of Chairman Mao: The Inside Story of the Man Who Made Modern China,* Chatto and Windus, 1994.

Mehta, Suketu, *Maximum City: Bombay Lost and Found,* Penguin, 2004.

Pei, Minxin, *China's Trapped Transition, The Limits of Developmental Autocracy,* Harvard University Press, 2006.

Pomfret, John, *Chinese Lessons: Five Classmates and the Story of the New China,* Henry Holt & Co, 2006.

Ramesh, Jairam, *Making Sense of Chindia: Reflections on China and India,* India Research Press, 2005.

Saran, Mishi, *Chasing the Monk's Shadow: A Journey in the Footsteps of Xuan Zang,* Penguin, 2005.

Sen, Amartya, *The Argumentative Indian: Writings on Indian Culture, History and Identity,* Penguin 2005.

Seth, Vikram, *From Heaven Lake: Travels through Sinkiang and Tibet,* Penguin, 1983.

Spence, Jonathan, *God's Chinese Son: The Taiping Heavenly Kingdom of Hong Xiuquan,* W.W. Norton, 1996.

——,*The Search for Modern China*, W.W. Norton, 1990.

Studwell, Joe, *The China Dream*, Profile Books, 2002.

Index

HarperCollins Readers' Club

Become a Member today and get regular updates on new titles, contests, book readings, author meets and book launches.

Join the Readers' Club today!

Post your reviews and build a literary network of your own.

Register at www.harpercollins.co.in